JOOK RIGHT ON

BLUES STORIES AND BLUES STORYTELLERS

JOOK RIGHT ON

BARRY LEE PEARSON

THE UNIVERSITY OF TENNESSEE PRESS / KNOXVILLE

Copyright © 2005 by The University of Tennessee Press / Knoxville.
All Rights Reserved. Manufactured in the United States of America.
First Edition.

Frontispiece: Do Drop Inn. Shaw, Mississippi. Photograph by Barry Lee Pearson.

This book is printed on acid-free paper.

Library of Congress Cataloging-in-Publication Data

Pearson, Barry Lee.
Jook right on : blues stories and blues storytellers / Barry Lee Pearson.— 1st ed.
    p. cm.
Includes bibliographical references and index.
ISBN 1-57233-431-2 (hardback)
ISBN 1-57233-432-0 (pbk.)
  1. Blues (Music)—History and criticism.
  2. Blues musicians—United States—Interviews.
  I. Title.
ML3521.P39 2005
781.643'092'2—dc22
                           2005001327

Blues is a story about real life. It's something that happens to you in life. I mean, just tell your story.

WILLIE COBBS

CONTENTS

ILLUSTRATIONS

ACKNOWLEDGMENTS

From my first interview to the final edit, this collection is over thirty-five years in the making. Up to now, I've interviewed 230 blues artists, 98 of whom are included in this collection. Looking back over so many years of fieldwork, I realize I can't recall everyone who has helped along the way. Nevertheless, I will attempt to acknowledge some of the many friends and colleagues who contributed to the production of this incarnation of what I think of as the best of blues stories.

First and foremost, I want to thank my family: my wife Elizabeth; my daughter Segrid, and son-in-law Jack; and my granddaughter, Dolly O'Dell. They have proved a never-ending source of encouragement and have provided invaluable help in the manuscript production. This book is dedicated to them.

I also want to thank my teachers, particularly Henry Glassie, John Cephas, Joe Wilson, Bill McCulloch, Bill Lightfoot, J. Otis Williams, Ralph Rinzler, and Archie Edwards.

As far as the manuscript goes, special thanks are due to Shirley Moody and Betty Wineke. Readers included Richard Burns, Adam Gussow, and Howard Norman. I truly appreciate their useful comments. I also wish to thank the University of Tennessee Press, particularly the editors Stan Ivester and Scot Danforth, and designer Kelly Gray.

Other institutional entities provided resources such as photographs and tapes. These include Prince Georges Community College's Blues Project and Bluebird Blues Festival; the National Council for the Traditional Arts and the National Folk Festival; the Smithsonian Center for Folklife and Cultural Heritage and the Smithsonian Folklife Festival; the Library of Congress Folklife Center; *Living Blues* magazine; the Chicago Blues Festival; and the University of Maryland.

I also want to thank various photographers for the use of their work. These include Brett Bonner, Jay Boyar, Robert Cogswell, Joseph Donaghy, Isa Engleberg, Lisa Falk, Carl Fleischhauer, Dexter Hodges, Kathy James, Alex Jones, Mike Joyce, Dave Penland, Rob Riley, Margo Rosenbaum, Nick Spitzer, Richard Strauss, Jeff Tinsley, Steven C. Tracy, Richard Vargas, and Joe Wilson.

ACKNOWLEDGMENTS

I would also like to thank friends I have not already mentioned who have assisted in so many different ways: Steven Abbott, Scott Barretta, Barry Dolins, David Evans, Lyle Linville, Jim O'Neal, Diana Parker, Richard Spottswood, John Vlach, and Andy Wallace.

Finally I want to thank the hundreds of blues players who have taken the time to share their insights and their stories with me. Whether their words are included in this collection or not, they are contributors nevertheless as teachers and caretakers of their tradition.

INTRODUCTION

Violinist, historian, and blues storyteller Howard Armstrong sat in harmonica player Phil Wiggins's[1] Washington, D.C., apartment recounting
his adventures as an American musician. Born in Dayton, Tennessee, in
1909, he had witnessed most of blues history from its introduction into
African American repertory to its present worldwide popularity. That afternoon he spoke of jooks, house parties, fish fries, and other blues venues. His discussion turned to personal anecdotes that underscored the use
of language as a tool, a natural subject for a man who had eight languages
at his command. Looking back to Chicago in the 1930s, he recounted the
perils of looking for jobs in the city's ethnic neighborhoods:

> Speaking languages . . . that kept us from getting zapped out.
> You see, we did what we called "pulling doors." As a matter
> of fact, that's how we ran into Mr. Lawrence Welk.[2] He had the
> instrument that all us door pullers hated—the squeezebox—'cause
> one man could take the place of four or five. But we were pulling
> doors. You get your guitar and whatever, fiddle and mandolin,and
> we black cats would light out for the North Side. It was nice on
> the North Side . . . pretty nice. We were accepted. But the South
> Side, you go into Italian Territory. You could hardly drag a black
> guy over there to go in and play. You know, freelancing, pass the
> hat. I pull a door *this* time and the man let us play or not. You pull
> it the next time, and sometimes you open the door and he throws
> a cuspidor in your face or something.
>
> So now we were going down the street and I saw a sign in
> Italian, "La Casita," which is almost the same in Spanish. Means
> the Little Hut or Little House.
>
> I said, "Let's go in there."
> They said, "No man, that's a dago joint. You can't go in there."
> I said, "Oh, I'll go," and they followed me in there. It was hazy
> with cigar smoke and everything, and these big, bare-bosomed
> Sicilian guys with hairy chests came around chewing on these little
> twisted cigars. They said, "You guys, you think Joe Louis is a nice
> a man, huh?" He had beaten this Primo Carnera.[3]
> "You think he's a nice fighter, huh?"
> I said, "No. I don't know no Joe Louis."
> "Oh, you know him."

I backed up on the guitar player; he backed up on the washboard player; he backed up on the bass fiddle player, and he blocked the door up. There I was trapped. So a little imp stuck his tail in my ear said, "Why don't you talk Italian?"

I whipped some Tennessee Italian on him and he stopped cold. The whole atmosphere changed. I told him I could play Italian music. He says, "Sonata, sonata la musica, presto." Play right away!

I almost tore up that little old raggedy case getting that Stradivarius out of there, and played, and the whole atmosphere changed. And they got pasta and polenta and lasagna and all that. But these other black dudes with me didn't know what it was, and didn't care what it was after they got a snoot full of that dago red, that wine. Then they got to where they knew more Italian than I did.

He says, "Sing-a that song 'Oh Marie.'" I started singing, "Oh Maria," "Oh Solo Mio" in Italian and these guys . . . that dago red was *talking* to them. Some of them would holler, "Oh my leg," "Oh, my everything." And some of the Italians were as drunk as they were. They hollered, "Ah, you boys sing-a nice Italian songs." So we played there for over a year.

Cincinnati piano player Big Joe Duskin, a former policeman and masterful boogie-woogie technician, sat on his bed in a Johnstown, Pennsylvania, hotel room. He was explaining various systems he had invented for interpreting the Bible, reading music, and teaching the piano. That evening he also talked about his attempts to learn blues and boogie when his preacher father would not abide such "devil's music." Little Duskin had to sneak some practice time when his father was out of the house and, like other musicians in similar circumstances, he learned to play in a key that he could safely switch to a religious song if need be.

My dad, he didn't know I was playing in those bars, but when I'd get home I'd start playing that stuff. Oh Lord, man, you talking about eating you up with that whip. And I told him, I say, "Dad, you got to get with it. I'm gonna be playing this stuff."

"Don't never play that devil's music in here." That's what he'd call it, and I'd get mad with him because he called it the devil's music. I said, "The devil ain't got nothing that good. I know better than that." So finally what happened, he caught me playing again. I told him I was sick. He says, "You stay home. You said you were sick, so don't bother that piano or let me catch you on it.

Because if I do, I'll tear your ass to pieces." Just like that. So, he never forgets his umbrella, but this morning he goes away and leaves it, the umbrella. He gets on the streetcar because the kids say, "Yeah, we seen him get on. He's gone." So around about a half an hour, here he come back because he forgot his umbrella. I was sitting there playing I don't know what it was, but it was something. I always play in B-flat so if he do come, the kids would tell me and I just swing into "Be Not Dismayed Whatever You Do, God Will Take Care of You." That was his favorite song. And I'd play it.

So he come to the window and all the kids was looking in and they didn't see him. And he's looking in. They all get away. I'm still playing, and I was down in it. And I looked and seen him. Oh my God! And I swing into "Be Not Dismayed Whatever You Do, God Will Take Care of You." He said, "I'm coming in there and take care of you right now."

Armstrong's and Duskin's narratives are "blues stories"; that is, narratives told by blues artists that also embody qualities found in blues, whether echoing the sound or language of blues songs, or reiterating situations or values central to the blues tradition. This book is a collection of some two hundred and twenty such stories taken from interviews with ninety-eight African American artists. Each narrative was chosen because it illuminated or reflected the blues in some way. For example, Armstrong's anecdote incorporates the core blues qualities of improvisation and transformation, illustrating the skills musicians need to get out of the scrapes their work can get them into. As a story about work, or as occupational folklore, it reflects the value musicians place on improvisational agility, and their respect for the mediating power of language and music.

Duskin's story likewise deals with improvisation but illustrates that sometimes you lose, a central message in blues songs. A story about learning, it exemplifies the dues musicians pay for the right to call themselves blues artists. It also employs the familiar motif of changing the "devil's music" into a spiritual, underscoring the musical relationship between secular and sacred songs. One of a series of episodes pitting wayward son against preacher parent, it has countless parallels in the autobiographies of artists ranging from W. C. Handy to John Lee Hooker.[4] As a final irony, Duskin's preacher father conned him into giving up playing blues and boogie altogether until after his death, then went on to live to be one hundred and five. Now *that* would give you the blues. But yesterday's painful memories also make for today's good stories, and blues has always been able to squeeze humor from hurt.

Both tales deal with transgression, improvisation, and the power of language; but where Armstrong turns language to his advantage, Duskin's words are turned against him. Both also show how malleable the world is, whether in regard to situations, relationships, or song genres. Armstrong transforms a hard time to a good time, Duskin a boogie to a sacred song. Blues songs similarly deal in change and potential, whether changing one's mind or changing one's partner.

Often such stories are set pieces used to answer common questions, to make a favorite point, or simply to entertain. They may even be elements of on-stage performance. Jokes or anecdotes are often used to introduce or explain a song or style. One-string guitar player Moses Williams, once professionally known as Haywire Tom, spoke to a National Folk Festival audience in a workshop demonstrating the instrument he called a "Yakkedy board."

> Now I know some people can play better music than me on the piano and guitar and things, but look, I wasn't raised up with that piano and I couldn't learn to read the book to learn to play the guitar like I really wanted. Of course I know a whole lot of people can learn without it, but I wasn't around a guitar as much as I was around this one string. But, I come to find out I'd break so many strings I couldn't get my tune. Every time I'd try a tune the string would break. One night I was playing for the little frolic and then the string broke." I say: "Well, one monkey don't stop no show. You got a good broom?" I said, "I'll get the wire off here and keep it going right on." And I started playing that thing and we frolic all night long. They say: "Ooh wee."
>
> Woman say, "Look a here, I didn't know I was sweeping the floor with the rock and roll."

Not every blues story shows the polish of a twice-told tale, but each teaches about the blues tradition. Some subjects appear more frequently than others, a reflection of their cultural significance, so expect some repetition. For example, making a one-string guitar, what Williams creatively names a Yakkedy board and on another occasion christened a "traveling loafer board," is so crucial to the story of blues that it can't be covered by a single version. Making something from nothing, making instruments, literally making music, is so central to the blues tradition, it deserves extra attention, and like a tried and true blues riff, each version of that story has its own flavor, coming to life with the storyteller's style.[5]

These stories come from interviews that took place over the past thirty years. Most are episodes from the speakers' life stories, the spoken word they use to document themselves and their accomplishments.[6] Ranging from several pages to several sentences, the majority of the texts are personal narratives. Taken altogether, however, they provide a panorama of blues history, showing blues from the insider's perspective, focusing on personal relationships and the deep ties between artist and community. Most are grounded in the South, particularly the Deep South and the Southeast, but others, like Armstrong and Duskin's accounts, document life after the great urban migration to Chicago; Cincinnati; St. Louis; Detroit; Washington, D.C.; or New York City. Some tales portray events, such as corn shuckings and other communal work parties, that have largely faded from African American life. Others make reference to older dance styles and musical forms such as the fiddle and banjo–based breakdowns and reels, the latter a term once commonly applied to blues. But blues superseded those earlier forms and has remained a continuous, albeit evolving, musical and ritual component of African American community events for a hundred years.[7]

Like the blues, the majority of the artists come from the South. Ninety-eight percent were either born or raised in the South and more than half were born or lived in Mississippi and nearby Memphis, bolstering that region's claim to being the home of the blues. Nevertheless, the contributors represent the blues tradition in the broadest sense and include many of today's best-known artists as well as individuals whose musical inclinations are known only to family and friends.

Making their way when segregation was the law of the land, they encountered the challenges of racism and economic hardship. Each musician dealt with obstacles in his or her own way by drawing from a wide repertoire of techniques. Because of the diversity of the speakers' backgrounds, it is risky to speak of a single blues culture; "blues cultures" is more appropriate. Despite some regional commonalities, there is no single blues life in the real world. At the same time, there is a relatively cohesive common understanding of what makes up a blues life, or what gives people the blues. Some artists may offer disclaimers that their experiences were atypical and that they personally never suffered from racism, poverty, or endless hard work. But the very need for such disclaimers testifies to a shared understanding of conditions or experiences that link the artists to their constituents.

Traditionally, blues cultures have been characterized as lower class, or working class, composed of rural agricultural workers or urban laborers. Blues artists supposedly share the same working-class background as their traditional audience, yet many come from middle-class families, and their real lives may not always jibe with the life commonly portrayed in blues songs.

According to stereotype, hard times, hard work, trouble, danger, mistreatment, and losing at love are core elements in the blues lexicon and credentials for living the blues, having the blues, and having the right to sing the blues. But many of these blues stories challenge such notions. Instead, they portray a variety of experiences. Artists lived in different circumstances or dealt with similar circumstances in their own particular manner. In their own words, some worked the system to their advantage or chose to portray themselves in a positive manner, victor rather than victim. Older artists, especially when looking back to their younger days, recall a time when the rules, however harsh, were easier to understand and test. They take pride in their survival and accomplishments, often saving their harshest criticism for misconceptions about their art form and what they perceive as limited media exposure.

While most play a range of musical styles, including ballads, spirituals, gospel, rock and roll, even country, and see clear connections between these categories, the majority choose to be called blues artists, demonstrating an allegiance to a particular artistic tradition. They believe in the quality of their work and assume people will appreciate it if they get a chance to hear it. Yet, in spite of massive CD reissue projects and the current popularity of blues-rock, it is not always easy to find recordings by these artists. According to Chicago vocalist Koko Taylor, the problem is largely due to promotion: "It's like anything else. Most people cater to what's being advertised. You know if you advertise chicken and steak that's what everybody's going to go and buy, you know, when neck bones is just as good. But they just don't advertise it."

As spokespersons for their community and as masters of the blues idiom, blues artists share a broad frame of reference with their African American traditional audience, embracing language, proverbs, familiar story lines, and common philosophical perspectives. In performance they use these reference points to discuss a range of common concerns from love and sex to economics, bearing witness to a shared vision of how the world works—sometimes touching on how it ought to be, but usually telling it like it is. In this way, blues addresses individual concerns in the context of a collective discussion of shared problems most often dealing with relationships. But blues also incorporates other life experiences: hard times, working conditions, or the good-time environment in which it is traditionally played. Rooted in a tradition of collective participation, blues employs antiphonal patterns of call and response, individual expression and communal support, offering artfully constructed lessons about human behavior. Blues songs provide models or examples of human actions and motivations keying in on power, pride, desire, dependency, and loss. They directly confront the power struggle between men and women, lovers, partners, and competitors, playing out on an open field of sexual politics dealing with motion, change, potentiality, and possibility. Contrary to popular opinion, the songs are neither intrinsically sad nor do they wallow in self-pity.

Instead, blues uses complaint to call attention to the way people behave, or rather misbehave. Offering advice couched in proverbs, blues performers encourage their audience to enjoy the good times but to also be ready for the bad times. In the blues world, change occurs for better or worse and, despite a generally stacked deck, both winning and losing can be in the cards. Moreover, blues songs and blues stories often employ quick turnarounds or reversals, where expected loss results in sudden victory. Although life is unfair and unpredictable, that very unpredictability offers provisional victory to the quick and the ready.

Like blues songs in which the singer invariably assumes the role of the protagonist, blues stories have blues artists as narrators as well as subjects. They share other qualities commonly found in blues songs, including traditional language, proverbs, story lines, and a certain characteristic attitude of affirmation, albeit couched in complaint. According to blues philosophy, certain qualities such as flexibility, the ability to improvise, perceptiveness, and mother wit are highly valued survival tools. Through a combination of world wariness and a predatory ability to spot an opening in a generally closed system, it's quite possible to benefit from life's instability. Not only can one win, it's not unreasonable to expect to win some of the time.

Blues songs also employ humor and irony to look at a problem in several different lights. Moreover, they often shift perspective in mid-song, moving from passive to aggressive or from complaint to action. These shifts contribute to the characteristic ambivalence commonly associated with blues. Blues ambivalence is most typically characterized in emotional terms, as reflected in the proverbial phrase "laughing to keep from crying." Squeezing humor from hurt resonates through blues, and such blues lines as "You may be beautiful, but you got to die someday" draws the sly tag "so give me a little of your loving before you pass away." Blues songs and stories alike turn to overstatement to destabilize credible complaint through verses like "I asked her for water and she gave me gasoline," or "if it wasn't for bad luck I wouldn't have no luck at all." In similar fashion, other forms of oral tradition, particularly ballads, tall tales, and lies, use much the same technique, eroding credibility and edging toward the absurd until pathos collapses in laughter. This characteristic blues quality can even take the teeth out of a good sermon. Thirty years ago, at the first Ann Arbor Blues Festival, Arkansas-born blues spokesman, disc jockey, and emcee Big Bill Hill lectured me on just who had the right to the blues:

> If you never worried nothing, you can't dig the blues, you just hear it. See, blues is a hurt. Now if you never had no problem, if you were born rich, everything you wanted was at your fingertips, you don't really dig the blues. You don't really feel it. But when you've lived it, when you have to suffer for this and that, small things, and you're denied; you want a shirt, your friend's got one and your mother and father can't buy it for you, or a little baby in the cradle wanted the milk bottle, he can't get the milk bottle, he's got the blues. Now, there's thousands of American people born with no hurt, go to college, big cars, money, a certain allowance. . . . you have no right to dig the blues . . . unless your woman quits you. A woman make a man sing the blues, especially when you been rich and got broke because your woman left with your friend.

Typical of the blues tradition, Big Bill's litany of complaint ends up with laughter. Blues humor also shows up in what may at first glance seem the most unlikely places. But often if we look more closely we see that these may also be where humor is most needed. For example, Memphis-born blues man Johnny Shines commented on his experience in Mississippi: "I spent some time in the Sip but not much. I spent maybe three hours there. I don't know anything about life in Mississippi. I know I was told by a white woman she didn't want me hanging around her place, and I said, 'Well thank you ma'am, thank you ma'am.' And I did appreciate it. She didn't want me hanging around her place 'cause it was a regular thing for blacks in Mississippi to hang around in trees."

Alabama harmonica player Jerry McCain used humor to confront his own personal tragedy after suffering a stroke that potentially could have ended his career:

Now in 1961 I got paralyzed from here right down in my face. Everything went bad just like a stroke. It hurt real bad. I thought it was an earache but the doctor said a nerve closed up and went bad and cut the circulation off, and I was taking Stanbacks and everything and it helped a little bit.

My mother would always get up and cook at four o'clock. Nobody was going to work but she, that was just her style. And she said, "How is your ear?" I said, "It's a little bit better, but it still kind of hurts a little bit." I went to the hydrant, didn't have no fancy house, had an old wooden table built there and the wash pan right there. And I got up under the hydrant, got some water in mouth . . . gonna rinse it out like that. But it just run down like that, feeling funny. I got some more water try to gargle my throat out and it just run out. Turn around, I said, "Mama," I said, "I'm having a light stroke."

She said, "Go away from here boy. You're too young to be having a stroke. Go away from here." I say, "Oh yeah, my daddy died with a stroke." Later on my sister died with a stroke. My brother died with a stroke and my mother died with a stroke.

And so I showed her and she looked at my mouth and it was twisted. She said, "Yeah, you're having a light stroke just like . . . We call my daddy Morris."

"Yes," she said. "It's just like Morris. Your mouth's done twisted."

I said, "Lord have mercy I won't be able to play my harmonica no more." So they had to hide the shotgun and all the stuff like that 'cause I was gonna take me out. If I can't play my harmonica then I don't want to be here.

But anyway, I didn't kill myself and I'm glad I didn't. I made a joke out of it. I told my mother—I wasn't supposed to cuss around my mother because she was a Holiness woman, a sanctified woman—and I said: "You know what mama?"

She said, "What?"

I said, "I know how come I got paralyzed."

She said, "How come?"

I said, "Shit, I done got so damn good with the harmonica, God just slowed me down to give them other asses a chance."

She said, "You . . . !" She was trying to get the belt so she could hit me. So I just turned it into a joke.

Each of these three examples illustrates variants of blues humor. Where Hill's blues lecture uses overstatement, Shines's historical quip recasts a potential adversary's threat into advice, using a pun and bitter humor to blunt the horror of Mississippi lynchings. Finally, McCain's account, a concrete example of the survival value inherent in laughing to keep from crying, employs irreverence, competition, and signifying, or bravado, to flip the script and turn tragedy to a joke.[8]

Blues artists are witness to a world that embraces hard times and good times, and as masters of transformation they can find humor in the least likely places. Truth tellers, they can format the truth in a lie, and a few artists were notorious for their creative approach to the interview. At times placing a higher premium on storytelling than historicity, several artists—but I won't call their names—have been known to embroider the truth for their own amusement or to entertain their fellow musicians or simply for the sake of an artfully crafted story. Like blues songs, such tales tell of things that could happen, although it pays to watch for the metaphor and it may call for a little wit to see the truth in a lie.

Blues stories come in many forms: Lies, legends, anecdotes, and confessions, although most of the stories in this collection are personal narratives or autobiography. In speaking of their lives, blues artists draw on their own experience to explain why they chose blues or, in some cases, why blues chose them. Like Big Bill Hill, most acknowledge the ethnicity of their chosen art form and, while they welcome a broader audience, most are also quick to point out that blues derives its essential meaning from African American experience. They encapsulate this relationship in the proverb, "You have to live the blues to feel the blues." Moreover, it is common knowledge that you have to feel the blues to play the blues. Often perceived as an extra-musical dimension, feeling cannot be learned in a music lesson, and artists differentiate between playing music and playing blues, implying it is relatively easy to learn the surface techniques of blues, even for musicians who have not been steeped in blues culture. But feeling, that is a more complex quality. Essentially it determines how effectively an artist communicates with an audience by combining authority based on experience, empathy, and intensity of expression. Simply put, to play without feeling means you are not playing blues. It is the ultimate measure of the blues artist. For example, Big Bill Hill gave his hero Elmore James the highest praise when he said, "he played the blues because he felt the blues and he lived them."

Musicians also say blues comes out of life, meaning, in part, that blues songs reflect and express experiences shared by many African Americans, experiences commonly portrayed as hard times, good times, or both. According to Alabama-born piano player Wilbur "Big Chief" Ellis, "Blues is a living thing. Every blues you hear a person singing, somebody has lived that life, it happened to somebody."

Artists from the Mississippi Delta, considered by many to be the birthplace of the blues, characteristically connect blues to farm labor and hard times. For example, Delta guitarist George Washington Jr. explained, "I used to sing the blues out there in the field. Looked like it made it more easy on me working. Well, that's the way people learn how to play the blues. It's hard times. A person have so hard a time way back, he just gets the blues and goes to playing the blues. I just went to playing the blues."

Blues may reflect hard times but, as Virginia guitarist John Cephas noted, blues also comes from the weekend's good times:

> Blues was born in a segregated society. In the black community this was an integral part of the whole experience of blues. Imagine, on a weekend after a hard day's work, living in a segregated society, having no money, not being able to go out to socialize into the whole society. People created blues as a form of entertainment where they had house parties. They would have food, they would have drink, and they brought their instruments there. And this was how the blues was actually born.

As Cephas contends, blues is part of a related sequence of life experiences bridging the hard times of the workweek with the good times of
the weekend.[9] To have the blues is to be down, whether brought down
by hard work, hard times, or personal mistreatment. But hearing the blues
can be a cure or source of strength and a healing ritual. As Joe Willie
"Pinetop" Perkins reminds us, singing blues can be a way to escape farm
labor: "My mother liked it that I became a musician. They didn't cold
water me about it. You know, I had to make a living some kind of how,
instead of plowing those mules which is what I first started doing down
there. Yeah, I would sing out in the fields. That's how I got that voicing.
Plowing those mules and singing."

Collectively, the following stories synthesize what it means to "live
the blues." I think of them as a blues quilt, an assemblage of colorful bits
sewn together to make a single thematically unified work, a collective
vision of a major American art form. And, like a quilt, blues stories are
not only artistic, they are functional. Cut from the same cloth as blues
songs, blues stories teach as well as entertain, providing valuable lessons
about the hard facts of life.

Following the introduction, the book is divided into five chapters:
(1) "Blues Talk," (2) "Living the Blues," (3) "Learning the Blues," (4)
"Working the Blues," and (5) "The Last Word." These divisions proved
loose enough to accommodate most of the best stories and at the same
time provided some sense of organization, although it is clear that many
stories could fit in several sections. As a whole, these narratives empha-
size the experiences that not only shaped the musicians' development as
artists but also shaped the blues tradition in general. However, after "Blues
Talk," the categories also imply a chronological progression, beginning
with environment and shaping forces—those institutions and traditions
that affected the artist—and ending with the artist as master craftsperson,
exerting a shaping influence on environment and community.

The first section, "Blues Talk," is not really a chapter or even a mini-
chapter. Rather it is a second introduction in which blues artists introduce
the reader to their art form. And, unlike the other three chapters, it is not
really an assemblage of stories as such. Instead, it is a dozen short bits—
illustrations, descriptions, comparisons, and even lists as to what causes
and/or cures blues. It can be read as a blues primer or even as a praise
poem dedicated to the blues. Since they are often asked about what they

do, or to explain the nature of blues, the majority of the artists I have spoken with have constructed responses that deal with, or at times deflect, such inquiries. Rather than elaborating the formal characteristics of blues songs, their definitions or illustrations focus more on what causes blues or how blues works to alleviate such conditions.

Their descriptions may involve personification and generally connect artist and art form, as when harmonica player J. C. Burris claimed: "Blues are more than music. They are a way of telling about life. Not everybody's life, just the lives of some people. You make them and sing them from life. They have a history for sure. They come from the cotton fields and tobacco patches and went somewhere else just like I did." Similarly, Alabama-born harmonica player George "Wild Child" Butler describes his relationship to blues in terms of a birthright:

> Playing the blues, well, we, I was raised up with it. Matter of fact, the people who I was raised up with, my parents and their neighbors and them, used to work in the fields when I was young, and they would bring their guitars to the field with them on their lunch. When they come off at dinner, they call it dinner down there, they would play, play and sing the blues and drink corn liquor and have a good time and then go on back to work. And I was raised up around with that. And it come to be a part of me.

Blues talk refers to blues as both a racial and a regional birthright, listing grievances or examples of mistreatment commonly described in blues songs. For example, Big Bill Hill's earlier lecture on who has the right to claim the blues is just such a list, climaxing with the blues' primary cause—mistreatment by one's partner. Blues poetry focuses on the ongoing struggle between men and women, or lovers or competitors in general, and blues talk follows suit, linking the speaker's experience to their art form's typical subject matter.

Blues has always had a close connection to the spoken word, dating back to hollers and work songs, and so-called talking blues, in which a vocalist talks over an instrumental background. Moreover, vocal qualities are applied to musical instruments as well. Blues talk highlights the link between the spoken word and song and, even without instrumental backing, evokes musical echoes. (It even reads well against a blues soundtrack.) For all its artistry, blues talk is also an important part of working the blues. Self-promotion and public relations involve dealing with the media through interviews in which artists are commonly asked to define or explain their craft. Using the language of blues to talk about blues, blues talk illustrates the ways musicians cope with the challenge of explaining what they do. While other definitions of blues as sound, feeling, a way of talking about life, or even a job, thread through the other chapters, Blues Talk provides overt, poetic descriptions of the way blues works.

The second chapter, "Living the Blues," illustrates what musicians mean when they say blues comes out of life, reflecting both the experiences of weekday work and weekend celebrations. It's divided into two sections, the first focusing on various kinds of work, presenting multiple images of southern life with an ear toward the soundscape of the workday world in the fields, the saw mills, or in the chilling confines of Parchman Prison Farm. The second half of the chapter is concerned with the weekend, highlighting the good-time events that also gave birth to the blues. While blues echoed and described physical work and helped pass the workday, blues rituals—the house parties, suppers, and jooks—were primarily weekend events that made the workweek bearable. Collectively these blues stories show both the rigors of life and the celebration of life; the conditions people lived through and the events they lived for. I have, however, left out the church, a major part of life and dominant institution. That belongs in another work. So, beyond casual references to church people or church attitudes, this book deals primarily with secular life.

"Learning the Blues," the third chapter, details process, what musicians do or go through to learn the skills they need to work their art form. It follows a roughly chronological sequence of inspiration, improvisation, determination, endurance, and acceptance in four subsections: "The Sound;" "Making Music;" "Small Crimes;" and "Turn Arounds." While we have already noted that the foremost blues lesson involves living the blues, this chapter shows in greater detail what it takes to actually master the idiom, proving that blues is much more than a simplistic natural expression of community life.

Live and learn, as the proverb goes, and so blues artists do by absorbing the sounds, language, and drama of their community, particularly the music and musical events. The next step is translating what's in your ear to something you can play, which means making music or making something that you can use to make music. You also have to be willing to take chances and to risk punishment by breaking rules in order to get next to the music. Although it was considered inappropriate for children to fool with adult art forms like the blues, over and over again blues storytellers recount the small crimes they committed as youngsters and the suffering they endured for their art. In the long haul, if you have the ear to catch the sound; the wit and the nerve to make, beg, borrow, or steal the music; the determination to practice; the courage to risk humiliation; the skill to make the grade; and the luck to be in the right place at the right time—in other words, if you study your blues lessons as hard as you can, you just might learn the blues and make it as a blues artist.

The next chapter, "Working the Blues," deals with the workday, or should we say worknight, and its social network. Blues may be an art form and a calling, but it is also an occupation with its own traditions. Occupational lore obviously includes the techniques of performing and playing effectively, but it also embraces the range of skills and the knowledge required in order to be admired by audiences, employers, and co-workers alike. Moreover, stories of the workplace provide a key into the musicians' value system, showing the kind of behavior they prize, the situations they try to avoid, and the things they consider funny. A premium is put on competition and artful improvisation, both dominant values in blues performance.

The chapter divides into five sections: "Money," "Names," "The Road," "I'm Not Dead, I'm Here," and "Winners and Losers." Initiation into the job of music means making money, not making music. While other rewards justify playing, nickels, dimes, and quarters allow the artist to support the music habit. Working the blues can be both a pleasure and a chore and, most often, money makes the difference. However, it is also important to remember that, in spite of the need to make money, the value of money changes in these stories, and yesterday's depression-era windfall adds up to today's chump change. And, depending on whom one is talking to, musicians may choose to present themselves as doing very well. We should keep in mind that, as a group, these artists may have been financially exploited, yet many consider themselves astute businessmen and ever competitive, they like to show how much better they are doing than their peers. Work may also mean choosing or creating a musician identity by taking a musician's name. Like their calypso or rap counterparts, blues players acquire alter egos that become their on-stage characters. Today, work means playing clubs and festivals, but years ago it meant playing country dances and the streets. Itinerant musicians hitch-hiked, hoboed, or walked to wherever a crowd could be persuaded to part with their hard-earned change in exchange for a song. They often competed for the money, and the better player pulled the other's crowd.

While musicians need to draw the attention of the crowd, they also need to beware of the dangers inherent in being the center of attention, especially when dealing with wives, lovers, jealous husbands, or other envious competitors. Stories of workplace dangers serve as examples, warnings to stay alert, to keep cool, and to keep one's charm under control. From jooks to barrel houses to the various "bucket of blood" clubs, blues has traditionally drawn a tough, hard-partying audience, and blues storytellers document workplace dangers with accounts of near misses and harsh violence often paralleled in blues songs.

"Winners and Losers," on the other hand, shows the playful, albeit competitive side of the blues business, reminding us that blues artists literally play for a living. It illustrates competitive traditions ranging from long simmering rivalries and on-stage cutting contests to the more typical signifying, hustles, and cons that musicians employ to beat each other out of their money or simply to claim momentary bragging rights. Work life, on stage and off, provides the arena for such ongoing contests, and for some longtime partners the games go on year after year, occasionally escalating to violence. But for the most part, the games are a traditional mode of interaction, a pastime and a source of entertainment. Musicians interact in a playfully aggressive manner, ever on the alert for a competitive edge, as illustrated in a set of exchanges between piano player Roosevelt Sykes, vocalist Willie Mae "Big Mama" Thornton (who originally sang the blues classic "Hound Dog"), promoter Big Bill Hill, and Chicago legend Howlin' Wolf at the 1969 Ann Arbor Blues Festival. First, Thornton approached Sykes:

> Thornton: "Roosevelt. Roosevelt Sykes. Man, if you don't come over here, I'm coming over there."
> Sykes: "Hey, you ain't nothin' but a hound dog."
> Thornton: "Look, I don't play. . . ." She then sees Big Bill Hill, "Hey, is that Big Bill? Hey, Big Bill."

Hill: "Who? Big Bill Broonzy. No. He's dead. Now I know who
you are. You ain't nothin' but a hound dog." Laughter.
A little later, Thornton challenges Chicago vocalist Howlin' Wolf:
"I got me another man. I done quit you."
Howlin' Wolf: "Look here. It takes two to quit me."
Thornton: "Well, look fella, I don't play."

Thornton's "I don't play," as in "I don't play the dozens," belies the fact that musicians do play, and not just music. Musicians' games are often illustrated in personal accounts of turning the tables on an adversary who once had the upper hand, the same type of reversal that dominates blues songs. Other accounts show the positive qualities of coolness, even to the point of playing so gracefully that losing with style overshadows winning. Again, the ambivalence of winning while losing reverberates throughout the blues ethos. Whether waiting for showtime or winding down after a night's work, blues artists drink together and entertain each other with jokes and lies, often reliving their own adventures or accomplishments. Joking relationships, in group humor and competitive word play, fill the incredibly long hours of travel time. Waterloo, Iowa, vocalist Will Campbell playing a festival in Clarksdale, Mississippi, alluded to this function of storytelling: "I don't know why musicians joke all the time, but we did it all the way down here. We left home yesterday about one and got here about three something last night, so I kept them all woke best I could. I didn't go to sleep at all."

Campbell's bandmate guitarist Etheleen Wright added: "We tease each other all the time. That's just something that we do, we try to have fun that way. We laugh all the time because we joke with one another and understand each other that way. Somebody might say something, you know, we have different words we say among ourselves that you might not even understand."

A self-conscious in-group, blues artists use their quick wit to signify, interact with, and entertain fellow musicians and audience alike. Wordsmiths by trade, blues storytellers appreciate the turn of a phrase and are often their own most appreciative audience. I recall musicians laughing with delight at their own verbal dexterity, as when Howard Armstrong said of a gifted musician, "He could play anything from a trombone to a hambone," or when Big Joe Duskin said of a man berating his wife, "He cussed her from a cat to a kitten," or when Mississippi guitarist

Eugene Powell said of showing off his Studebaker, "I would crank it up. I'd tell the boys, 'Listen at that motor frying like ham and eggs.'" Such down-home speech is a mainstay of southern humor, and blues songs are drawn from the same well.

The final section, "The Last Word," serves as a brief goodbye, modeled on the way many blues songs end.

Blues stories, like blues songs, are oral literatures, part of a broader African American oral tradition. Nevertheless, a secondary literary tradition has developed based on transcription of the spoken word that often combines personal autobiography with explanation of the blues.

Over sixty-eight years ago, John and Alan Lomax published *Negro Folksongs as Sung by Leadbelly* (1936), including a collaborative autobiography supposedly based on Huddie Ledbetter's spoken life story as well as transcriptions of his songs. Nearly twenty years later, in 1955, Mississippi-born Big Bill Broonzy, who had just learned to read and write, was determined to expose the inequities in the recording business through a series of letters to Belgian jazz researcher Yannick Bruynoghe. He began a project he initially titled "The Truth About the Blues," which eventually came out as *Big Bill Blues: The Big Bill Broonzy Story*, also a combination of autobiography and song texts, commentary, and some discussion of the blues recording business. A remarkable work, it included an array of tales, lies, and anecdotes proving Broonzy one of the all-time great blues storytellers.

That same year Nat Shapiro and Nat Hentoff's *Hear Me Talking to Ya: The Story of Jazz as Told by the Men Who Made It* expanded the format by using multiple speakers. As the title indicates, it was written as transcribed, the spoken word presented in musician's vernacular. Drawing on dozens of their own interviews, augmented by some print sources, they produced a book in which multiple voices tell a collective story of their art form while detailing their own lives and telling stories about their co-workers. Despite assembling a remarkable cast of speakers, the authors downplayed their own editorial presence. Writing the book was "the story of jazz as told by the musicians whose lives are that story,"[10] connecting individual artists' lives to the general history of the art form. But as they noted, the art form was jazz and they paid limited attention to blues: "But there are parts of the story of jazz that are not covered in full detail. There are the blues. The blues weave through this work—as they inevitably must in any expression of jazz—but the blues deserve and need their own book."[11]

Ten years later, British music scholar Paul Oliver published just such a book, *Conversation with the Blues* (1965). First published in England, the book employed multiple musicians' voices drawn from the author's wealth of interviews. He presented commentary from major blues players in a single, ongoing conversation connected by topic in which multiple voices addressed a limited number of subjects. The result was an artfully constructed collection of narratives supplemented by contextual detail and photographs. Moreover, he paid attention to oral tradition in general, tying blues to the spoken word in the larger context of African American spoken-word performance.

Ten years later, Robert Neff and Tony Conner published *Blues* (1975), which also used musicians' voices to stress the tie between the spoken word and blues song, noting "we hope that the reader will find, as we do, that the remarkable blues men and women in this book literally make the pages sing." A more balanced collection of commentary and photographs, it shared this book's commitment to let the musicians' commentary stand on its own—or as they put it, "to let musicians speak as the music speaks—directly to the listener."[12]

Jazz Anecdotes by Bill Crow was published in 1990, and although it relies primarily on printed sources, it treats musicians stories' as narrative, jokes, or anecdotes that reflect musicians' occupational folklore as well as music history.

Alan Lomax's prize-winning collection of Mississippi traditions, *The Land Where Blues Began* (1993), also drew upon multiple speakers, several of whom also contributed to this book, including Sam Chatmon, David Edwards, Jessie Mae Hemphill, Jack Owens, Eugene Powell, and Joseph Savage. Lomax's ambitious assemblage of song text, social commentary, legends, lies, life story, dance description, and analysis derived from a lifetime of field work and presented transcribed interviews, bits written from memory, and in some cases materials collected by other folklorists.

In 1998 James Fraher published *The Blues Is a Feeling: Voices and Visions of African American Blues Musicians*. A remarkable collection of photographs, it also includes what the author refers to as quotations designed to share with the reader the musicians' "feelings about the music they make—where the blues came from and where it's going—and offers insights into the evolution of a blues artist."[13] Once again, it features a half-dozen artists also in this book and has several parallel accounts, primarily what I refer to as "blues talk," as well as several home-made guitar stories. The primary difference is that his emphasis is on his photographs, which tell their own story, and his quotations are relatively short.

Other scholars and journalists have published traditional tales from blues musicians Big Joe Duskin, Mississippi John Hurt, John Jackson, Mance Lipscomb, James Thomas, Wade Walton, and Booker White, while other artists including Howard Armstrong, John Cephas, Archie Edwards, John Dee Holeman, and Lightning Hopkins have had their storytelling skills documented in film or video format. A number of books, particularly regional histories, have also relied extensively on oral history or the spoken-work format.

Several of the best of these studies are Roger Wood and James Fraher's *Down in Houston Bayou City Blues* (2003), Steve Tracey's *Going to Cincinnati* (1993), and Nathan W. Pearson Jr.'s, *Going to Kansas City* (1987). Dozens of blues artists have published "as told to" biographies; in fact several, including Muddy Waters, B. B. King, and James Brown, have more than one biography to their credit. Other artists who have collaborative autobiographies or biographies which employ the musician's spoken-word commentary include Ruth Brown, Bo Diddley, Honeyboy Edwards, Willie Dixon, Buddy Guy, Wynonie Harris, John Lee Hooker, Elmore James, Louis Jordan, Mance Lipscomb, Eart Palmer, Yank Rachell, Henry Townsend, Little Walter, and Howlin' Wolf.

Finally, since the 1960s, literally hundreds of interviews with blues artists have been published in a wide variety of magazines and journals, including *Downbeat, Cadence, Rolling Stone, 78 Quarterly, Blues Unlimited, Juke Blues, Blues and Rhythm, Blues Revue Quarterly,* and especially *Living Blues,* a thirty-three-year-old publication built around the interview format. As an off-and-on contributor to and full-time supporter of that venerable periodical, I share its editorial policy dedicated to the premises that first, blues is an African American tradition that remains alive and well, and second, those most qualified to interpret the art form are its own traditional practitioners. In the same spirit, *Jook Right On* presents transcriptions of African American artists' own words, devoid of commentary and subservient to no higher critical authority. But at the same time, as this brief survey demonstrates, the stories in *Jook Right On* don't exist in a vac-uum. Whether presented as conversations, quotations, biographies, or stories, they are collaborative efforts involving storyteller, audience, tran-scriber, and reader, each of whom brings their own frame of reference and interpretative skills.

I have been writing about blues autobiography and blues story tellers for over thirty years, addressing such issues as the role of the blues artist in black culture, white stereotypes about blues, and the inter-view tradition. I have also published articles on subjects ranging from jook women to the Appalachian blues. The bulk of this work relies on blues musicians' commentary drawn from interviews with over two hun-dred and thirty artists. *Jook Right On* is the third in what I initially envi-sioned as a connected series tying together spoken-word autobiography and the blues tradition. The first book, *Sounds So Good to Me: The Bluesman's Story* (1984), dealt with the motifs musicians choose to portray their lives as blues artists, and how these subjects work as a shared frame of refer-ence in the interview process. Moreover, it considered the broader cul-tural significance of such topics as homemade instruments, parental and church opposition, and first paying jobs, and examined how the process of repetition shaped such narrative accounts into spoken-word perform-ances, artistic representations of past events, or what I simply call stories.

The second book, *Virginia Piedmont Blues: The Lives and Art of Two Vir-ginia Bluesmen* (1990), was a regional study of two artists, Archie Edwards and John Cephas, both of whom I worked with closely for over twenty-five years. It presented more detailed versions of their life stories and included their repertories and artistic philosophies as well. Where *Sounds So Good to Me* was concerned with the musician's role or the performer's on-stage mask, *Virginia Piedmont Blues* considered the men behind the masks in a more deeply contextualized manner. *Jook Right On,* on the other hand, is a collection of stories pure and simple, and they are intended to be valued for their own sake. I have, however, added brief biographi-cal portraits of each of the contributors that readers can refer to whenever they wish. In a sense it is a "best of" collection designed to highlight blues artists' storytelling skills and is less concerned with questions pertain-ing to either biography or history. Nevertheless, these accounts do have historical importance as personal history, as individual perceptions of blues history, and as a collective story of the blues. As this collection evolved, several related projects, written with my collaborator William H. McCulloch, drew our attention to the wide variety of ways in which people envision or represent blues and blues history. First we contributed thirty-six biographical entries to *American National Biography* (1999), a reference work with a pronounced bias for facts. Here we wrestled with the concerned queries of their fact checkers who wanted details as opposed to the more artistic personal reminiscences the musicians preferred. A second project, *Robert Johnson: Lost and Found* (2003), is a historiography that traced a sixty-plus-year paper trail exploring the ways blues icon Robert Johnson has been represented and elevated from man to myth. Here too we were struck by the multiplicity of representations of the past. Yet in the end we concluded that, despite their differences, history and story are mutually compatible and offer complementary ways of looking at blues lives and blues as an art form.

I hope the reader can "hear" these voices through the medium of print. I have tried to reproduce the speakers' words in a format that does justice to their storytelling skills, yet I realize the difficulty of confining such animated performances to the printed page. Like blues songs, blues stories pose editorial challenges. I hope the reader will bear in mind that what is written represents the final step in a process that began with an interviewer burdened with his own set of preconceptions asking musicians to talk about themselves. Despite my desire to remain in the background, I am deeply involved in the process of putting this book together. I am responsible for collecting the materials, for transcription, selection, and placement. Having worked with these and other transcriptions for years, I know I have made mistakes. I have been talking to blues musicians for well over thirty years and even worked briefly as a musician, witnessing some of the musicians' occupational traditions. Yet I remain an outsider with an outsider's capacity for misunderstanding, and I apologize for mishearing, misspelling, or other transcription errors. My work has been to seek out blues experts and to listen to what they tell me about what they do, and over the years I have become a much better listener. These interviews date back to 1969. Even before that, during the 1960s, I talked with such artists as Sleepy John Estes and J. B. Lenoir, and today I deeply regret not having taped our conversations. I guess I thought they would always be around. As a result, I have overcompensated, and today many musicians would not recognize me without a tape recorder.

I have been allowed into the backstage world of the working blues musician and have had more than my share of fun along the way. I have worked to return favors when and where I could, writing articles, liner notes, or recommending artists to festival promoters or other employers. I have worked with several contributors for as long as twenty-five years, others only briefly, and have unfortunately written too many obituaries. But whether business partner, friend, festival acquaintance, or stranger, all the contributors gave their time generously, passing along the lessons learned and the wisdom earned. I owe them all a terrific debt of gratitude, and I thank them once again.

Clearly these are the words of strong personalities who, for the most part, are not shy about relating the history they lived or sharing the opinions they hold. Expect diversity from this remarkable chorus. At the same time, notice the commonalities, coherence, and harmony of their voices. This cohesiveness stems in part from common experience and participation in similar institutions, but it also derives from a shared commitment to the blues, an art form that has not been given its due respect. But let the stories speak for themselves.

BLUES TALK

The blues was here when the world got here. When Eve and Adam come from the garden. The blues was in them since they got together, man and woman.

JOHN LEE HOOKER

THAT WILL MAKE YOU HAVE THE BLUES
YANK RACHELL

Yank Rachell. Largo, Maryland, October 2, 1993. Photograph by Alex Jones. Courtesy of the Blues Project.

I just liked the blues. It was just a gift for me I guess. And I just would have the blues. When you come from where I come from you would have them way back. You can't hear nothing but the hooting owl. You go to town probably once a month. Get one pair of shoes a year. Man, it's something. You got to get out there and plow all day with two mules.

It wasn't no tractor or nothing. You got to hoe that cotton one row at a time. You hoe two or three rows a day, well, you done a days work. You come home, you got to go draw water, pack water to the house. You got to make a fire to heat the water to take a bath. You got to take a bath in one of those old tin tubs. Didn't have no hot water to turn it on and take a bath. Had to get in a tin tub and tote the water and get it warm before you take a bath. You take a bath and that, well, by the time you do that, you go to bed. You get up the next morning; you got to make a fire in the stove. Didn't have no electric. You got to make kindling, make a fire in the stove to cook and eat. Come back, you have to do the same thing. You got to cut up wood at night to keep the heat going for the fireplace. You got to do all of that, man. That will make you have the blues. Make you have the blacks, to tell the truth.

BORN WITH THE BLUES
PINETOP PERKINS

Yeah, the biggest of the blues come out of Mississippi and Alabama and places like that. You know the thing about it, blues is something just like you're worried about something or another, you can't get it off of your mind. When you were born 'round the Mississippi Delta, you were born with the blues down in there. That where the blues come from. You can't get what you ought to, or what you want, and it seems like everything is going on wrong. You got the blues even if you can't sing them. Like when I was little coming up; I didn't know nothing about no girls or nothing like that. But when I did get up big enough to get a girl and you like her and she goes off and leaves you, man you got the blues so bad then its terrible. Now, if you were to marry and your wife quits you, oh, man, you got the blues even if you can't sing them.

PROTECT THE INNOCENT
JAMES "SUPER CHIKAN" JOHNSON

I asked an old man once, I said, "How do you write a blues song?"

He said, "Well, being you're born and raised in Mississippi, you just write what you see."

So I tried that and I got in trouble.

I went back to the old man he said, "No, you don't write other people's business."

He said, "You write the things you see around you, and use some other name if it looks like it's getting into somebody else's business." He said, "Don't use that person's name, use some other name to protect the innocent."

LOW RUNNING BLUES
SILAS HOGAN

When I made "Trouble at Home,"[1] that verse about the rats and roaches, what made me make that was sitting down at my own house, big rat run across my foot and I jerked it up. And I looked over there through the kitchen and I seen some roaches crawling up there and I started singing "I got rats in my house, I got roaches too."

I made that by looking at what I see. I can make them from what happens to other people too, like when I made that record. See my wife went on vacation and I made "Got a suitcase in her hand and she won't be back no more. Ain't it sad when your love's walking out your door."

You make them, by looking at what people are doing. I could probably make one about us here eating dinner if I wanted to. I like them low down blues; that way back yonder blues. Something that worried people's minds. Yeah, it worries your mind, them low running blues. Like you got a girlfriend and somebody takes her away from you it don't take you long to take the blues. You can take the blues just terrible then.

WHY ME?
J. OTIS WILLIAMS

I was liking this girl who was nineteen. I must have been about fifteen. I knew I didn't have a chance, but she was so friendly and nice and so beautiful. And this Sunday afternoon, I was hanging around up there in this cafe called Belle Sykes Cafe at the time. I'd hang around and talk with her. And she left and went to Greenwood with this grown man.

He had a nice car, Chevrolet with monotone gutted mufflers on it, had that nice sound to it. And she came and told me, say, "Well I'm fixing to go to Greenwood. I'll be seeing you."

And it was just like my world came to an end. I remember standing at that juke box and at that time you could put a quarter in and get six plays and I played Little Walter's "This Is a Mean Old World," fifty cents worth. Stood there and listened to it over and over again:

**THIS MEAN OLD WORLD TO HAVE TO LIVE IN BY YOURSELF,
CAN'T GET THE ONE YOU LOVE HAVE TO USE SOMEBODY ELSE.²**

I'll never forget that Sunday evening. Her name was Lily Frances. First time I met the blues was one Sunday about four o'clock.

And the blues walked in and I said, "Blues, why me?"

And the Blues said, "Why not you?"

SOMETHING'S GOT TO GIVE
JAMES "T-MODEL" FORD

T-Model Ford and friend. Clarksdale, Mississippi, August 7, 1993. Photograph by Barry Lee Pearson.

My real name is James Ford but everybody calls me "T-Model Ford" and the "Tail Dragger." I waited until I got fifty-eight years old before I picked up a guitar. I'm sixty-nine now. Well, my wife, she had bought me a guitar and amplifier.

So I come in one night and she say, "You see your present."
I seen it, I say, "Yeah."

I went over and tore it open; she had bought me brand new guitar and amp. I couldn't play it. I didn't know how to, but then my wife left me. When she left me I grabbed a hold to it. I been playing ever since. So don't nothing like that worry me. When the blues get to worrying you, something's got to give.

THE CAT AND DOG LEAVE
EDDIE CUSIC

Eddie Cusic. Clarksdale, Mississippi, August 2, 1997. Photograph by Barry Lee Pearson.

What really gives you the blues, you go out there sharecropping and you think you're gonna get so much at the end of the year. And the end of the year comes, and the man asks you did you need any more of whatever you need and that's it. Well, you done worked for him all the year. You have to do the best you can. A lot of times you had to work by the day, or pick cotton by the hundred or something to have you something for Christmas. Anything don't go right, that you can't get lined up right, that give you the blues. Then look like the blues, it's good for you. You can sing the blues and look like it solves the problem. It don't, but it helps. In other words, you just sing the blues and it get the sadness off, it look like. Like you know your wife or something, your old lady can leave, the cat and dog leave home, don't nothing be right, look like. You can sing the blues and that pacifies you.

NOT DEPRESSING
KOKO TAYLOR

Koko Taylor performing at National Heritage Fellowships program, Washington, D.C., September 2, 2004. Photograph by Michael G. Stewart

A lot of people that don't really have the experience to know, or aren't used to listening to blues, they think, they describe blues in their mind as old, slow, drawn out, depressing music, you know. You hear a lot of people say, "No I don't like blues because it's too depressing." I'm sure you've heard folks say that. But, you see, blues is not depressing. My blues is designed to make people look up, to look forward and not to look back. A lot of people come up to me after a concert and say, "You know that song you did, 'You Can Have My Husband,' aw, it just made my day."

LIKE BEING A GOOD MINISTER
BIG JESSE YAWN

Big Jesse Yawn with Archie
Edwards. Largo, Maryland,
September 14, 1996. Photograph
by Barry Lee Pearson.

Blues is a deep, deep feeling where you let out how you really feel inside
through a song. What I do, or when I go on stage to do a performance,
this is a normal setting. Anything that's inside of me, from days gone by
even, it all comes out through a song . . . the good, the bitter, the ugly.
It all comes out. Consequently, when I'm done, I'm usually just like a
man that's been born again. I'm completely relieved of all frustrations. Oh
they will reoccur, most of them, but temporarily I'm floating. I don't care.

Well, I try to reach the people in the audience. Being a blues singer
is almost like being a good minister or preacher. You got a congregation
out there, we'll just say for the benefit of what we're saying, an audience. You try to reach somebody. If you don't reach them, I think you
defeated the purpose. But if you can communicate with them, and they're
feeling what you feel even if it's not as deep as what you're feeling,
that's it; you've accomplished something.

What I'm gonna say now is a little far fetched but, a preacher has
a job to do. So do I. In some weird way or the other I feel like a lot of
times in singing to audiences I reach them, and very possibly relieve
them of some of their bad feelings, ill feelings.

I've had people say, "I just feel better all over. What you said was
what I wanted to hear and I just feel better about it."

NO PSYCHIATRISTS
NAP TURNER

A lot of the young people say, "I don't want to hear no blues," because they think that the only thing it's about is sadness. But it's not. The blues talks about every day living, things that happen every day. Like they got an old blues song, the dude says his woman has left him and he says he's gonna go and lay his head down on the railroad track. But the kicking line is, "but when I hear that train coming, I'm gonna snatch my head back." So even in that there's a kind of hope and a kind of surviving. See what I'm saying. I mean, they got all kinds of lyrics about different life situations, but the amazing thing is how we were able to survive with that. You know there was a time when black people didn't have no psychiatrists and psychologists, therapists and all that; wasn't no going nowhere and sitting down on no couch. You had to sing the blues or go to church or get you a rabbit foot so that you could survive.

I'M THE DOCTOR
ROOSEVELT SYKES

Now some people don't understand. They think a blues player has to be worried, troubled to sing the blues. That's wrong. It's a talent. If every man with worry could play the blues, why another guy's worried to death and he can't sing it. So blues is sorta thing on people like the doctor, I'll put it this way. There's a doctor, he has medicine; he's never sick, he ain't sick, but he has stuff for the sick people. See, you wouldn't say, "Call the doctor."

"I'm the doctor."

"Oh, you're a sick man."

"No. I just work on the sick people."

So the blues player, he ain't worried and bothered, but he got something for the worried people. Doctor, you can see his medicine, you can see his patient. Blues, you can't see the music, you can't see the patient because it's soul. So I works on the soul and the doctor works on the body.

LIVING THE BLUES

I'm from the lowland, the swamp. I'm from
where the blues came from, and that's
where I'm going before it ends up and
something happens to me. I'm going back
to the lowlands. . . . that's where the blues
came from, right off that old country farm.

GEORGE "WILD CHILD" BUTLER

WORK

PARCHMAN
EUGENE "SONNY BOY NELSON" POWELL

After I got nine, I moved on to a place called Lombardy, up there near Parchman, Mississippi, on to the free part. Not in the prison. See, now it's a railroad coming through there, and one side of the railroad belonged to Parchman, one side belonged to free people. So that's where momma went and she raised me.

I heard people singing at work in Parchman Prison;[1] now that's where you hear your good singing at. Them boys would be, well, them men would work them so hard, beat them up and he would be sorry he done what he did do that caused him to be in there. The blues mostly come from prisoners feeling down in heart. Know he got to work. Know if he don't work, he gonna get beat up and all such stuff as that. See, if you broke the rule some of them would take a chance on running out from under that gun. Some of them get killed. Some guy would shoot him down.

But some, they got to the place just like if I was going to tell you, "Tomorrow, I'm gonna let you go home. You think you could get away if I allow you a chance?" You might say, "Yeah."

But then you out in the fields working or doing something; then he'll break for the near side where there ain't many guards and try and cross where the man that had told him "You come by me" was, "I ain't gonna shoot you." Guards start shooting at you and miss, you know, let him get away. Some of them, because they like you and you don't lie to him about nothing and don't steal and treat him right, he'll come to like you, say, "I'm gonna let you go home one of these days."

But now if you get one those mean son of a guns, he'll kill you if you just bat your eye. Kill you. Beat your ass until blood run down your leg. I've seen that when I was a little boy. Yeah, I've seen that. They had a dog in the penitentiary, a bloodhound. His ears would hang down on the ground. They liked that dog so good, he caught so many prisoners for them, that they had a gold tooth put in there and a gold tooth put over there in his mouth.

THEY HATED TO SEE ME LEAVE
DAVID SAVAGE

Then they'd make you try to run because you got about six or seven guys standing out there with thirty-thirty Winchesters; and they was hard to miss, too. They see a rabbit running and shoot it. You *know* what they'd do for a big man. So I stuck with that until I got away from up there.

Sometimes they'd plant so much cotton up there, wintertime would catch that cotton in the field. A lot of butter beans, them little bunch butter beans, them things would have ice on them and you had to get out there and pick them with your bare hands. And if you build a fire, the guards, they shoot it out.

Of course you got treated according to how you carried yourself. If you was one of the best you got the best deal. If you acted all right, they'd treat you all right. I guarded up there seven and a half years and the sergeant told me, say, "You catch them fellows out there with a fire in the field, shoot that fire out."

There was a bunch of trustees around carrying guns; and I waited until he got through talking and I eased over to him and I said, "Look, Sarge," I say, "I been picking cotton out there with them fellows, too, in that ice."

I said, "And their hands get to hurting. How they gonna pick cotton without a fire?"

"Well you don't have to shoot the fire, just scare them."

And that's just what I'd do . . . just scare them. I wouldn't shoot no fire out. So me and the guards got along all right. They hated to see me leave them up there. But I was glad to get away.

I BELIEVE I'LL LET YOU GO HOME
JOE SAVAGE

I fooled around after I came out of the Army. So I fooled around and got in trouble and they put me, took me to jail. And I took me a spoon and made me a file and I broke out. And took out across the cotton field. It took them a long time before they could catch me but they did catch me. Then finally they sent me to Parchman. So they beat me pretty bad when I first got there. I headed the row. So the sergeant looked at me one morning, he heard me singing.

He say, "Joe, Why you got so long?"

I say, "I killed a man and I was wrong."

He said: "I'll tell you what I'm gonna do." He said, "I believe I'll let you go home."

After I had been there two and a half year, he says, "You too good a man to be bound down." He say: "So I'm gonna let you go home." He let me go. I went free.

BABY, PLEASE DON'T GO
J. OTIS WILLIAMS

My mother used to take me to the cotton field in various places in the Delta. We'd go on the truck. You had to get up before day in the morning get on the back of a truck and usually stand up all the way out there. And when you get in the field the dew would still be on. But one thing that a lot of good cotton choppers used to do would be singing; and this one guy who I patterned after had been on Parchman, and that means you can chop as fast as you can walk. So I used to be ashamed of myself because when I first started chopping cotton my mother had to come back and catch my row up because I'd get way behind. And this guy started going to the field with us who hadn't been long come out of Parchman. He wore a red bandanna around his neck and one on his head, and he would usually sing "Baby Please Don't Go."[2] And I realized that "Baby Please Don't Go" gave the right beat; it had the right cadence.

My father, he'd tell me how to chop cotton, he said, "You got to get you a steady gait. If you get a steady gait, then it won't be hard to you." But I would hit a lick and stand up, hit a lick and stand up. But I followed this guy and he would sing "Baby Please Don't Go," and he put all these different verses in it. But he'd be rocking on it. He worked right with the beat. And I just started doing what he was doing, and I got to the point where I could chop as fast as I could walk almost. It's all in the technique. I didn't have the same kind of pressure that he had to learn to chop fast because, see, they would beat you at Parchman if you were too slow. But it was a habit of mine to get me a good song and just go at it. And I learned to chop cotton. I forgot it was work.

HE WOULD TELL ME TO LEAD TO THE FIELD
CORA FLUKER

Cora Fluker. Clarksdale, Mississippi, August 7, 1993. Photograph by Barry Lee Pearson.

When I was a little girl, my daddy had us out on a plantation. So, well, when we used to go to the cotton fields, I would lead the field. The white man, the boss in the field, he heard me, and he would tell me to lead the field. I was the leader of the singing of all the songs. Mr. Poole always put me there. So, I'd get to hoeing and get in the front of them, oh, I was little girl about twelve years old. I started at twelve, singing all them songs like "Bring 'em Down Lord." And they would be chopping behind me; "Sing Low Sweet Chariot" and all that.

I would sing,

GOT ME WAY DOWN HERE
GOT ME WAY DOWN HERE

**BY THE ROLLING FORKS
AND TREAT ME LIKE A DOG.**

I was singing "Baby, Please Don't Go," and I got interested in it. So I got some screen wire, got me a piece of plank, and I made me a guitar.

PLOWING AND JAMMING
DAVID SAVAGE

Before I left Mississippi I used to sing the blues out there in the cotton fields. My dad, he was a preacher, he didn't want to hear that. No, man, I'll tell you why. He said anybody in his house had to be a Christian, and I'm gonna tell you if he came in the house and we had the radio on, blues on the radio, we had to cut that radio off. If we had a hi-fi or something like that, when he walked up, we had to cut that off. Get on out of there. But when I caught my dad going to his hunting traps—he'd go for his traps every year in the morning—and while he was gone, well, that would give me a chance to sing a couple of blues songs. My mother, she was a midwife. She wouldn't be there one half the time, going delivering babies. My brothers Joe, Daniel, and Cleve [and I], we were out there in the field, picking cotton, or chopping cotton. Then sometime I'd come and get the mules and plow. And I'd be plowing and jamming. I'd be behind the mules there walking along and I'd be singing them songs.

QUITTING TIME WOULD BE GETTING CLOSE
JUNIOR KIMBROUGH

Junior Kimbrough. Clarksdale, Mississippi, August 6, 1993. Photograph by Barry Lee Pearson.

We worked hard, lots harder than these people work now. We'd have to go to the field and plow mules; we'd have to pick cotton by hand; go out and bale hay. Now that was work. Now I done all of that. Pick cotton, bale hay, pull corn, plow mules, all that. And I would sing. Most of the time the singing would be late in the evening getting close to quitting time. We'd be picking cotton or either pulling corn, and then we'd start in singing, I would. And there'd maybe be somebody else there singing too. They'd be getting glad because quitting time would be getting close. Then they start in singing. Then I'd go home, take a bath, and get my guitar and put it on my shoulder and go over to my girl's house. Play there until around about, well, we weren't allowed to stay there no later than nine o'clock. That was the girl and parents' bedtime. So we'd play around there like that through the week. Then on the weekend they let us stay up a little later.

WHOA MEANS STOP
DOUG QUIMBY

Frankie and Doug Quimby. Cuyahoga State Park, Ohio, September 21, 1984. Photograph by Dexter Hodges. Courtesy of the National Council for the Traditional Arts.

When I got in the fields I could sing the blues. The old folks would say I could really "whoop" them. But you're just singing a song while you're out there working and it seems like it makes your work more easy. You sing and it makes you more happier while you're working. So that's what I would do, sing the blues or maybe a spiritual, crying behind a mule; so that's how I learned.

When you get to singing you talk about the "gee" and "haw" to the mule. "Gee" means right, "haw" means left. "Giddy up" means go forward, and "whoa" means stop. Any word that sounds like "whoa," a mule will stop because it thinks you are saying "whoa." You could say, "oh," "no" or "so and so." But when you're singing most of the time you say, "oh," like that, and the mule will stop because he thinks you're saying whoa. So I'd sing a lot out in the fields and I could just picture myself as I was singing, that one day I'd be singing before a big crowd. I didn't really think it would happen but then it finally did.

A MULE CAN SING THE BLUES
LAVESTER "BIG LUCKY" CARTER

In the evening time, long about sundown, my daddy used to sing "Smokestack Lightning" and all those tunes like the "Wolf."[3] The "Wolf" would of had a problem with him when he sang those blues, I'm telling you. But you know, when you start singing the blues that old mule will lay those ears down like that, and it's a moan that a mule can give. Brother, don't nobody know this but he [Eddie Cusic] and me. Honestly, yes, sir, he will moan to the blues. He would actually be that sound that he would make, would blend in with what you were singing. I was a little boy I used to listen to it. I said, "Well I'll be doggoned."

I thought about it the other day. Man, that's something. A man think I'm lying when I say a mule can sing the blues, but shoot. And you know they know exactly when they're supposed to quit. And if you don't take him out to the yard, he'll take you, plow and all, when it come time. That's how you can tell time without a watch.

MULES AND MEN
EDDIE CUSIC

Later on in the evening, man, if that old mule don't like you, you can't do nothing with him if you treat him wrong. But that old mule, later on in the evening, well, when the sun get low it's time to work then. You get one of those mules and he like you, you like him, and you go to singing the blues, a lot of times he'll wear his last damn pair of shoes out. When I go to hollering the blues that mule says, "Hoo, hoo, hoo." Late in the evening, that's right. But get one of those young mules that ain't been around, that son of a bitch will carry you to the lot when he gets ready. You talking about "Whoa," you better not be letting him go, he'll drag you home. And then what's gonna happen if you think he's all right and you go to take a leak or something, he'll have gone and tore up half the cotton all across the field.

But that mule is something else man. You know he ain't dumb when you can talk to him. You and him getting along, you can throw down the line. But if he don't want to do anything he gonna act crazy as hell and two lines wouldn't do no good.

HE'S GONNA QUIT AT QUITTING TIME
CLARENCE BUTLER

The mule's the smartest animal in the world. See, a horse will work for you until it falls dead. That mule will work until it gets tired then he will sit down until he's rested. He won't work anymore. Sometimes if he doesn't sit down, he'll stand still. You can beat him and beat him but he ain't moving until he rests.

I plowed mules myself, and we had one would work his heart out; but if he got tired, and you couldn't pass dinnertime, because he would quit. But he's the strongest, the best worker. When you work him hard all you got to do is at rest time, rest. But if you work on and on and try to work him, I don't care, you can sing to him all you want to. You can blow your harp to him all you want to, but he going to quit at a certain time. And he's going to quit at quitting time. Like, if we gonna knock off at five o'clock because we go out there before day. When day break, we done plowed almost a half field. Yeah, we start out there with lanterns. We start out there before the sunrise. Start about five o'clock. It's still dark.

I'M GONNA FIND MINE
ALGIA MAE HINTON

I was raised in Johnson County, North Carolina, and I done a lot of work. We picked cotton, picked up corn, shell corn, shuck corn, you know, prime tobacco. We done a lot of work in the field, pulling up peanuts.

Algia Mae Hinton. Vienna, Virginia, July 12, 1980. Photograph by John Putnam. Courtesy of the National Council for the Traditional Arts.

It didn't bother me because we would dance in the field. See, we always danced, honey.

My daddy would get in the field, say, "Algia, what you doing?"

"Nothing."

But I'd be just dancing and we would sing this here song about "I'm Looking for the Man That Don't love Jesus." That was a spiritual. And my sister would say, "Lord, I'm looking for the man."

And we'd come in, "I'm a-looking. I'm looking."

I said, "Lord, I'm gonna find mine."

I'VE BEEN A MAN EVER SINCE I WAS NINE
JOHNNY SHINES

I left home when I was nine years old because I felt I wasn't cared for. My stepmother, I could hear her and my father fussing all night. My step-daddy, every time he said something it was, "That goddamn boy; that goddamn boy." And I just figured neither one of them cared for me, and I got out of the way. Went my own way. And I've been a man ever since I was nine years old.

I left my home and worked my way down to Louisiana and I got a good job as a driver on a sawmill pulling slabs from the carriage. There were these big knots that you cut off a log, limbs, you know, had been sawed off. I had a hook and I had to throw this hook in that knot and pull it away from the carriage and keep that knot from turning the carriage over and killing the men that were on the carriage. And I had to do it in due time. And I was only nine years old, and some of those things weighed a thousand pounds. My hands would be so raw and bloody sometimes it would stick to the hook. But I had to eat and I had to sleep so I didn't give up.

Finally one day the boss man, the big boss, come through say, "How long has this boy been here?"

"About three months."

"How much you pay him?"

Say: "About seventy-five cents a day."

"Well, give him a dollar and a half a day like you do the rest of the men. He deserves it."

So they decided to pay me a dollar and a half a day, three meals, and a place to sleep. In the timber camps they had a place where you could gamble and things like that. Then on payday if the women would come out to meet the payday, some of them would go back filthy rich, some of us just go back filthy.

RED RIVER BLUES
ARCHIE EDWARDS

We would go out in the wood and cut down trees and you could hear those guys singing the blues all over the woods there. They would sing while they were working cutting down a tree, sing while they were cutting until the tree drops. It was a musical thing. You hear one guy over there singing the blues and the other one answering back. They would sing all along the line. Somebody would be singing all day. It kind of makes you think of the old songs from the levee camps, but they consisted mostly of prisoners. In the sawmills the guys had the same spirit—sing while they work. Of course, they didn't have any guns, any dogs on them but they would just sing the blues alone by themselves.

So I'm listening to all this and I said, "Well, I'm gonna sing these sawmill songs one day." You know, they sang "Red River Blues" where it has the verse,

I KNOW, YES, I KNOW, WHY THE POOR BOYS DON'T DRAW NO MORE, BECAUSE THE LINE STARTS AT THE PAY TABLE AND GOES STRAIGHT TO THE COMMISSARY DOOR [4]

Well, I know about that because this is what really happened. They work all the week and they would buy cigarettes and candy and what-not on credit, you see. And when the foreman sets up his pay table in a little tent, you go there to the door and call your name. Everybody lines up like they do in the Army. Line up and call your name. You walk up and they hand you a little envelope.

Well, the first thing they do then after they deducted out what you owed them, the rest of it they would take and go straight to the commissary and buy cigarettes and sodas and candy.

So this is why they say, "I know why the poor boys don't draw no more, because the line start at the pay table and goes straight to the commissary door."

I COME UP HARD
HARRY HYPOLITE

They used to sing songs in the sugar cane fields. I got an aunt in an old folks home now, my aunt worked in the cane fields. At them times, they used to pay you in the field. They used to pay you when the grinding season was over with. They wouldn't pay you, like every week or anything like that; they pay you when the grinding's done. So my aunt, my mama's sister, worked the whole season, the grinding season. Her money what she was supposed to have made, they took it and give it to the doctor for me, for when I was born. Took her money for when I was born. I go to see her now and we talk about it. I bring my guitar and I go play sometimes over there. But I cries, too, because it brings me memories of my mom and her.

Then, when I come up, I was working in the field. I used to cut sugar cane for a dollar a ton. I come up hard. Nothing was given to me. But I learned experience. Now I have more sense about life than I had before. A few things they pound in my head and beat in my head. I learned how to speak French before I learned how to speak English. See when I started going to the Notre Dame school, the Catholic school, that's when learned how to speak English.

You know things change. Life is not the same way like it used to be; I could go in some places and, man, everybody knew each other. I could play some dances, boy, and everybody knows you. It was not much money. I used to stop at the baker shop and get what you call a Washington Pie. It was a big old piece of cake, but it had raisins and all that stuff in it to eat. And it was five cents. A nickel. Nickel is big money. You think I'm joking. The guys laugh at me now. A nickel was some big money; mister, a quarter, twenty-five cents was some *big* money. But they laugh at me now because I be talking about it. But I know what a dollar is.

FROM CAN TO CAN'T
"UNCLE JESSE" WHITE

I was born in 1920 and I was raised up in the country. I wasn't raised up around no town. We lived about five miles from the little old town Terry, Mississippi, and my daddy had me in the field picking cotton when I was five years old.

Now my grandkids, they don't know what a field is. And the older I got, the bigger the sack he put on me. That's the way I come up. He learned me how to pick cotton by telling me, "If you pick one hundred and fifty pounds you can knock off." I got so I could pick that by twelve o'clock, one hundred and fifty pounds of cotton. So that was my life coming up. And then I went to plowing mules in 1937. I was plowing a mule, and I tell you I was getting fifty cent a day plowing them from can to can't. That means when you can see to when you can't see. That's what we call plowing from can to can't. Plow them all day long and get out there at night and do that, well, I was young then; it didn't bother me. That's right. I was making two dollars and fifty cents a week.

My kids tell me: "Now Daddy, I wouldn't have done that."

I say, "Yes you would have worked for that; you'd been glad to work for that two dollars and fifty cents a week."

See wages was cheap. I was making two dollars and fifty cents working a week and then I was getting five dollars to blow the harmonica. That's all I was getting. But that sounds like good money back at that time though. Five dollars does.

We was playing at some little old jook houses like out, they had one out from the little old town. A guy that was on the plantation was running a place out from the little old town. We'd go out there and party out there at night. But, see, back at that time we didn't have no amplifiers or nothing, but you know it's funny; back then, it seemed like those harps sounded louder. I could hear this guy Ellis Johnson used to blow harmonica, you could hear him coming down the road, you know, blowing that harp. It just sounded that good. Now, if you were playing one of those harps away from the amp, you can't hardly hear it at all.

MY DAD MADE THE BEST
ARCHIE EDWARDS

Corn and tobacco was about the only field work that we did because they didn't have cotton in Virginia where I lived. So corn and tobacco was the two things that we had to help take care of; the wheat would grow by itself, but we did have to harvest it later on in the year. We'd plant plenty potatoes, white potatoes, sweet potatoes, and in the garden we'd put the beans, cabbage, beets, whatever. I did pluck a lot of tobacco. We grow tobacco. Call it priming tobacco, pick off about eight or ten leaves. The rest of it, take a tobacco knife and whack it out, call it cutting tobacco.

Franklin County, Virginia, was the corn liquor capitol of the world, and my daddy, he made the best. Oh, back in the thirties, that was the only thing that he could do for survival to keep the family going; because we had several droughts there during the thirties and it was just so hot and dry until you couldn't make anything. So, during the time that he couldn't grow a crop, you know, he would make whiskey. So that was kind of a shaky survival, but he made it. The law was around every day looking for people making moonshine, but somehow he got lucky enough to make it and get out of the hollow before the law came. So he was never caught. He was always able to get in these hills, hollows, and make just a little corn liquor. He used to work for other people but, after that, he started making some for himself. He kept a little liquor somewhere around in the bushes there where a man could come up and if he wanted a half a gallon or a gallon he would sell it to him. It kept him in spare change to buy a little groceries with.

Back in the country the only thing you need to buy was sugar, salt and pepper, and a little seasoning for your food, you know. And so he made it pretty well. We used to buy coal oil then. We didn't have any electricity. They'd have this big old lantern with the chimneys on them, you know, shades on them. Fill that with oil and it would last you for about four or five months. You only light it when it gets dark. Most of the time in the country you go to bed before it got dark, so it was a very inexpensive life in the country. So we came over pretty good; sell our little corn liquor. And me and my brother, we would carry wood for them, and they would give us a little bit . . . half a gallon, a big old gallon. Next thing you know, we would have two or three gallons of the stuff saved up.

We bought our first old Model-T Ford—not a Model-T, but a Model-A Ford—selling whiskey and working in a sawmill. Yeah, we lived a pretty decent life in the country, pretty decent. I call it good times when times were hard, because we used to have fun. So I started off knowing how to handle corn liquor, but we didn't drink it like the older guys did. I didn't start drinking the stuff until I left home. Now I get mad with myself every time I get a taste of corn liquor. My God Almighty, I was down there where it was and I didn't drink it! And here I am now, crazy about the stuff.

SOMETHING TO TALK ABOUT
DOCTOR ROSS

Well I come from a little country town they call Tunica, Mississippi. It was five boys and six girls, so I come from a large family and I'm the baby of that family. My father's name is Jake Ross and my mother's named Lulu Ross and we was farmers. They was farmers. And my father and them used to work over a hundred and seven acres of land. And they make a lot of cotton. I was a little boy coming up, I used to be the water boy. I take water to the fields for them. And my sisters and them used to chop, and some of my brothers would plow. My father was mostly a new-ground man. He'd clean up the woods about hundreds of acres.

On the farm there always was someone having a birthday party. Well, this was just a good time, showing appreciation, you know. They say, "Well, you come over, we gonna have a horn of home brew." The boys I played with, they loved that beer. We'll have a horn of home brew and corn whiskey; they call it "white lightening." We'd have all that plenty to eat. I wouldn't be drinking nothing but a pop. We'll have you plenty of pop, soda water. So we'd go and play from seven-thirty maybe on up through eleven-thirty. Eleven-thirty come we all go home. Next day get up go on back in the fields. Then we have something to talk about.

CHRISTMAS MONEY
HENRY DORSEY

I been working cotton ever since I was big enough. That was when I was three or four years old. I was out there with my family, you know, ever since then. I had a little old pillowcase. I'd pick some cotton, put it in there, and pour it in my mama's sack. She would pay me a dime or fifteen cents. Then I had money; I was about five or six. I would hear people singing old cotton field blues. They would do hollering songs like a prison song like:

IF TIME DON'T GET NO BETTER HERE
I'M GONNA MOVE ON DOWN THE LINE

Oh, yes sir, people sang in the field old Delta blues. It was hard work but didn't nobody complain. Back then it was the only way they had to make a living. They just get out there and work hard and sweat, come in get their bath, eat supper, which was fried hog meat, molasses, mostly, and biscuits. That was one of the main meals. Well, you milked the cow you had milk and bread, corn bread. Most everybody, see, had a hog and they raised corn too. And sometimes, Christmas time, they just, they take the corn put it in like a corncrib until around Christmas time. Then they sells the corn to get some Christmas money. You didn't have to have too much money then. Most all you had to buy was like flour. You didn't have to buy no lard because you raised your hog, milk the cow, just about everybody milked a cow. We did. That's where I learned how to milk. I can do it with both hands. And we had butter, bread, corn bread, grind some corn, you know, have a meal. Good old milk and bread, sweet milk, clabber milk, buttermilk, all that's good. Them was the good old days for me.

THEN WAS GOOD DAYS, THESE ARE BAD DAYS
BIG JACK JOHNSON

I had to pick cotton, chop cotton, saw wood. I had to work at the gin, run a cotton picker, run a combiner. I plowed mules. I put in corn, lima beans. I did all that stuff. You know, a lot of people can't take it. "Plow those mules. You did that?"

Well, somebody had to do it. Man, it ain't no big thing to plow no goddamn mule, or chop cotton or pick cotton, that ain't no big deal. Somebody had to chop it. They all got to live. That's how our living was made. If we don't pick cotton or chop cotton, what are we gonna do? Wasn't no big factories like there are today or all this other stuff. Or cotton pickers or combines. Wasn't none of that kind of stuff. So a man worked with his hands in the soil, know what I mean, called a dirt farmer. He's out really dirt farming.

Back then, all the food was planted. The only thing you had to buy then was like black pepper, salt, and coffee. You raise your hogs, got your meat, salt meat. You make sausage out of the hog, you get your lard from the hog. Then you had your chickens. Chicken lay all the eggs you wanted. You had your cow; you had your milk, your butter. Well, shit, you hear what I'm saying. That didn't cost you nothing. And then you go in the woods and cut wood, all the wood you want you rack up. Now you got to pay your oil and light bill and gas bill. Everything you put your hand on, you got to pay. You had everything out there; you had your chickens, your hogs, cows. All that's gone bye-bye. That was the good days then. Don't talk about bad days. Then was good days, these are bad days.

A ROUGH TIME
DAVID "HONEYBOY" EDWARDS

David "Honeyboy" Edwards.
Washington, D.C., June 1991.
Photograph by Richard Strauss.
Courtesy of the Smithsonian Center
for Folklife and Cultural Heritage.

In the towns, the little cities like you stay in, they had something they call the "Hog Law."[5] Like if you was a farmer and you didn't have enough labor on your plantation to keep your farm cleaned out, well that farmer go to the city hall and pretty soon one of them comes out, say, "We'll get them niggers out the city, they ain't doin' us no good." Then they put on something like the "Hog Law." If they caught you anytime that day, they'd lock you up. You supposed to be working somewhere, you understand?

So the days when I wouldn't work, I had a girlfriend. She cooked for white people, come home with my dinner in her hand, all this stuff the white people left from dinner. The white people down south have always eat good. They had steaks, chicken and stuff, and throw away more food than we could get 'cause they was gettin' all of it. You know what I mean?

So she would bring home the meal and say, "Honey, here's your dinner."

I'm layin' in the house, see, I wouldn't come out until six o'clock 'cause they might pick me up and arrest me 'cause I ain't choppin' no cotton or pickin' no cotton. I wasn't going out there. I stay in the house, put a fan on, stay in the house all day long. Stay until six o'clock. When I come out, they don't know if I had been in the country or not.

And sometimes when the levee breaks, high water breaks, they'd pick the boys up out of the streets and they wouldn't ask you nothing: "Come on, go on to work."

Stacking them there sacks down at the levee, stop the water from comin' in the city. They wouldn't say how much they give you or nothing, just "Come on, get on the levee, get them sacks and stack them up over there."

"Yes sir."

And after you get through they might give you a couple of dollars. But you *got* to do that. That was a rough time down there, a rough time.

YOU STAY OUT OF THE GRAVEYARD, I'LL KEEP YOU OUT OF JAIL
EUGENE "SONNY BOY NELSON" POWELL

Well, my boss man he liked me so good. He knew I wouldn't steal his stuff and he would always give me a break.

He'd say: "Now Red. . . ." He called me Red. "Red?"

"Yes sir."

Now me and him were about the same age. Now I was calling him "W.T." at first. He didn't tell me not to call him that. So I got to looking at him one day, I said, well, he's a white man, he wants somebody to "Mister" him. I believe I'll do it. And so when I started to "Mister" him, there wasn't nothing that I wanted or asked for that I couldn't get it, his car or anything. He was just nice to me; the whole family of them.

His mother, when I got mad and left the place, well, she come and found me and told me, said, "Red, you get ready, and come on back home."

Say, "It just don't seem like home no more. You come on home. You know you're welcome here. Come on back. I'll make W.T. give you some money."

I go back and W.T. just as nice to me as can be. Me and him go out sometimes shooting targets, killing rabbits, I don't know what all. I had a pretty automobile.

Sometimes he want to go off and he say: "Red, lend me your car and you take my old tractor and drive that."

I say: "All right."

I'd do it, and he liked that. He used to tell the other white folk, "If it wasn't for that nigger I don't know what I'd do. God damn it! I don't want no son of a bitch to bother him. He tends to his own business and he don't mind working."

Me and another fellow got into it gambling. Me and him got into it and got in a fight. He talking about killing me and I'm talking about killing him, and Mr. W.T., I went up there and told him about it.

I said, "I might have to kill a man." I said, "I want to know can you help me?"

He say, "Oh yeah, who is it?"

I told him.

He went down there and cussed that nigger out, and told him, "If you lay a weighted hand or shoot a pistol in the air around him, I'm gonna put you in the penitentiary."

And he told me to sell all the whiskey and beer I wanted. He say, "I can't keep the revenue man off you. I can't do that. But now, if you keep the revenue man off you, I'll keep the police off you."

And he did. You know how people will get jealous? They got jealous of me, a lot of them colored guys back there, say, "Go on, God damn you. I believe that's your brother anyhow."

I say, "He is." Yeah it was good to me and didn't nobody bother me. No. He say, "You stay out of the graveyard, I'll keep you out of jail."

DOWN IN THE BOTTOM
TED BOGAN

It used to be around there, it's like a guy would come in town and see a lot of guys idling say, "You all want to work?"

Say, "Yes."

He'd offer to pay. If you made a dollar a day at that time, you was doing good. He'd come up and tell you he's giving you five dollars a day. Aw, they'd just jump at that you know. You get them down there in the swamp. You get 'em there, then they'd have shotguns. Slave labor. Make them work for them. That's what they call it, "The Bottom." "In the Bottom." Take them out like in the swamp. On the chain gang they have heavy chains, stripes, and have your legs chained. But the ones that got the chain on, they went to trial. But the ones in the bottom, they didn't know what trial was.

SOMETHING ABOUT MISSISSIPPI
LITTLE SAMMY DAVIS

Yeah, I'm from Mississippi. I left there when I was fourteen years old and I ain't been back. And I'm sixty-seven now. [*Laughs.*] I never been back, not even to play a gig. I didn't tell nobody I was gonna leave, but I just got out of there because there wasn't nothing there. Its nothing left, man. You know you gonna work yourself to death. I'm gonna tell you the truth, man, if you want to know something. I'm gonna tell you something about Mississippi. My aunt was cooking for people. My aunt was cooking for people and when she got ready to eat her dinner, she had to go in the fucking outside and get it. She couldn't eat in the house. She could cook in there, but she couldn't eat. Now that's just how it was. I said, "Shit, I ain't got no business in a place like this."

PLAY: THE WEEKEND

ALL THE WEEKEND
JOHN CEPHAS

John Cephas at home in Woodford, Virginia, 1988. Photograph by Nick Spitzer. Courtesy of the National Council for the Traditional Arts.

After work you come home, change your clothes, take a nice hot bath and dress up and put on your weekend best clothes. You get your instrument and you always know there would be some central place, somebody's house where everybody would kind of meet up. It may be a family member or maybe a friend, but invariably there was someplace where something was going on. People would come and go. They'd be coming in and out all the time maybe fifty or sixty people. Start on Friday and last through Saturday. They'd be sitting on the couch asleep until they get a little rest then wake up and continue with the party. And that would go on all night long, all the weekend. And we're talking about *every* weekend. Fridays and Saturdays is when the parties were going on. Sundays is the time you go to church. Yeah, you go home and clean yourself up and you go there with your bloodshot eyes and sit up in church.

HOUSE HOPS
FLORA MOLTON

When I was a little girl they used to have something they called house hops. Like on Saturday nights, you know, they had worked through the week after the crop and things so they have little parties. And the different people would have them at different houses. And we would go there. They would be singing and dancing at these houses, then we young girls, we'd be in the other room, we'd be dancing too.

My mother would fry some chicken and different things they would sell. You know, real cheap, anybody could buy it. And it was a lot of fun. They would sell the chicken and things but they just did it to have some fun. They would sell lemonade and stuff like that.

They had some kind of square dance they called it. And then we had a dance they called "stealing partners." That was a fun dance. Several of us on that side, several on that side, and always have an odd man; and like I would steal your partner and then somebody would steal mine. You know, each one would have a partner. And they'd be singing and there would be all kind of little dances they would do then. The musicians, they would be the country boys. We all knew them and they would be playing, they called them harps in those days, play guitar. And then they had another thing they call set dance. Dance in sets. They had a lot of fun, play a lot of games, and we used to enjoy it. I said sometime I'm gonna sit down and write a story about it.

They didn't have them every week, but pretty often in the winter and the fall. And then in the summertime, revivals and things were going around. But in the fall of the year, when the people would end up the crop, they would have the parties. We didn't have no trouble. They would do a little drinking, but everybody was very friendly. Every now and then people would have those little guns shoot them off, but they weren't shooting at nobody. They just get together and have a little fun. And at that time they didn't call that so much wrong, they just call theirselves having a little fun. The church didn't bother them. Well, I reckon some of them didn't know about it because they lived kind of far apart. But then if they wanted to come, they could come. But the church didn't bother the people there. My mother she and all of them were Baptist people. They were Christians. Of course, my father, he didn't approve of it. But he wouldn't know nothing about it if it hadn't been for my big mouth. My father was a preacher then. My father wasn't home; he was out in West Virginia working. He came home and so my mother didn't want him to know they had had the party. So I don't know why I told him because I wanted them to have the parties. But I told him.

So papa went off somewhere and I said, "Mama, after papa's gone," I was real small then. "let us have the parties again."

She say, "Uh huh, I'm gonna tell him what you said." So when he came back she told him.

He said, "Why did you say that for?"

I say, "Papa you know I was just picking Mama."

But I wasn't, I meant that.

IT WAS NOTHING TO WALK TWENTY MILES
JOHN JACKSON

On the weekend they would all get together and sing music and some would dance. There wasn't no kind of club or anything to go to then. Someone would bring instruments if they could play and set up in one corner of the house, and somebody would start in playing. And the next thing you know everybody wanting to dance would be dancing. And some would be telling tall tales and everybody would get together and have a good time. They would have music going all the weekend. Some-body would cook a ham; somebody would cook a pot of beans; somebody would make some cakes and pies. We'd climb down in the icehouse; get a great big chunk of ice. You know you would fill the ice-houses in winter cutting ice off the pond. Wash the straw off it, bust it up and put it in a can, cut up some lemons and make a big thing of lemonade. We'd have plenty to eat and plenty to drink all the weekend. And play music all the weekend, that's what they'd do. One neighbor would have a dance and maybe it would be a year before it would get back to him. It would go from that neighbor to the next one and next one. And it would just go all the way around in a circle. That's the way it would do. Why it wasn't nothing to walk twenty miles on a weekend to where a dance or party was going on. When I lived in southwestern Virginia, why I used to walk thirty miles with a guitar on my back play-ing house parties on the weekends and just get back in time to go to work Monday morning.

SATURDAY TO SATURDAY—CHRISTMAS TO CHRISTMAS
DOC BARNES

What we used to call them back in my day was either frolics or breakdowns. Have a "frolic" or either a "breakdown" or a "fish fry."

Yes sir, I have played from eight o'clock in the evening—that would be at night when the day gets short till 'round seven-thirty or eight on a Sunday morning. That's right. And if I got three dollars that was big money then; oh lord, I reckon it was big money. A person wouldn't give you a nickel then. Uh, uh. I knew I was doing pretty good, 'cause since that time, since I been a man, I have worked for three dollars a week. Sure have. So back when I was a boy coming up, way young then, I'd make three dollars playing, you know. Good God, I was money rich then. Let's tell it like it is.

They'd wear me out dancing and going on, swing cotillion, they used to call it. That's an old dance. They'd get a bunch of 'em, you know, in a place big as this here room and all. All of them take hold their hands and everybody stop then and swing their partners, and promenade as they call it. I don't expect you ever heard tell of that but that used to be their word, you know.

ALL RIGHT EVERYBODY GRAB YOUR PARTNER NOW, PROMENADE, MAKE ME A RING, GET ONE MORE AND 'ROUND AND AROUND THEY GO.

Yes sir, that's been a long time ago.

They'd have food. Otherwise they used to have a dance they call dancing on sets, well, all right, I'd have a girl friend or either a lady friend or my wife something like that, I'd take her and dance awhile, then when that set was out, then you take your wife, girlfriend, sweetheart or whatever, you take her to the table and treat her to what she asks for. Whatever she asks for and you had to pay for it. That's right. That was for the people that give the party. See, otherwise that's the only way they could, you know, that's the way they had to make their change. They just do that to pay for the party, you know. They try to get expenses back. That's the way they done that. Nobody was making no money 'cause there wasn't much to be made then. Call it "hot suppers," call it a "frolic" or either a "fish fry" and that's three names I know they had back when I was a boy. They'd dance, have drinks, and so on. Just like one person have a big dance here, I say over here on this Saturday night, next Saturday night the one over there have one. Next Saturday night the one over there. Just from time to time and about from hand to mouth, from one to another one you might say, from Christmas to Christmas.

SET THE WHISKEY IN THE MIDDLE OF THE CORN
ETTA BAKER

Etta Baker. Largo, Maryland, September 19, 1993. Photograph by Alex Jones. Courtesy of The Blues Project.

It was always in the fall of the year in harvesting time, everybody would set a corn shucking,[6] and they had big dinners good home-cooked food. Then after the dinner at night, after all the shucking was over, then they had this big dinner. Then after that was over, everybody played music and danced until daylight.

They done buck dancing, and what they call the "sixteen hands up," which is a reel; and each one would come up with different steps. But nobody then knew anything about this late dancing, clogging and things like that.

Daddy Edwards always called the figures and he would say, "Seven hands up circle to the right, drag your partner with great delight." And then from there everybody starts.

I never did care for dancing. In fact, I never did have very much of a chance to dance because I was furnishing the music for someone else to dance. And I have played for my daddy and I know he has danced three and four hours at a time. He was just that smooth with dancing. He didn't tire out. Of course, the supper was cooking while they was shuckin' the corn. Then they would get a gallon jar of good apple brandy or corn whiskey and set it in the middle of the corn pile where they'd just sit in the middle and whoever got through the corn, shuckin' corn, would get the first drink.

I'LL BEAT YOU DANCING
JOHN DEE HOLEMAN

They would give these woodcuttings in the fall of the year, chop wood. Gather a large crowd in to cut wood, maybe fifteen, twenty, thirty men. Then we'd have the woodcutting, and then a big eat, dances, tap dancing, blowing the harmonica. So it's the same thing with a corn shucking. Start that, go through a pile of corn, jar of liquor be on the other side waiting for you. Have to go all the way through it first. So the time you get to it, you had went through all that corn. So then we get to feeling good, start slapping, tappin' and have a good time.

Mostly it would be on weekends when I played at those corn shuckings and woodcuttings. A group of people amongst the neighborhood would go, like I help you, and you come and help me.

And when you finish here, everybody try and outdo the other one. I'll beat you dancing, you beat me dancing; I'll beat you playing the guitar, you beat me.

BLUES, THAT'S JUST ABOUT WHAT WE STAY WITH
J. T. ADAMS

Me and my brothers, we had a group and I played violin for years. But my main instrument was a guitar. I learned guitar. I played ever since I was a kid. My dad played; my mother played. I just fell in love with it. Yeah, my dad was a banjo picker. He played guitar too, but his main instrument was a banjo. He could really rap that old thing. He enjoyed playing at dances and dancing. You know, get out on the dance floor. When he was a younger man, he played different types of old songs on banjo and he clowned a lot with that thing. He'd throw it out like that then bring it down and hit it. He was a good banjo player, but he'd play guitar too sometimes. He had about three brothers, three uncles: Uncle John, Uncle Charlie, Uncle Jim. All of them was banjo players and could play banjo and guitar. Play some damn good music, just like me and my brothers. We played for dances. Hell, we played all over down there in Kentucky. We played amongst each other and we had lots of fun with it. We played mostly blues, but we played anything, any kind of music. I played at suppers, dances. I played for white folks down there. They'd have dances and I played for them quite a bit. They mostly liked those popular songs. Then they liked what we called old breakdowns; old breakdown music sort of like a square dance. We played that for them too. But us colored people, we like blues. Blues, that's just about what we stay with.

WE MIGHT AS WELL START RUNNING
HOWARD ARMSTRONG

Music was in my family all my life. You know, there were four members of the family older than I was and four younger. The older members were playing when I was just a little tot. Then they married off and what not and my Dad and Mother quit serenading as we called it. They used to go out and serenade in Tennessee. They called themselves serenading the white people. And we little birds would stay in the nest until they came home on the weekends.

After my brothers got married, I trained the other brothers under me. The next largest member in the group was a brother who is passed now; he was a minister some years ago. Roland, he played the bass. My dad made that bass for him and he also made me the first fiddle ever I had. Whittled it out with a pocketknife. And those two young ones, I taught them to play. We had a pretty nice family group. Now, we played for, as black people say, upper crust blacks. We called them the "saddity"[7] blacks and upper crust whites; we called them the elites. But we played for them at their social gatherings and proms and things.

But we had to be very selective in our music. We had a type we played for each group. We played for the upper crust whites; we played pop music and things like that. But no blues! The only blues we were allowed to play were the "St. Louis Blues" and "The Memphis Blues," and that was all accepted. But if you played old low down dirty black blues like we are today, we might as well just start running ahead of time. You know what I mean, move on.

Then when we played for the "saddity" blacks we'd have to play practically the same thing, a carbon copy of what we played for the whites. But, when we got to play for the "rounders," and the "low lifers," as they called it, then we'd go out there and play whatever we wanted to play. And we never played without playing blues. And what was so paradoxical, black preacher would sneak in the back door and jump in and sing a verse or two of the blues.

And I've heard old church sisters and brothers say, "Honey, that sounds so good, I'm gonna sing one verse anyhow. I don't want my pastor to hear me 'cause he'll put me out of church."

But they didn't know that the pastor was in the next room getting squizzed on home breeze or home brew. That's the type of thing I was exposed to.

COAL OIL BALLS
JUNIOR KIMBROUGH

Back in them days, they were having such a thing as coal oil balls. Take a bunch of rags and make them into balls. Get a tub and get five or six gallons of coal oil and pour it in that tub. Throw them balls over in there. Sometimes they'd make a hundred or hundred and fifty, something like that. And put it in that coal oil for them balls to soak. You take and reach in that tub light you one and throw it. Let it start to burn good and then reach and throw it. When they throw that ball it would be a veil of fire as long as my arm trailing behind that joker. It would be real pretty at night, real pretty. And they'd try to dodge them, but a lot of them would get hit. And when they get hit by being wet with that coal oil, it's gonna just splash on you. It's gonna splash all over them and it's gonna blaze up on them and set them on fire. So they jump in the pond there. Coal oil balls, that was a fun game. But you always have to have it around a pond.

PICNIC AIN'T SPELL NOTHING
IF THE DRUM AIN'T THERE
OTHA TURNER

I give picnics there at my place.[8] When I give a picnic I dress a hog in the morning. Clean and put it on at noontime. It goes around until five or six o'clock that evening. I clean my pit out; I dig a pit out and barbecue. I'm talking about barbecue from the real way it's supposed, dig you a pit. I'll say about half deep as here. Put you some broad cloth and put your screen on it. Put your meat on. Cook your meat. Parboil it. Put your season in it. Don't let it cook until it falls off the bone. Take the meat, the quarter, and lay it up there and take your pitchfork and sock it to it. Lay it up there, mop it good with your flavor all the way in to it. When it gets brown on that side, turn it over on the other one and just keep on. When you get through with it, every time you cut down there, you cut slugs out of it just like that, that seasonings all the way through. That's barbecue.

Get through with that about sunset or sundown and then they start to walkin'.

"Where you going?"

"I'm going to Otha's."

"Man, we's giving a 'fry' tonight. Goddamn we gonna have some fun. We going balling."

And they did ball. Yes sir, me and my wife and, man, shoot, I'd cook them, dress that meat, and fix it at that end and she'd cook about three or four tater custards. Got cold drinks in a tin tub, ice crushed down there, man, sell every bit of it. Yes sir, we'd have some fun and not a squall in it all.

Now where I'm at now, I give a picnic right outside, outdoors. I don't have no problem. I go across to the main man.

He say, "Otha, I know you. Go ahead, you know how to do it. You get ready to go just tell 'em you gonna call me or call me and I'll drive out there too."

They love to come. They come in. I give 'em a place to sit down in and buy what they want and then they laugh and talk and get out and dance. [We] play the drums outdoors. If it's raining you go in the house and tune 'em down low. Play it low. But as soon as you can, you go right back on out. Just like I started marching. That's the way I learned. When you start the drum, that drum is the leader of anything that's supposed to start out. Like, when I give a picnic, say tomorrow, I start to get everything together. This evening while I'm cooking my meat.

I say, "Boy, you take them drums out there."

They take them drums out there and tighten them up and play them. People would be there that night.

Say: "Otha giving a picnic man. Let's go."

"We going."

And that Saturday from I'd say three o'clock three-thirty on until twelve or one o'clock that night, they'd be there. They coming, oh man, just lined up. That's the way it is. Don't have a bit of problem.

So them drums, when you hear them drums that Saturday morning, take them drums out there and play a round or two, out there and man, what you talking about, they coming.

"I don't hear your drum, ain't you giving anything?"

"Man we didn't hear no drums. You oughta line them up there."

Let em get on those drums, man. People don't know it. Reckon they get out with them drums they know they coming too. Yes sir, they coming. That drum, that's the call. That's the leader, yes sir, sure enough. And the picnic ain't spell nothing if the drum ain't there.

SHOUT, CHILDREN, SHOUT
ARCHIE EDWARDS

Long about 1926 things started to roll pretty good in the West Virginia coal mines. That's what my uncle did; he worked in the coal mine. That's about the time that Blind Lemon Jefferson started recording about "Ain't Got No Mama Now."[9] And the boys that came from West Virginia sang a song about "I Ain't Got No Mama Now." So that was when people began to get hold to a little money. A little money was in circulation because of the coal miners and they were bootlegging a little bit, a little country corn you know. That was sort of in the middle of the "roaring twenties." There were dances. My dad would give a little house party to pick up a little chump change. They would come in there and they would buy them a little twenty-five-cent shot; a little glass of liquor. My daddy would make maybe fifteen or twenty dollars during the night.

This white guy, not only one but three or four, would come in there from time to time and ask my dad if he could stand inside the building there along the wall and watch them dance the square dance and listen to them pick the banjo. In other words, picking up on black culture. And so my dad said, "O.K., if you want to."

So they sat around and learned it so later on in life they were square dancing and buck dancing and flat footing too. They were doing it all. It came from my dad's old house parties.

They did what you call the four hand, swinging the four hand, they did that. Four people do it, two men and two women would do a little rug cutting. But it wasn't any of that swing and jitterbugging. That didn't happen until the mid-thirties. That came out of Harlem, New York.

. The white that played the banjo was Clifton Ferguson. Yeah, he was a pretty good banjo picker. My Uncle Archie, named Archie Spencer, he played the banjo. We had lots of banjo pickers around there. But my dad, he was a heck of a banjo picker. He could whip the hell out of a banjo. But Uncle Archie could too, and Uncle Archie could dance. He could buck dance, flat foot, he could do all kind of dancing. My daddy could dance a little bit. I saw him dance a couple times. And boy that guy could blow harmonica, and he could pick banjo. He kept some kind of banjo most all the time. He'd whip that five-string banjo to death. . . . Well, anytime he got without a guitar he could play anything he knew on the five-string banjo; take the five-string banjo, play the same thing. He was better on the five-string banjo than he was with the guitar because he could get more out it.

Yeah, my dad could make that banjo ring. And I'll always remember he had one saying that he would always say, when he was playing. He'd holler:

SHOUT, CHILDREN, SHOUT
CAUSE YOU AIN'T GOING TO HEAVEN NO HOW

My dad was a crazy little old fellow. Boy, he was a good man though. He was one of the most inspirational persons to me that I ever had because he told me one day. He said: "Boy you play a good guitar. Don't waste your talent like I did mine." He said: "Get out there and let the people see and hear you."

I said: "O.K. Daddy, I'll go. I'll whoop and holler until the good Lord stops me."

ALABAMA WOMAN
SANDRA HALL

At age five I was singing at my mama's fish fries, so I was born in show business. The fish fries was every Friday and Saturday. She'd cook up a batch of fish, and sell Black Label beer. Back in those days everybody partied in their homes. All black people, that's what we did. That's all we did . . . cook out on Fridays and Saturdays, and serve fresh fish and coleslaw and beer. My grandmother played piano and my sister and I used to sing. And she built this little, like stage, in the middle of the room for the performer to stand on while she played the piano. Because she was always there, it was just so much fun growing up in show business. Well, I had a very strong-willed grandmom. She was an Alabama woman, so can't too much get out of hand with her, because she could see out of all the corners of her eyes.

HUSH, HOLLERING JESSE
JOHN "JUNIOR" HURT

There was a man by the name of Mr. Willie Hill. He say, "Hurt, come play for me Saturday night. . . ."

And we would have so much fun, and daddy would play all night long. And all he would earn was about five or six dollars. You pass the hat around, you know. They drop in pennies, nickels, dimes, and that stuff.

It was like people gathering up on Saturday evening.

> "Who's playing tonight?"
> "John Hurt."

And people start gathering up. And there was a white dude called Willie Narmour; he drew the bow on the fiddle, you know. And they played "Carroll County Blues"; man, you talking about fun.

And then daddy never would say a bad word but he'd say: "Hot dog. Let's get down."

Mr. Willie Narmour would draw the bow and daddy would second behind. That's what I would like to hear. They would be doing that two-step. That's what it was daddy played for them to dance.

And when my mama would be dancing, she say: "Whooh."

And daddy would say, "Hush that, Jesse. Hush hollering, Jesse."

And every time daddy would play "Spoonful" somebody would get to fighting. But after that, you could play anything else and nobody get to fighting.[10]

SHOOT OUT THE WINDOWS
YANK RACHELL

Oh man, way out in the country see there wasn't no place nowhere to play. I'd play out in the country like this time of year, now getting ready for fall. People gathering and harvesting cotton and stuff. They pick their cotton, carry it to a gin, a little place called a gin. They gin that seed out, they'd have a bale of cotton. Well, everybody gonna have a supper, they call it a supper. They'd go on a Friday and buy fish, carry it home. In the kitchen women put the table across the kitchen door. They'd be in the kitchen cooking fish, frying fish. Well we'd be out there playing music. Well that's a fish fry.

Tomorrow night, he gonna have a supper, we'd go out and play for him. Next Friday night he have one, go out and play for him. Sometimes they break the floor in; sometimes they get to fighting and shoot the windows out. I've been in places where they shoot the window out, shoot the light out and everything. But I was there. I didn't have no sense. We out there drinking that old white corn whiskey. They'd be making whiskey, they'd be gambling, out in the crib gambling. They'd be in the house, his wife dancing. He's coming out, he done lost his money, he's gonna come in there mad.

"What's you doing dancing with my wife? What you talking with my wife about?" Well, blah, blah, blah.

"All right." Boom, boom.

See all that happened. I been through it.

At a country supper, a dance, or a fish fry, we'd be there picking and they'd dance. Well, the women in the kitchen cooking fish and you'd get a fish sandwich. They'd set it down on the table and you would stand up there and eat it. We eat chitterlings and fish and drink that white whiskey and we have a big time all night long; sometimes all that Sunday. That Monday morning we go to work.

Next Friday night, such and such a one having a supper, well, they come get us. I had a band, me and Sleepy John Estes, and say another bunch have their band. Those guys get this band.

"They playing such and such a place."

"Such and such a one playing over there."

"Yank Rachell and them playing over there, I'm going where they at. They make the best music."

Yank and Sleepy John. That's the way it went all the time you know. People go around and do that. They selling white whiskey and them police try to arrest you, or catch you selling it. They were buying it for me to sell it, but they arrest you for it.

HE JUST SPIT THE BULLET OUT
JOHN JACKSON

This was near down in the country, a little place that they call Paoli Mills. They was having a little party at this school selling cakes and pies and things like that, and the people come they would charge them ten cents at the door. And it was six great brothers came. They had this big man on the door named Jim Lee and he told them, said, "You all have to pay ten cents before you come in here."

And they said, "We ain't paying."

He shut the door on them. And this John Ed was a big man. He hauled off and kicked the whole door down and come in and they got to fighting. Honest to God, Jim Lee knocked all five of them down. But this John Ed was the big one, he was down on top of him beating him, just beating the daylights out of him. And he had some kind of old piece of pistol and he shot him right in the mouth. Knocked out them two teeth. And he never paid a bit of attention. He just spit the bullet out and kept on fighting. And he nearly beat that man to death. It took ten or twelve people to get him off of him. And they never did fight no more around there after that.

BREAK THE HOUSE DOWN
EDDIE TAYLOR

I used to go out at night to where they were playing. Sometimes they wouldn't let me in because I was too small. I'd crawl under the house and lay there listening to the music. One time they got to dancing and broke down the floor. Yeah, break the house down. I was under the house and the snake, cats, dogs, chickens came out from under the house with me. POW. I was laying in there, and that floor crashed down and I didn't know what it was, a bomb or something. But it was the house broke down right in the middle of the floor. I took off from there, dogs and cats flying.

The truth is the truth. The only thing that saved me, I was sitting over in the chimney corner right up under the piano. Roosevelt Sykes was playing that night, and Brother Montgomery and a whole lot more. Yank Rachell, I think. They had a big thing that night.

THAT DIDN'T STOP THEM FROM DANCING
GEORGE WASHINGTON JR.

They dance so much that the weight and jumping on it, and dancing around, and jumping up and down, well, see, that's what make the floor break in. The floor is probably rotten too. Then that would make it break right on in with too much jumping on it. That happened once when I was playing over there at Gunderson, Mississippi. Kirk Metcalfe used to run the place called "The Hall." The floor in there, in "The Hall" see, the house broke about that high up off the ground. It fell in there. But I'm gonna tell you when they fell in with it, they got back up out of there and went to dancing, shaking their leg on the floor. That's right, that didn't stop them from dancing when the floor broke in.

JOOK RIGHT ON
JACK OWENS

Jack Owens. Clarksdale, Mississippi, August 6, 1993. Photograph by Barry Lee Pearson.

They give jooks all around in that country, every which a way. And I played for them; me and Skippy James would play for them. Then somebody else would play what could play. It was a few good players around there.

I went to many a dance playing all out in the country. And now there'd be so many folks there, they'd break the house down, break the house down, and the house just fall down on the ground.

And they say, "Well they done done it now. Mr. so and so gonna get on us about breaking this house down"

I say, "Well ain't nothing to do but put some blocks under it and put it back up."

So, all right, we left there. They got scared that the man was gonna say something, you know. But he didn't say nothing, but go up there and fix the house. Told them to jook on. Yes sir. He let them jook right on.

RUBBING ELBOWS OR WHATEVER ELSE THEY WERE RUBBING
HOWARD ARMSTRONG

A jook, you know; you've seen those machines that you put nickels and things in, now they call those juke boxes, but I think that's a corruption of the word. After they quit picking up stray musicians, now I remember when you see, back years ago, you talk about apartheid in South Africa, well, we had something similar to that. We called it "Jim Crow" in Tennessee and Alabama and those places. I don't care.

I had friends who had amassed quite a bit of wealth, black friends, and they used to tell me, "Bill, you know, it's a shame," he says. "Even though we've got money to go, pay our way anywhere, we can't even join a simple yacht club or anything like that."

So, since the black people became aware of this, not to be left out, a bunch of them pooled their little resources, went into the woods, chopped down some trees, and built a great big structure and cut it off in to cubicles, a big dance floor and a place for the musicians.

And then they had upstairs and downstairs and they had a big kitchen. Oh, that was the black man's club, and they called it a "jook." See, jook,[11] not j-u-k-e, but j-o-o-k. And so it was a place that opened its doors to, you might say, all comers. It was no place for snobs and what we black people call "saddity" people. It means snobs, elite, upper crust,

Howard Armstrong. Vienna, Virginia, July 1972. Courtesy of the National Council for the Traditional Arts.

and so forth. Well, everybody rubbed elbows or whatever they were rubbing, on common ground, you understand. I know the first ones I played in, they had a wick stuck in a Coca-Cola bottle with oil, coal oil, or kerosene hanging around on the walls or even out on the trees, a line near the trees for light. Nobody wanted a lot of light in the first place. Well, there would be every strata of society rubbing elbows or whatever part of their anatomy they were rubbing on that dance floor. You know what I'm talking about.

Some guy might be dressed in his old plow clothes and brogan shoes. And here, maybe, one of the good Reverends, you understand, was there. . . . they sneaked away with one of the choir sisters and things. They were all on common ground. And everybody seem to have a good time.

J.O.O.K.
JOHNNY SHINES

It's jook, not juke, because jookin' was a way of dancing. They all out there jookin' all night. That was before the jukebox came out, juke. They'd be out there gambling and letting steam off; get drunk and have a good time. And the guy that have the best time of all was the one that come in and got him a half a pint and drunk it down. And sit over in the corner and slept the rest of the night. Now he'll get up and tell them more about what fun he had on a Monday than anybody else.

WE JUST CALLED THEM GOING TO JOOK
MAMIE DAVIS

Mamie Davis. Washington, D.C., June 1991. Photograph by Rick Vargas. Courtesy of the Smithsonian Center for Folklife and Cultural Heritage.

A jook house or a jook joint is unlike the clubs. It's just a joint. It might be a big old building, and they got some homemade chairs and some tables in there and they got old raggedy shades. It's not sophisticated like at all, but it's where people go and they just have fun. They are places that when you go in you wouldn't suppose that it was a beautiful place because it's not; but once you are in there, you have a beautiful time. So you forget about what it looks like.

So that's what a jook house is. But then also a jook house was called that because it was before they had a lot of joints. They were called jook houses because it was always in somebody's front room of their house. They would have like a juke box in them, they would have a stove where they'd have a refrigerator full of beer and pops and stuff. And all of this was going on in one room.

They'd have somebody over here shooting dice, somebody over here making music, and that was called the jook house. Then, when they started buildings away from the house, then they were called jook joints. We still have a lot of those. We have some jook houses out in the country and we have jook joints at the same time.

They had the house parties, but we just called them going to jook. My understanding it's from "jook," means you're going to have fun. You're going to party, dance and get drunk or whatever. We don't have so many of those now, but we have some, and believe it or not you have more fun at those places than you do if you go up in to the city into a night club. You have more fun and it's much safer.

Then we also had a store out in the country. We had this one store they call it "The General Store." In the store you could find anything that you were going to need, so I guess that's why they called it general. And this store had a porch, and on the weekends my grandparents and my parents would always say, "We're going 'store porching' on Saturday; we going 'store porching.'" And what they would do, it would be somebody there that would play music. They'd sit on one end of the porch and play the music and the other part of the porch was for dancing. And they called that "store porching." Everybody danced on the porch of the store. We did this on maybe Friday nights, but basically Saturday nights. But on Sunday there was none of that because you had to go to church all day Sunday. Sunday night they had to stay home. Then they had to go to work on Monday. But Saturday night was the jook night.

DON'T GO TO BIG MARY'S CANDY SHINES

Candy Shines. Washington, D.C. Photograph by Richard Vargas. Courtesy of the Smithsonian Center for Folklife and Cultural Heritage.

My father, he died when I was about three years old, and my mother was on like welfare. And she didn't have enough money, like sixty dollars a month did not take care of my family. She had five girls and one boy. Two of them had grown up, but she had the whole rest of the four kids, and she just didn't have enough income.

So she started making home brew first. And she got so popular making it that people would come from miles around to get the kind they say that has that blue smoke coming off the top. And then after a while she had to move out of the project that we was living in and she went to a single house. And then she got her a Rockola and opened up a jook joint, what you called a jook joint back then.

And that's where I started trying to be an entertainer and listen to the jukebox, all the music. People like Blind Bud Bailey and stuff that was playing at that time. Matter of fact, Blind Bud Bailey a lot of people don't remember, but he was one of the like Delta blues sounding men back then. He would pull the crowd into the jook joint. My mom's jook joint got so popular they started talking about her on the radio.

Talk about, "Don't go to Big Mary's house."

They call her Big Mary even though she was a very slim lady.

And they say, "Don't go to Big Mary's house. First go to the party, then go the dance and then go to the house of Big Mary. She'll still be open. And we'll meet up."

And that's what the deejay used to talk about. I can still remember it. He used to talk about it. I remember his name it was Jiving Johnny and he used to holler all the time, "Jiving Johnny gonna have a little beer."

You know he's going to Big Mary's house tonight.

I'M GOING TO THE JOOK JOINTS
FRANKIE QUIMBY

My daddy used to go to the jook joint. That's what we called them. And we would say when I was a child, because everybody didn't go. It wasn't like a flux of people, it was a certain, in those days, as Bessie [Jones][12] would say, it was "those kind" that went. You know the "flaggers." The "flaggers" would go to the honkytonks and to the jook joints. That's what we called them there on the coast, jook joints. And they would go there. And when I was a child my daddy drinked, so he went to the jook joints. Well, my mother was dead, but my stepmother that raised me, she didn't go because they had it like the nice ladies stay at home. And my family was the Sullivans, which we're supposed to be up-to-date people because they owned their own houses and stuff. So they didn't go. My stepmother and my aunts and my aunt-in-laws, their life seemed so dull to me as a child.

And I would say, "My God when I get grown I'm gonna be like my daddy. I'm going to the jook joints."

Because it looked like when you go by the jook joints, like walking to town, or going somewhere by them, they would be having so much fun. They didn't have air conditioning so the doors and windows were open. And it just seemed like they were having such a good time.

And I said, "Oh, when I get old, get grown, I'm gonna go to that jook joint."

I WAS SMOKING
EDDIE CUSIC

I used to go up on the hill and play at Kinloch Plantation, Kinloch, Mississippi, out on Sunflower River.[13] They used to have country jooks. Everybody leave town come out. You could hear them walking down the road picking guitar. Sometimes it would be a couple of them. One will play a while then the other one play a while; wasn't no electric then, just acoustic guitar. And you talking about people after hard work, five or six days a week, after all that, they would get out in that country and have a time. They would leave town and go out in that country. Go to them jooks. They could get out there and have a quarrel or something like that. One of them would shoot a pistol out there and every light go out in the house. I remember when I was out there one night; I had to take my guitar try to get down get out there and get out, to keep from getting runned over. And man, they running so fast in the fall of the year, cigarettes in their mouths would be lightening up going across the cotton field. And I'd be right with them. I was smoking. That's the best fun you could have after you turned that mule loose. [*Laughs.*]

THE LIGHTS GO OUT
EDDIE BURNS

Jook joints, they was nice. They had gambling and fish fries and all kinds of food to sell. And just clean dancing and stuff like that. But whenever they did have some violence, it was some mean stuff going on. It was tough, you know, like shooting scrapes and whatever. And sometimes they would do that because some mean people come from Mississippi. Very mean. Treacherous. Mississippi was a rough place.

I've seen them gamble and everybody would lay their guns up on the table in the lamplight. You know, there wasn't no electricity back then. So everybody get to shooting in there and the lights go out 'cause the lamplight got a tendency to don't stay lit. A lamp don't when they're shooting in a house. Everybody'd be in the dark.

CLOSE UP THE PLACE
DAVID SAVAGE

There were jook joints all around Greenville, a nightspot they call Leroy Grayson's, Bay Jennings, Big Ruby's Night Spot in Leland. Rice Miller,[14] he used to play over there with the King Biscuit Boys, and Robert Junior Lockwood. Willie Love, he's dead and gone now, he was a bad boy. He played with Lockwood and them. He played piano; he was really from Greenville. Yeah, we used to rack 'em up. Yeah, they played them country jooks out in the country, drinking that white whiskey, shooting them big-eyed dice. Sometimes the Sheriff's Department come in there late at night and make 'em close it down, all that kind of stuff. Close them from gambling and whiskey selling too. Make them close the whole joint. He tell him to close the place up. He put everybody out, whether they had a ride home or not. Be about six or seven miles out in the country. Hitchhike, come back to town. That's just the way it way back in them days.

I'LL ACCOMMODATE YOU
JOHN "SO BLUE" WESTON

I used to run a jook and it was out in the woods, and I had a real bright light. You know, where there's alcohol and people, you gonna have some misunderstandings and quite probably fights, you know. So what I would do when they start, I had about a hundred-and-fifty-watt bulb in there and I would flick that light on and blow this police whistle. That was the end of it. Well you know police means you're gonna hit the power structure, that money, they gotta pay see.

Then there was a guy that wanted to fight me there one night. And I told him there was nothing to gain for it.

I said, "I've done nothing to you but made you welcome here." I said, "Come on outdoors." I said, "If you just want to fight, I'll accommodate you. So we'll get in my truck and we'll go to this plowed ground just across the road here and I'll fight with you."

I say, "And if you whip me, I'll come back over the P.A. system and I'll make an announcement, well, whatever you name is, and say, 'Ladies and gentlemen, he really tore me up good.'"

But, I said, "If I get the best of you, won't nobody know it but you and me, so let's go."

You think he wanted to go? No.

I said, "Well do you just want people to see you clown? This is what you want? You ain't gonna get no credit for it. You gonna make confirmation that you're a fool."

Well, I had to use a lot of diplomacy, man.

KEEPING ORDER
CANDY SHINES

My mother just didn't play. I remember a time we had like a fireplace that was in the Rockola room and these couple of guys came by there this particular night, and I was standing there in the doorway watching them. They'd sit there and they had some old chewing tobacco or snuff or something in his mouth, and then they sit there and they spit all around the fireplace and stuff. And my mom wasn't that kind of mother. You just couldn't do anything.

And I walked in there and said, "Mom, those people just spit all over your place, all up against the wall and the fireplace."

She walked in there and looked at that. She walked back in there and handed them a bucket of soap and water and two rags. Torn from old sheets or something, and she handed each one of them one and said, "Now clean my fireplace back the way it was."

"We ain't gonna clean nothin."

She stood back in the hall. I didn't even know she had a shotgun. All these years she had a shotgun. It was old and had a real long stock to it. And she just stood right there with that shotgun and they cleaned it. Honest to goodness she did. I couldn't have been over five years old.

THE YELLOW DOG
J. OTIS WILLIAMS

I lived in Grenada County, and it was a dry county, meaning you weren't allowed to sell alcohol on a commercial basis. It had to be bootlegged. And the adjacent county was Carroll County and depending on who was in office it was a wet county or a dry county. So the Yellow Dog was like right on the county line; so a lot of people would say, "Let's go to the county line." Because you could always go out there and buy beer in the quart, set it on the table and everything. You didn't have to sneak it. So there were several joints across the county line but the Yellow Dog was one of the main ones.

Now I thought it was going to be something fabulous before I went out there because I had been to Greenwood to clubs there, some nice nightclubs with juke boxes. You dress up and go there. But the Yellow Dog was just the opposite. It had dirt floors like sawdust on the floors. It had a little bar and stuff set up there, and a little makeshift stage. There was nothing fabulous about the Yellow Dog. And cars would park all around the place and they had lights. And them guys, pulpwood was one of the main jobs in that area, pulpwood cutters. And the guys who cut pulpwood made pretty good money for that area and they would always have the smell of this pulpwood in their clothes. And these guys would come in right off work with that money in their pockets on a Friday night, on a Saturday night and they wouldn't change clothes. They were wearing their overalls. The women would be all hanging on to them. And they'd be, we called it "wrestling," you know, "slow dragging" to Muddy Waters and them. You know that beat, and they'd be hanging on to them for the money.

And if it gets a little too rough, then you just got to get up and get on out of there. The bouncer, I can see this guy in my mind right now. He always carried a couple of pearl handled pistols, and occasionally people got shot out there. But the main thing about the Yellow Dog is that it was, if Carroll County went dry for a spell, then they would have the liquor. They would move the liquor to the other side of the county line because the place was built right on the county line. But it didn't even have windows; it had croaker sacks hanging, when the wind blows. It was nothing fabulous about the Yellow Dog, but it was happening. People come in from the city. You see cars there, you know, tags from Michigan, Illinois, and everywhere. I mean that was the place. Because people come home, see, and they'd sit there. They'd have three or four quarts of beer on the table, big time, you know.

THAT'S YOUR HOME
BIG JACK JOHNSON

We had a lot of fun at the house parties: White whiskey and hot buffalo fish, lot of gambling going on a cloth table. And sometimes it would be muddy down in them old fields. Here come a rain and you all get stuck, but you didn't care. You were full of that white whiskey anyway. You didn't care. Good times there, man, real good times. All those times have gone bye-bye now. There ain't no more houses in the field no more. The ones in the fields have burned down or were tore down. But anybody care about their plantation, anybody care about the past, would let some of that stand. But most guys tear it down.

Some of these people left home at eighteen, nineteen years old. Now they're sixty, eighty some years old, go back home to see where they used to live, they can't find it no more. All they know, they were born somewhere close around that town, but they don't know where. I think that's real bad for you. The place you was born at, that's your home.

LEARNING THE BLUES

My folks always knew that I was
musically inclined, because, well, I'm
gonna tell you a little story that
happened to me when I was four.

MAMIE DAVIS

THE SOUND

THAT'S ALL THE LESSONS THAT I EVER HAD
ETTA BAKER

Well, when I lacked two months of being three years old, my mother
and father never did have to say: "Etta, it's time to get up;" I was awak-
ened by my daddy on the banjo or either the guitar. So that's all it took
to get me out of the bed. And I would get up at four o'clock, four-thirty,
and sit and listen to my dad. And I was such a nuisance to him until he
would take time to show me the different chords on the guitar. And I
would follow him around. I'd stand up between his knees, come up
between him and the guitar and watch over the top. And before I was
large enough to hold the guitar, I could make the basic chords but I
couldn't hold the guitar. So he'd sit me up in the bed and lay it across,
and I could note the three basic chords from the top. And he knew I
was in the right place, but I wasn't getting very much sound to it. But
he was real patientable. When I got large enough, then he bought me a
little small Stella guitar; and so I had one in the home ever since. And
that's all the lessons that I ever had about my music was from my father.

I WOKE UP TO THAT MUSIC
HENRY TOWNSEND

Henry Townsend with grandson Robert. Photograph by Kathy James. Courtesy of the National Council for the Traditional Arts.

My daddy was a musician. He played an accordion, and another man, we called him Otto, his name was Willie Davis, he played a guitar. And late that night they'd put me to bed. I remember, this was in Carruthersville [Missouri]; they'd put me to bed and they got started out on their instruments and it woke me up. And I woke up to that music, and I guess when you're asleep and you wake up to music it sure enough sounds pretty because you get it all. And it remains to be the thing that really pushed me over the cliff towards playing the guitar. That was the beautifulest sound ever I heard. And that was a thing that could never leave me and that hasn't left me. That was my first sound of the blues.

My daddy, he done vocal. I remember the old song he used to sing something about:

HURRY DOWN SUN DOWN AND SEE WHAT TOMORROW BRINGS
IT MAY BRING SUNSHINE, AND IT MAY BRING SHOWERS OF RAIN.[1]

WE COULDN'T GO IN THERE
ALGIA MAE HINTON

My Mama had a lot of young ones. She had fourteen and I was the baby girl. She played a lot of blues and spirituals. She did them both. She'd blow her harp, she'd knock her spoons, play guitar, play jews' harp, piano, organ. She played everything. You name it she played it. And my mother, she played for parties around the house on Saturday night. Oh, we had a lot of dances. We'd have parties sometimes of our own. Her uncle, her brother, so many people would come and Mama would be playing. But we were a lot younger than them so we had to be sitting down on the wood floor in another room. We could hear it but we couldn't go in there. But we'd be stomping on the floor to it but not too loud. We'd be in there and I'd be doing the "fishtail" and everything. And if I heard Mama coming, right down on the floor I'd go. But that's where I got the idea of it, and I've been dancing ever since.

I WOULD HEAR THE SOUND IN MY EAR
JOHN CEPHAS

I can remember they would have house parties, and they would send us upstairs to bed. All the kids would be upstairs and they would be partying downstairs. We couldn't help but hear all that music and stomping and frolicking that was going on downstairs. We could hear it. A lot of times you couldn't go to sleep for all of the music and frolicking that was going on. But we weren't participants. That didn't come until later years when they kind of loosened the reins on you. You know, the older people used to have the reins on you. They wouldn't expose you to too much of what they were doing during that time. But I would hear the sound in my ear, you know, the words that they were singing and how they would be affected by it. And it kind of affected me in the same way. Even though I was going to church, I always had that aspiration to go there to be with that other crowd. Of course, the people in the church, especially my mother, kind of frowned upon that even though they were doing the same thing. They would go to church on Sunday, but on those Friday and Saturday nights they would gather at each others houses for those country breakdowns and hoedowns where they dance and drink corn liquor and just have a good time.

HE WAS MY IDEAL
BOOGIE BILL WEBB

William "Boogie Bill" Webb.
Washington, D.C., June 28, 1985.
Photograph by Lisa Falk.

The way I got into it was back at that time, my mother used to go and get the blues singer Tommy Johnson[2] from Jackson, Mississippi, and bring him to New Orleans. He played for house parties for her. And that's the way I got the idea with guitars, by looking at Tommy Johnson. My mother used to get him and guess what the fare was? One dollar. And guess what she would pay him? She gave him six dollars and carfare and he had made plenty money. Tommy Johnson was playing his "Canned Heat Mama Blues," "Cool Water Blues," "Maggie Campbell Blues," and "Big Road Blues." That's the type of music he was playing at that time. In fact, he never did get over playing that. That's all he could play, was that. But that was enough at that time because there wasn't too many people playing, you know. And he had an acoustic guitar, not electric. But, good gracious, how loud it sounded at that time. He was my ideal. I used to look and see my mother when she'd go get him. I'd see her coming, you couldn't hold me no more. I'd run to meet them.

SOUNDS SO GOOD TO ME 1
DAVID "HONEYBOY" EDWARDS

Tommy Johnson, Clarence, they all come to Wildwood in 1929. 1 was fourteen then. They come from Crystal Springs, Mississippi. They stayed in Crystal Springs. They had a old T-Model Ford. They come up picking cotton by the hundred, and they had a big double house they stayed in. A great big old house and they'd pick cotton all through the day and at night they'd sit around and play the guitars. They were cotton pickers, day hands. Course in the hills there wasn't nothin' to do. See, they come out of the hills, around Crystal Springs, raise them truck patches and all that corn—wasn't no cotton in the brown hills. And they came up to the Mississippi Delta 'cause that's some flat country. They'd pick cotton, gather corn, make a little money and go back to the hills later in the fall.

So Tommy Johnson, Clarence, Mager; there were three brothers and Peg Leg Sam. Peg Leg died about seven years ago. He was in Chicago. He was playing with them too. I know them all. I was fourteen years old and I used to go over there. He was playing "Canned Heat" then before he made "Canned Heat," "Big Road," and he was playing "Bye and Bye." And I used to stand around in the house right around the corner here and every night I would listen at them play. Sounds so good to me. Drinking that white whiskey, that moonshine.

MAN, THAT MAN COULD PLAY
JOHN JACKSON

They were building the first blacktop road up through from Charlottesville up through Rappahannock County, and they just had hundreds and hundreds of convicts with dynamite, mules, wheelbarrows, sledgehammers, and stuff like that, and they build a road. And this one particular convict used to tote water from my spring. . . . we never did know his full name. All we knew, everybody call him "Happy." And he was the happiest man you ever saw. He was whistling, laughing, or singing all the time. And so I was kind of small, and he'd come get a bucket of water, and I wondered why he made so much noise when he walked. And so when I met him at the spring, I come to find out he had a little chain on his leg. And he got to talking to us, and he wondered what you do around here? And I told him my father worked on the farm and played the guitar, banjo, mandolin, ukulele, and my mom played harmonica and accordion.

He said, "If you bring your daddy's guitar down here, I'll play you a song."

So I would take the guitar to the spring, and he'd play me a song and then he'd go. In a little while he'd be back and he'd do the same thing. It went on like that for four or five weeks.

And so my mother heard him playing one day when she come down there, and she told him—he said he got off in the camp at six in the evening—and she said, "I'll send the kids up there, and you come on over if you want to play some for us. The old man plays some." She was talking about my father, and she said, "And I'll fix you something to eat."

So us little ones went up on the hill where we could look right down at the camp, and he got off at six o'clock. We walked him back to the house, and he eat dinner and sat there and played for us until time to go back to the camp. And us little ones walked him back to camp. And it got that way every night pretty near. He'd come over and play, and then he'd sit me on his knee and try to show me how to play some. Man, that man could play. And my father got so amazed at him he wouldn't play with him. It was one spiritual he did that my mom used to sing to him. I can't remember what it was; I declare I don't. But anyway, he was around there for about a year and half or two years. But the first six months, they took the chains completely off, and made a trustee out of him. And he would come over to our house every evening, and then he spent every weekend over there; you know, they didn't work on Sunday. And he would spend Sunday until time to go back to camp on Sunday evening. And then in another six months they set him free.

And he got up one morning; he stayed with us for a couple days. And he said, "I have to go away, but I'll be back."

We took him to the nearest little town and put him on the mail truck. And never did ever see him again. Now who that man was I don't know; I have no idea where he was from. Some people said most of the convicts that was working on that road was from out of the South, but whether they were, I don't know.

But I really got into it when I heard the convict play. He really had a lot of influence on me because I couldn't leave the guitar alone after hearing him.

SOUNDS SO GOOD TO ME 2
EDDIE CUSIC

My name is Eddie Cusic and I'm from Leland, Mississippi. I was raised on a farm when I was small coming up. My mother's name was Lily and my father was Eddie Cusic, so I'm Eddie Cusic Junior. So we was out there making cotton, you know, living in the country and all that. My older people used to give them there house parties in the country. Call them jooks, Saturday night jooks. People used to go to town on Saturday to get paid off. People leave town going back to the sticks. Well, they used to go to my mother's house, go to her place and she used to have them guys playing them guitars. They had lamplights and they would lead them out from the country store. They come out to the country and they'd be walking down the road singing the blues and I was crazy about that.

I was a little old boy about twelve years old and I used to hang around there and listen to them guys years ago that played them acoustic guitars with no electric because there wasn't none. Man, they come out there and start to playing; man, it sound so good to me. I say, if I ever any kind of way can learn how to play I'm gonna do it. So I would. Anytime they put the guitar down I would grab it and try to play.

"Boy, let that man's guitar alone."

He say, "No, one day that boy might be somebody. He might come up playing himself."

So they wouldn't mind. People had a wonderful time in them days. They come there and they start to playing; my mother and them make us go to bed. Man, get up the next day, some of them hang around there all night. And one of them kind of taking a liking to the family, he would let me play his guitar. Play around with it and I hit it and I thought it sound so good.

MY MAMA WAS A BOOTLEGGER
MARY JEFFERSON

I was born August 10, 1926, on a hot Tuesday morning, so I'm a Tuesday's child. I was born in Washington, D.C., at Freedman's Hospital, and brought home to the alley behind the Howard Theater going into where the restaurants were. I was raised on that block of S Street. We had a house on Wiltberger Street, and that's right next to the stage door of the Howard Theater, so consequently all my life I heard music. My grand-daddy cleaned out the theater, and my daddy worked the backstage, and that gave me a kind of "open-sesame" kind of thing. So I was always in the theater. That was my pre-school learning. And my mama was a boot-legger, and we had house parties every Friday and Saturday night; so when they came over to the house to get a drink or so, we had a piano. We always had a piano, and Claude Hopkins was a piano player for mama. Duke Ellington was a piano player for mama. So consequently, I just heard all of the music. When Fats Waller would come, we had a stoop; you go up three steps and it was like, you know, a platform. And he would come and we would pull the piano up to the door, and he would sit on the stoop, and chorus girls and everything came up. That was one of the most enlightening times of my life because I met just about everybody. Earl Hines, Gene Ammons, and people of that ilk, and I was able to see them and get the opportunity to sing with them because I was so young, but I always had a deep voice.

I COULD HEAR HIM LEAVING HIS GIRLFRIEND'S HOUSE
BILL HARRIS

My first memory of the blues was George Dautrey, five-foot-eleven-and-a-half blues shadow. He didn't know that he was my teacher, but in my waking hour, three-thirty in the morning, I could hear him leaving his girlfriend's house singin' the blues. Yeah, George Dautrey was hollerin' and whistlin' and screamin' the blues to keep the hants off him. You don't know what a hant is? But if you walkin' 'round one of them dark North Carolina roads about three-thirty in the mornin' and see about twenty-five of those white hants gathered 'round a cross, you'll get your hat because you know North Carolina ain't the home of Casper the friendly ghost.

THE DEVIL'S GONNA GET YOU
LONNIE PITCHFORD

Lonnie Pitchford. Clarksdale, Mississippi, August 6, 1993. Photograph by Barry Lee Pearson.

It all started when I was real young. Like, I didn't have no instrument so I was always fascinated by the guitar. So I didn't have no money to buy nothing, a kid coming up at that age wouldn't have no money at all; so I just made me an instrument. I made my own out of a piece of broom wire and a snuff can and a couple of nails and nailed it upside the wall. Stretched the string and nailed it. I had fun with it. When I made it, to me it was just child's play. I was just doing something to amuse myself. It just came naturally to me I guess. But I seen my brothers, they used to do it, but they would put it on a board, make it on a piece of board, and they used to put maybe two or three strings on sometimes. I tried to put two or three strings on one time but I couldn't get no sound out of it, so I always wind up with just one now. Sometimes with that one-string deal, you out there banging on it I used to like get some static from the other end. Like momma would tell me sometimes, "Stop with all that noise."

They always told me, "The Devil's gonna get you."

BOING BOING BOING
JAMES "SUPER CHIKAN" JOHNSON

I wanted to play guitar so I made me a one-string diddley bow.[3] A couple of nails, and a string of baling wire with a Prince Albert can or a salmon can, slide it under it and tighten it up to give it the acoustic sound that you want through that can. "Boing, boing, boing."

I wanted to make me a guitar and I knew it had wire on it. I made it on the wall of the house first. Then I had trouble out of my grandma. I had put it on one of those big country houses we used to live in back then. I don't know, I must have put it in the right spot, it would echo all through the house. The inside of the house would be like the inside of a guitar, because I had a pretty big piece of wire on the side of the house there; and I would hit that thing and it would vibrate through the whole house. "Boing, boing."

My grandma didn't like it. She'd holler out there at me, "Boy, there, quit beating that doggone wall."

She thought I was beating on the wall. But I had me a little old stick; I'd pluck that wire. I had that wire pretty tight, you know. I'd pluck that wire, "boing, boing, boing"; and I'd slide something else on it, a glass bottle or something make the sound "boioioing," you know. I plucked it with a stick and I noted it with a bottle.

MY MOUTH WAS MY MICROPHONE
KOKO TAYLOR

I cut my eye teeth singing gospel in the church. That was my main choice. But my second choice was to make sure I would listen to the blues. And then I would get experience singing the blues at home. We had this little shotgun house, and of course I grew up on what we call a sharecroppers' cotton farm. And every day, we'd come home from the field, me and my sisters and brothers, and we'd go behind our little shotgun house and we'd have jam sessions. And my brother and myself and others, we couldn't afford guitars and things. So my older brother took some hay-baling wire and wrapped it on to some nails that he had driven in the house. And my younger brother made himself a harmonica out of a corncob. And of course, I didn't have no mike, my mouth was my microphone. So we would get back there and we'd played and jam and have a good time.

PULLY DUM
STERLING "MR. SATAN" MAGEE

I was just given to make that instrument; it was a barn instrument. Imagine the wall up here, but a crib for corn at harvest time. I would take a piece of wire approximately so long and nail it and get a nail and nail the other end. Then I'd take me like a brick on this end and maybe a can of some sort on this end. Then I'd take a coke bottle and roll it. Then I wouldn't mark it, I'd just go for the sound. I'd hit it and I could slide it and it would sound good. And it would be on the side of the crib. And because of the low frequency of the crib people would be coming by telling my mother: "Your boy sounds good over there."

I never tried to put two strings on there, it was just one. I called it a "Pully dum." I'm gonna pull it, and it sound "dum-dum, dum-dum." You pull on it and it gives you a "dum-dum" sound. That's a pretty name, "Pully dum." Pull it until you're dumb-founded. A one-string crib-tar.

HE MADE IT OUT OF A CIGAR BOX
BOOGIE BILL WEBB

Well the way I got into it was the time I had a cousin, he made him an instrument you understand. And I used to take his instrument and play something like "Stormy Weather";[4] and guess what? I always say he's the one that learned me how to play, but he never did play nothing. He couldn't play nothing, but he made that instrument. He made it out of a cigar box. Yeah, and screen wire strings, and I was able to get "Stormy Weather" on it at that time.

So, well, my mother saw, you know, that I was very interested in it so she bought me a guitar. So I started to whanging on it. At first I was playing in a tune that nobody couldn't play in, 'cause my box wasn't tuned. Well, they had a friend of my mother's come from Jackson, Mississippi. His name was Roosevelt Holts.[5] He lives today, but he's real old, but he lives today and plays today. He tuned my guitar for me. He stayed with us two weeks. That's the onliest teaching I ever had.

And he said, "You ain't gonna never play none the way you got this thing tuned, you ain't gonna never play." He said, "But I'm gonna tune it for you." And he say, "If you let it stay like I got it tuned, C natural, you may play, but I doubt you'll ever play."

But I done made him eat that up a plenty times.

HE HELPED ME MAKE ONE
ROBERT LOCKWOOD JUNIOR

Robert Lockwood Jr. Washington, D.C., June 1991. Photograph by Jeff Tinsley. Courtesy of the Smithsonian Center for Folklife and Cultural Heritage.

So Robert Johnson,[6] he was right there in the house with me so every time he set the guitar down, I'd pick it up. So he finally asked me did I really want to learn. That was the keynote. He showed me where to put my hands at, where to put my fingers. That's the first thing I learned. And I played that all night, and I played it all day, and my mother took a stick of stove wood and chased me out of the house. I played it all night and all day. When I wasn't asleep, I was playing the guitar. That's how come I learned so fast, because I slept with the guitar. Then he acted the fool and helped me make one. They sure enough didn't get no rest then because I had my own. We made one. It stayed together about six or seven months. We didn't have the kind of glue you have to have to really put the thing together, but it stayed together pretty good. But when it tore up, then my auntie bought me one. Then everybody was in trouble.

NOBODY SHOWED ME NOTHING
GEORGE WASHINGTON, JR.

George Washington Jr. Clarksdale,
Mississippi, August 5, 1995.
Photograph by Barry Lee Pearson.

When I first started out playing music I was nothing but a boy. I started playing these here drums; I call it a drum, upside the wall of the cotton house. Took a snuff bottle and put it up under there, take one and put it down there, and take a castor oil bottle and go to playing up and down that string. I'd tear up every one of mamas brooms, you know, get all that wire off of that. I got a whipping about that many times. But that's the way I did. I first put baling wire up, but it didn't work so good. Then I put broom wire and broom wire worked good. But I got some good whippings about it. But I went on and did it.

So the old man told her, he slipped up on me one day. I was playing my drum down there at the cotton house and mama say she gonna whip me.

He say, "No, don't whip that boy. That boy's gonna come to be a musician. Let him play."

So that's the way I got my start. Nobody showed me nothing. I just learned my own self. A white man, his name is Mr. Johnny Hall, come down there one day and he seen me playing that drum. And I was playing "Baby Please Don't Go" on that drum, one string of wire.

He say, "You know what I'm gonna do George? I'm gonna get you a present."

He didn't tell me what it's gonna be. When I come to find out, he slipped me a guitar at home. That's the way I started. So I kept practicing, going over and over and doing it until and I learned how to play.

IF THEY CAN DO IT, I CAN TOO
EDDIE CUSIC

We out there making cotton, living in the country, and we had old cotton houses that we put cotton in. Put it on the wagon, and we'd cash it in. So when my daddy and them carried their cotton to the gin, man, I'd get up in one of those cotton houses and get me a hoe. In them days them there cotton hoes, they had a lot of steel in them. I'd take the handle off and get me a pin and get in there and listen up, listen up, listen to the ringing in my ear.

Well I stopped that, and put me a one-string upside the wall. I was going to school when I had time to go and that wasn't too many months a year. I'd have to stop and go to plowing a mule, you know. I was about twelve or fourteen years old then. I used to get that old baling wire what you bale hay with. It felt, in my mind, that it didn't have a ringing sound; it had a dull sound. I put me two bricks in one, one down in the bottom, and take me a bottle and hit it to like make a sound.

Well I stopped that. And we used to get these old brooms with that wire up on there, these sweep brooms. And man, I'd be glad when one was old. I'd get the wire off it. And I'd have more than what I need; I'd save me some. And I would put it upside the wall. It was a little smaller wire, so it sounded better. It had a little steel in it. Then I started pressing it with a bottle. I wouldn't fool with them bricks no more. Break me a neck off a bottle, you know, and slide on it; and I could take that thing and make sounds with it. I don't know how I did it but I did.

My mother used to hear me she say, "Boy I don't want you up here. I want you to go to church. I don't want you playing no guitar."

So I went on with that and I went to school. Everywhere I'd go I'd have one of those wires up. And I had one of them not too far from school and I remember I like to got expelled from school. I'd be stopping those school children just before they'd get to school, make them late for school.

So after then, I went on. I'd be in the field plowing the mules and thinking some, "I'm gonna get me a guitar." What happened, it got so I could order me a guitar out of a catalogue, a Gene Autry guitar. I got that darn thing and I started to trying to play. I didn't know nothing about no tuning or nothing like that. I just learned. But they was playing up there at a place called Sunflower River. They used to have them houses out there, them Saturday night houses. Jook houses we called 'em.

I used to go out there. I was getting up about seventeen, eighteen years old, getting out then, go up there and listen to them guys play. Well I had been trying to play mine but my fingers was so sore I said, "I don't believe I want to do that." I put that thing down. Then I go back up there and I say, "God, if they can do it, I can do it."

It was a guy could play a fiddle, and a guy, played that guitar. Man, you talking about sounding good. I sit down and listen. I go back and get mine, my fingers hurt, I throw it down again. So late one night I laid down and well, something weighed on my mind. It was something like a dream; look liked something come to me in a crossroads. Boy, they were playing that guitar, man, playing that guitar and it look like its a crossroads. Man, it sounds so good.

I got up the next day, and got that guitar and started to make me some sounds on it. My fingers got kind of tough to it and the next four, five months I was up there doing the same thing they were doing, playing in that country jook. That's how I started.

I GOT EIGHT FINGERS AND TWO THUMBS
PINETOP PERKINS

I got started in music by putting a piece of wire upside the house down in Mississippi and playing it with a cake-flavor bottle. It was a one-string upside the house. Took me a wire off a broom and stretched it up there. I could play "Rolling and Tumbling"[7] better than the boy that did it. And from that in later years I picked me up a little old guitar they called it a Stella. Started playin' on that. It looked like, I didn't know I was going to be a musicianer, but people always come get me for to play parties and things. I said: "Well, look here I'm gone now."

But every time I'd go somewhere, you know, to play on my little guitar; you know, where a piano was; it would drown me out. I couldn't hear the little old thing. Shoot, I looked at my hands and said, "Look here, I got eight fingers and two thumbs; I ought to be able to play that thing too."

And I went to work on piano then, yes, sir, just by ear. I don't read nothing.

I BEAT ON A LARD CAN
HEZIKIAH EARLY

The way I come in to music, my father he was a fice blower.[8] In other word, we were born and raised on a farm way out, down in Mississippi; I say about twelve or fifteen miles outside Natchez in the country on the farm. And they would have outdoor picnics on the weekends, you know, like drum beating and fice blowing. So my daddy he did it, he did that. And so eventually he got out of it and joined the church and later decided he wouldn't do it anymore.

But I liked it. That was in me; it was in me the music, I loved that. Then later on, when I got big enough, like my mother would take us out on a Saturday evening to hear the guys play the drums, you know. When I got back home, I liked it so well that I would get me a couple of sticks and go to beating on a can. That's the way I learned how to drum. I started beating on a lard can, anything I could find to beat on, lard can, tub, bucket, or anything. My folks, they didn't have a lot, and were trying to make it, you know. And I never worried him about buying no instrument or nothing like that. So I beat on the bucket, tub. And I learned how to play drums.

I AIN'T GOT A THING TO DO BUT TO TRY IT
OTHA TURNER

Otha Turner. Washington, D.C., June 1991. Photograph by Joe Wilson. Courtesy of the National Council for the Traditional Arts.

My calling was, and I started out young, keeping around the picnic stand. Just like this place, might be a big gathering, and I'm looking around there watching. These old men was playing drums. It was twins Bill and Will, old people. They lay down, play a drum flat on their back and kick their heels up and holler and cut up.

And Mama says, "Son."

I said, "Ma'am."

She said: "You come on and get close to me now; I'm getting ready to go home now. It's getting late."

I said: "Mama, please let me stay over here." I'd stand around and watch and she come and got me. I didn't want to go.

She say, "Come on, I'll bring you back next picnic." She did.

So, it was an old man called Will Edwards, his name was Will Edwards, he owned a set of drums. He was playing drums. I looked at him.

"Son what you looking at?"

I say: "I'm looking at them fellows playing them drums."

"Reckon you'll ever do that?"

"I believe I will."

He laughed. He knew I didn't play no drums. He said: "I believe you. One day I'm gonna let you try. If you play drums or learns how to play drums, you got you a job. I'll see you."

"Yes sir."

But he heard me play the drums. I played the drums like I played on that stand over yonder. They rared back and every body say, "Hoorah, Hoorah"

He said: "Son, now you're one of my hands."

I said, "Oh no."

"Yes you is." He said, "You play as good as them old drummers."

When I started to playing drums, an old man they call Ira Williams he made the first fice I ever seen. He was standing out there on a rainy day. He came by the field we was farming. He stand out there blowing his cane. I was feeding the hogs, walking around.

"Howdy Mr. Ira."

"Howdy son."

"Uh, Mr. Ira."

"Son."

I said: "What's that you blowing?" Kind of studying him.

He say, "Son it's a fice."

I said, "Will you make me one?"

He say, "I don't know. If you be a smart boy I'll make you one."

I said, "I sure would appreciate it. I'm gonna pay you."

He made the cane, told me, he say, "Otha?"

I say, "Sir."

"Come here. I got your fice I made."

I run and grab it I said, "What I owe you?"

He said, "Nothing. You be smart now. You ain't gonna blow it?"

I said, "I ain't got a thing to do but to try it," said, "I'm gonna blow it."

"All right, son"

Start to blowing the fice, and the same man that let me play the drums, that's the one that the 'cause of me blowing the cane today. I'd go around the stand and hear some good drummers. And they told him say, "Will, you don't need nobody blowing no cane."

But another fellow, the old man they call C. L. Williams he couldn't get up with him. He say, "Otha can blow that cane just as good as C. L. Williams. He may not hold on to it but let him try."

I blowed for him that day, and I been playing drums and blowing the cane ever since.

HE'S GOT A TALENT
R. L. BOYCE

When I was younger I heard drums back then, you know, playing at picnics and things. I just wanted to get in there. Back then you'd hear drums all over down that way late in the evening when they were picking cotton. And later, on Saturday evening, people get off work, you could hear Otha and them drums cutting up. Now, it's so much noise so if you start playing late in the evening you can't hardly hear them unless you're sitting right there.

When I first started playing drums I was about fifteen. I used to walk two miles across a ditch to L. P. Bueller's to listen to Otha Turner play every weekend. I'd go on Saturday about this time, get there, and they'd be getting down. Come back, I'd get me a good whipping.

I said: "Mama, one day I'm gonna do like my uncle. I'm gonna play music."

"You ain't gonna do nothing."

Come Sunday I'd go on back across the ditch.

She say: "Where you going?"

"I'm going down there to get me something or other." But I'd go over that ditch to hear him play; get home that Sunday, she'd whip me. She got where she'd whip me every night. Went on again. They give a picnic, all of us had to go in the house back at that time. I'd sneak out the back door go under the house.

Say, "Uncle, one of these days I'm gonna play one of those drums with you."

My mama had some tubs. I'd get back home, I'd get them tubs and go to beating on them. My Uncle Otha come over say, "Annie Mae, you need to stop whipping that boy. He got a talent he's trying to do."

I say, "I'm gonna learn it one day."

So I got in along with them and been in the band ever since.

THEY WOULD PUT ME ON A COCA-COLA BOX
JESSIE MAE HEMPHILL

**Jessie Mae Hemphill. June 1987.
Photograph by Robert Cogswell,
Tennessee Arts Commission.**

My mother, her name was Bertha Virgalee Hemphill. They was playing "Bullying Well" all the time; my aunties and her. So my mother said, "Now you want to play 'Bullying Well'?" "We gonna learn you."

So she learned me how to play "Bullying Well," and my Aunt Rosie Hemphill, she learned me how to play "Roll and Tumble, Cried All Night Long." And so from that I learned all my granddaddy's pieces. Then I would learn pieces from records, and then I would go back to the house and learn them to my granddaddy. He thought it was wonderful. And everybody thought it was wonderful for me, so little that I couldn't even get my arm over the guitar.

So by nine years old I was really playing, really good. I had about seven or eight pieces I could play real good when I was nine. I play the organ. We had an organ. My auntie had a piano and I would play that, too. I learned boogies and things on there. Learned one piece on my granddaddy's fiddle that was "Tennessee Waltz." I learned that on that fiddle and I had myself something. Yeah, I used to love to play that. My mama and them get out there and dance that "Tennessee Waltz." They could dance like that. So I play it and they would dance.

Then when I was coming to be ten I was playing these drums, fice and drums. I was going with them to play in the fice and drum band. I couldn't hold the drum up. Some man would have to hold the drum up for me. And then they would put a Coca-Cola box down there for me to stand on and I would beat that drum. I would beat that drum have all them people, they be up in the trees and things trying to see me beating the drum. I was so little but I could beat that drum; I made my granddaddy proud of me. And I know he would be double proud of me now. He wanted me to be like that. He wanted me to learn whatever I wanted to learn. He wanted me to be like that.[9]

OH LOOK AT IT
NAP TURNER

When I came to Washington in 1942, just wandering around in the summertime when I wasn't in school, I got all kinds of education about music. And it was all kinds of music. I mean guys were down at Six and a Half Street playing the washboards and harmonicas. A lot of people that lived in those streets were migrants from the Deep South: North Carolina, South Carolina, Georgia, Alabama. You know, with the traditional ways of coming up the coast. And if you went down around Six and a Half Street in the summertime, people would be barbecuing out on the sidewalk and you would see them guitar players and stuff and they would be playing them rural blues. And that's where I learned to play the tub bass. There were some guys that played in the streets, and one of them had a bass that was made from a big old, I guess it must have been a five-gallon syrup can. And you take the top off it and put a hole in the center of the bottom of the can, take a piece of rope, real thin rope like clothesline rope, put a knot in the bottom of it, put the other end through the hole and get a long stick, take the string and nail it to the top of the stick and when you tighten the tension, hold the stick against the bottom of the can. And when you change the tension of the line it changes the sound of the rope. So I said, "Oh look at it."

So that wasn't hard to do. All I had to do was go to the drugstore and get one of them cans and get a piece of rope and a piece of flooring or whatever and I had me an instrument. So I learned to play that. And I remember I was playing in a group out in the street, and my mother was coming home from work and she saw me out there doing that and took her pocket book and "Whap!"

"I see you out here embarrassing your family, boy. You must be crazy."

PRINCE ALBERT TOBACCO CAN
"WILD CHILD" BUTLER

I was small; I stand and watch them. So I used to beg them, "Let me blow some. Let me blow the harp."

They let me blow, and you know, I'd strike a little tune or something on it. So they told me, say, "You going to be a big man blowing this harp one day."

They gave me an old harp. So I kept that harp for a long time. I blowed on it and I blowed till the harp went bad. I took me a Prince Albert tobacco can and beat, put some rocks in it and closed the mouth where it made some holes in the back of it, and I used to hum and sing and stomp my foot. And I, when I became thirteen year old, I wrote my first song, blues. I wrote a song that I used to sing about, "I Had Trouble Way Down on Old Jack Wilson's Farm."

THEY'D TAKE A CAN AND TUNE IT
HOWARD ARMSTRONG

I know black guys that were too poor to even buy [any] kind of instrument. Guys would play washboards, jugs, stovepipe, cue sticks, broomhandles, washtubs, and all those things. And get music out of them. That right. I've even seen guys get music out of bottles. Get so many bottles and put a certain height of water in there and play it, play real music on it. And of all things I've ever seen before or since, I've never seen this since I left Tennessee. My mother never had a can opener. It was common for those housewives, black and white, to open a tomato can, big old tomato can, or they had a lot of canned kraut, you know. You know how they would open it? They make a cross, one straight cut across the top like this and then almost exactly across the middle of the other one form a cross, then they pull the prongs out, pull them back, you know, that they'd cut. And then empty the contents out in a pan or something. But some smart guy, guess what I've seen him do? Take a kraut can or either tomato can and they tuned it. They take the prongs of these cans, the four prongs on the side, four on the other can, stick one under this arm, one under that one and play "Casey Jones," or just like you could pick on old five-string banjo now. Try it sometimes; tune it similar to how these black Jamaicans do these oil drums, what they call the steel drums. They tune those things with blowtorches, hammers and things and the pipe organ has nothing on it, when they get it together.

PLAY LIKE THAT
CHARLES BROWN

We had a roll piano. And my uncle didn't ever know anything about music, but he was very smart. He learned to play the piano by the roll piano, by slowing it down. He would come over and he saw that; that grandma, his sister, was interested in giving us music. And he said, "You got to learn to play like this."

Charles Brown. Washington, D.C., July 4, 1993. Photograph by Joseph Wilson. Courtesy of the National Council for the Traditional Arts.

So he'd get on the roll piano and pump it and put us between his legs and try to pump the piano, say, "Look at those keys boy, you got to learn, Don't that sound good to you?"

I say, "Yeah"

Say, "You got to learn to play like that."

LIKE RIDING A BICYCLE
JOHN "JUNIOR" HURT

What happened is that I asked my daddy, I said: "Daddy, Please show me how to play the guitar, please sir."

And my daddy did not show me but one time. And my daddy told me, he said: "Son."

I said: "Yes sir."

He said: "It's just like riding a bicycle."

He said: "If once you learn it, then you'll never forget it."

And I asked him the next time. That was the second time, you know. And he did not show me anymore, so I just had to take it up on my own.

STEALING THE MUSIC
ARCHIE EDWARDS

So one day, along about 1934 or 1935, me and my three brothers were sitting around talking about buying a guitar. We had this brand new Sears and Roebuck catalogue. So I said, "Look man, here's one for five dollars." So my brother said, "How do you know we have enough money?"

Five dollars was a lot of money back then. Sometimes you work a long time to get five dollars. If you have five dollars in your pocket, nobody in the world could tell you that you weren't rich. But me and my brothers, we all grew up around there in the country where they made a little corn liquor. So the ones that was too young to drink saved theirs and sold it. And the ones that could drink, they drank most of theirs. So I had two older brothers that drank most of theirs. So me and my brothers had some money from selling moonshine.

I was the mastermind of everything we wanted to do there, so I said, "Well, the guitar cost five dollars and with four of us, a dollar and a quarter a piece ought to do it."

So we all chipped in and bought this new guitar from Sears and Roebuck, an old Gene Autry guitar, with Gene Autry's horse and a dog on the front of it. So I wrote the order and took it down and sent it. They sent us the Gene Autry guitar with a little case. They sent that to us with some instruction books and what-not. I could read and understand a little better than the rest of them, so I was the one that tuned the guitar and started picking out a few chords out of the instruction book.

Then back in 1933 or 1934 my brother borrowed that record "Stackolee" and "Candyman,"[10] and he brought the recording to the house and put it on the old record player and played it. But the speed he was playing was a little too fast for us to catch all the sound and all. So we improvised a method of slowing the old record player down to where the man would talk just above a mumble. Then we would listen to the guitar, trying to follow the guy. If I made a mistake my brother would tell me where I made my mistake at; so I'd give him the guitar and he would fill it in. So we did that for a couple of weeks and when my brother carried the record back to the owner, my brother and I had stolen all the music.

I'D TORTURE THEM TO DEATH
BIG JOE DUSKIN

Joseph "Big Joe" Duskin.
Photograph by Steven C. Tracy.

When I first started to ever even think about a piano, it was down South in Birmingham, Alabama. My father was a Baptist preacher, and they used to have a old big upright piano. You had to press the pedals and I couldn't bother with the pedal part of it because I was too little to sit on the stool and pump it. So what I would do, I would just sit up at the piano and just bang the devil out of it with my fists. Sometimes I'd hit it with my fingers, you know, like that. And the old man would come get me down from it and I'd bawl like the devil. And when he'd go, I'd get back up on it.

So, finally when we come to Cincinnati, then I could mark down on the notes what would be what. I didn't know whether it would be A, B, C, or D, so I just put a two down if it was hitting twice, I'd put a two. I'd slow it down like that, and three and so forth. And then when I learned how to do that, I used to just work on down the piano and then back you'd go. So the old man said, "Get this kid out of here. This kid is gonna run us bananas here in a minute."

And they'd be talking and they'd raise sand. Finally they'd get me down and I'd bawl so much my uncle Louis would say, "Let him come on back in. He ain't gonna bother us."

So the old man say, "Come on back in here boy," and I'd get back there. And I'd get where I thought it would worry them the most, I'd get in the basement, play, oh boy, that really got it. And then finally I went to sleep at the piano and they got up and brought me [up] and put me to bed.

And I grew up to where I could play one song. And it was one of the most beautiful songs I thought that there was because I could play with both hands. I used to think that was the loveliest thing because I could do that with both hands and I didn't know I was torturing people to death.

And what they said, they said, "God, will you run that kid out. That kid's gonna run somebody bananas with that song."

So finally he said, "Will you please get up and get out of here."

And I'd get up and say, "Well, since you don't like music, I'll go to the Kirklands' next door. They love music."

He'd call them up, "Here comes the instrument of torture. You let him in, you gonna be bothered with him."

So they said, "Ah no, Little Duskin, No more tonight, Get away."

Then they wouldn't let me in. So finally the next day when they'd get up and let me in, man, I'd torture them to death. I'd stay there all day just playing that one song.

BEAT THAT GUITAR TO THE DEVIL
BOB LOWERY

Quite a few people in my family could play music. Well, there were some that called it "the devil's music" and all that mess, but I had two uncles who played. And my daddy played a little bit. My uncle he used to play house parties. Then I had an uncle by my mother's side, a stepfather, he could do pretty good. But I learned how to play better than he did right quick because he could only play in one key. My dad played and I would get him to tune the guitar for me and then I would just whale away with it. And when he wasn't around, we lived close to some white folks and they all played music, the old man and the whole family did. And I used to go up and sit and listen to them play like hillbilly or bluegrass music. And I used to take my guitar and get them to tune my guitar up and I would try to sit in with them. But I knew when that guitar wasn't in tune. If it was out of tune I would get them to retune it before I'd leave. And I'd get back home and sit me on a log or a stump out in the woods, and I'd run everybody crazy and beat that guitar to the devil.

I WOULDN'T EAT
HARRY HYPOLITE

We used to have a, what we call at home, was a "Baza."[11] Had a card game to play some cards and it was something like this, like a Baza, they tapping it at it, Baza. [*Claps.*] And there was a man could play the guitar, God knows. You know, you'd be a block away you could hear them playing and singing. And I'd come in and watch them. The floor wasn't so stable as the floors are today, you know, and as they dance, it would rock. Just rock.

And the old man happened to die. That guy happened to die and his niece had the guitar. Well, she had the guitar hanging up in the house on the wall. And her grass was yay high, long. She say, "If you cut the grass," she told me, "I'll give you the guitar."

I said, "Wow."

Because I used to hear the old man singing, and I said, "One day I'd like to sing like that old man be singing and be playing. And oh man, the guitar sound so doggone good."

Well, I cut the grass and it took me about two days; two or three days because I had one of those mowing machines that you push. So I finished cutting the grass. So there was some old man sitting out on the porch, old people, real old. They was in their seventies and I was maybe a boy maybe twelve, thirteen years old. Because I had the guitar, man, I'm going home with the guitar. So the old man's hollering said, "You not gonna learn how to play no guitar because your feet is too big." But he was just talking.

So I brought the guitar home and I had my grandfather's rocking chair on the porch. I was working at a hardware store in St. Martinsville. I was riding a bicycle; the bicycle they give you with the big baskets with little small tires with a big tire in the back. So I'll go on home go to get my meal, go to eat, but instead of me going to eating, I wouldn't eat. I'd just bang on that guitar. Didn't know nothing about playing no guitar. Didn't know the chords, didn't know what key it was in, didn't know what A was, didn't know what B was; nothing like that. Noontime then comes, at one o'clock time for me to go back to work. I hadn't eaten nothing yet. My mama tell me now to put the guitar up and go on get on my bicycle again. But boy, soon as I get off from work, I'm going after that guitar.

DO YOU KNOW ANY BLUES
J. OTIS WILLIAMS

J. Otis Williams. Largo, Maryland, April 17, 1993. Photograph by Alex Jones. Courtesy of the Blues Project.

My uncle was running a barber shop on Doak Street, and what they used to do most of the time was sit there and drink corn liquor. And he had a resident guitar player that would come in there and play some blues. He had two or three old guitars laying around there. They would sit there drinking liquor.

He had a guy that would come in there and play guitar for him two or three days a week. He'd give him a few dollars and some corn liquor and he and his buddies would sit around there and drink corn liquor; had their own little private blues session going. And I never knew all those years that my uncle was so crazy about the blues. I know I was in there one day with my guitar messin' around and sang a couple of songs for him and I thought it was the blues. I was picking and playing a little bit there and I thought I was rolling. He was smiling. So when I finished he says, "Say, Otis, do you know the blues?"

I said, "What do you think I been trying to do?"

I BORROWED HIM THE GUITAR
OTIS "BIG SMOKEY" SMOTHERS

When I was coming up I used to listen at Sonny Boy Williamson. Old Sonny Boy Williamson and Elmo James.[12] They had King Biscuit down in Mississippi. It was about fifteen minutes they'd be on. I'd listen at them. They had Sonny Boy, Rice Miller, not the original Sonny Boy. They sound so good. I was a young fellow then. And I met Elmo James down there. I had my little old guitar, it was a Gene Autry guitar; [I was] picking on it and playing and Elmo walks up and everybody they say, "Elmore, Elmore, Elmore."

I had my guitar and I hit one tune. I didn't hit but one tune over and over again. I'd end it, do it over again, see. Elmore James grabbed my guitar and tuned it up and started playing it. It didn't sound like my guitar no more. He played all these songs, "Caledonia," "Just Like a Woman," and all them. And then I took it from there. I say, "Hey, I borrowed him the guitar." So I got the mention.

SEE HOW THEY'RE WORKING
CHARLES BROWN

My grandmother told me, "If you learn to play music one day, you won't have to get up early in the morning and go to work at eight o'clock."

She'd take me down to the wharf and we'd watch those guys on those ships—the salt boats and the sugar boats and the sulphur boats. She'd say, "Now you see how they're working and sweating and all that stuff; and they ain't making no money." Say, "What if you get your education and learn the music, too?" Say, "You could go work four hours a night and make some money."

And that stayed in my mind.

WHY CAN'T I
LITTLE MILTON CAMPBELL

Little Milton Campbell. Largo, Maryland, September 14, 1997. Photograph by Jay Boyar. Courtesy of the Bluebird
Blues Festival.

The first music that I heard, I'm sure it was the radio and I think it was probably country and western. I know we had one of those battery radios because we lived right outside of town in the country and we didn't have electricity out there where we lived. So they had the coal oil lamps and if you had a radio, it had to be operated by the battery. That had to be what it was because I remember me being a young boy I used to listen to the "Grand Ole Opry" every Saturday night. Then the next thing I remember was Gene Noble with the Tarzan holler thing.[13] That was on WLAC playing the blues and what have you. And I guess that was my awakening to music that I really loved dearly and wanted to perform; because I figure like there just had to be a better way to make a living than chopping cotton and plowing the mules and harvesting the cotton and the crops and stuff. I said there's got to be a better way. If the boss man can ride around in an air-conditioned truck, why can't I? That was always my thing.

I GOT MY GIRLFRIEND BACK
WILLIAM "BOOGIE MAN" HUBBARD

A dude blowed a saxophone to my girlfriend; see, I was tap dancing at school, but man, that tapping wasn't nothing. You had to blow something or play something to get your girl, you know. And man, a dude named Willie Winston, he taught me. I had to give him but a quarter, and he started showing me how to play the boogie-woogie on piano for a quarter. And so I had to learn how to play piano to get my girl back. It took me about two or three months to get a good boogie-woogie. But anyway, I found out dancing was out of style. You had to do something else. You can't dance and get nothing. So I started playing a little piano. So, see, they had a program every Friday, so I put in for piano on Friday morning. The teacher told me say, "Hubbard, you know you ain't gonna play no, you don't know piano."

I wouldn't let them know I had been taking my little lessons. I don't let them know nothing. Oh man, because I was getting right. See, a lady named Miss Liza had a piano next door to us but she didn't like nobody to bang on it too much because she kept her headache; she's kind of old. But I went over there, to her house and I knocked me out a boogie-woogie. When I went, I got to school that Friday, I didn't know but one number. But I wore that boogie-woogie out. I played it and well, them folks, the girls started shouting. And they want me to do another one. I didn't know nary another one. I just did that first one a little slower. That was the other side of that boogie-woogie, I guess. I did it slow and I did it fast. And I got my girlfriend back, and about three extras. I had a little on the shelf, tired of sleeping by myself, and all that stuff; lipstick on the little paper. Man, I was in business.

NO BASEBALL
ROOSEVELT BARNES

When I was about ten or eleven years old I used to play at a little old store up at a little old place they call James Crossing. Some white friends of mine lived close by and they used to take me to that store and I used to play my harmonica for them without any amplifiers or anything. I'd just take it out and blow it and people'd throw me quarters and fifty

Roosevelt Barnes. Largo, Maryland, September 19, 1993. Photograph by Alex Jones. Courtesy of The Blues Project.

cents. I was happy; I'd sneak and drink me that beer. So that's how I got started out. My brothers, all of them are professional baseball players. They played baseball and I stuck to the music. I could drink and play music, but I couldn't drink and play no baseball. That's why I started playing music.

SATURDAY NIGHT HOP
ARCHIE EDWARDS

Archie Edwards. Washington, D.C.
1986. Photograph by Lisa Falk.

My older brother, Willie, he had met a few old professional blues artists. So I got around to play a few chords. I kind of ran them together and made a little something that sounded pretty good. So my brother would go to these house parties, get him a shot of corn liquor and tell all the other old guys, "You guys can't play no guitar, I got a little brother at home in the bed sleeping beat you playing."

So they all said, "Go get him."

So he'd come and get me, see, every Saturday night around two or three o'clock in the morning. I'd hear the old Model-A Ford coming out in the front yard idling, "Tick, tick, tick, tick, ticking."

When I hear that I say: "Uh-oh, gotta go help my brother out."

I'd jump up, put my little coat and trousers on, get that little old guitar, go play the guitar for them. So I called that song "The Saturday Night Hop," because I had to hop out the bed just about every Saturday night to go save my brother, you know, get him straightened out.

But my brother Willie turned out to be a preacher. Oliver, he's a little preacher, too. He's clean, but Willie, with all the lies he's told, now if he's saved, I'm saved. I'm still playing the blues, but he's a preacher. God knows anything can happen. My oldest brother used to be a devil. He was the craziest boy you ever saw in your life. Anytime a man would drive down the highway in an old 1930 Chevrolet, driving as fast as he could, eighty miles an hour with the speedometer needle bumping as far as it would go. He would take his old thirty-two out and, "Bing, bing"; look like a cowboy in the Wild West.

I said, "Oh my God." A crazy boy but he turned out to be a preacher. Well, miracles can happen. Yeah, everything works out good for those that trust God.

MAMA'S NOT GOING TO BLOW EVER NO MORE
BIG BO MCGEE

I was born in Emmelle, Alabama, and Porterville, Mississippi. See, I was born in a house where the state line goes straight through the house. The bedroom was in Mississippi. The living room and the kitchen was in Alabama. Well, that makes me part of both of them. That's where I was born. So my dad always said one half was Mama's, the other half was his. So they put both halves together and they come up with me.

But my grandmother was my inspiration, yes, sir. My grandmother was a blues harmonica player. When I was a little kid, I always wanted to grow up, well, you know some kids is a daddy's baby, I always was a grandma baby. So grandmother bought me a harmonica, I believe it was the key of G, when I was six years old. And she made me play on this thing until I was ten before she let anybody hear nary a note or anything I was doing. See they had a pantry where they keep food. Back then it was no refrigerators, so we can up all the foods and stuff you know, and put it in this pantry. So she used to tell me to get in there and play where I wouldn't disturb nobody and where the sound wouldn't get away from me. She said, "When you get good enough I'll let you know."

I thought she was getting rid of me, you know; I had no idea that it would turn out like it did. But eventually when I was ten years old, on my tenth birthday she told me one Saturday afternoon, she called me, "Hey Bo."

I say, "Yes ma'am."

"Come here."

I went to her.

"Go in and put on those clothes, Sonny, those clothes I laid out on the bed for you."

"Where we going Mama?"

She say, "You're going with me." And she said, "You're good enough now. You're gonna take my place and Mama's not going to blow ever no more."

So we went down to a place called Electric Mills, Mississippi. It was a sawmill community. It was a place there called Keil Hall. And boy, I really blowed. I had to show them what she had learned me. And we had one dude on a wash rub board, and one blowing the jug, and one on the guitar, and they had a fellow, called him Dent, was on piano. Man, was he good. And I hung around with those dudes until I was about twelve or fifteen. And I owe everything I know to my grandmother and the good Lord.

SMALL CRIMES

YOU EAT THAT
YANK RACHELL

I was going down a dusty road; it wasn't no street in them days, nothing but dusty roads. People didn't have no concrete when I come up; dust was knee deep. You go down the street a car come by it cover you up in dust. Well, this man was sitting on his porch and I was going down that dusty road. He had a gold mandolin; one of them old striped-back mandolins. That's what you call a tater bug. He's setting on his porch and I went by his house. The man was named Harvey Ross. And I said, "Mr. Harvey, what is that you got?"

"This is a mandolin son."

I looked at it. I was used to a guitar you know. I said, "I like it. Let me see it."

And he handed it to me. I said, "I like this."

"Let me sell it to you."

I said, "What you take for it?"

"Five dollars."

Well, five dollars was like five hundred to me then; out in the country way back. My daddy didn't give me no money and he didn't have no money either. Well, I didn't know where I'm going to get five dollars. I said, "I'll tell you what I'll do. I'll trade you a pig for it."

"All right, go get the pig."

My father raised hogs, them fine blood Poland China hogs. I said: "All right sir."

I went home and got me a tote sack and went to the barn, called a pig out give him some corn, grabbed him and put him in the tote sack, went around that thicket and give the man the bag. The man give me the mandolin.

I come on home. I was happy, and he was too because he had a pig that was worth something when it grew up. But I didn't care. I wanted that mandolin. I brought it home, couldn't play nothing, no tune or nothing, just banging on it. Then they had all those strings on it and I thought I was doing something, "Blam, blam, blam."

That old man, he didn't like it, he said, "Boy put that thing down and lets go to bed."

"All right daddy."

He go to bed. When he has to go to work, I get up and get it. I'm going to work on it. Mother wouldn't say nothing for a while, but later that morning the old lady got up, had a head rag on, sat there by the fire place. My name is James but everybody calls me Yank, my nickname. Because my grandmother named me "Yank."

She says, "James."

I say, "Ma'am."

"Where's your pig? I ain't seen him in a day or two."

I said, "I ain't either, Mama." But I kept on stroking on that thing you know. I knew where the pig was. The man had the pig, you know.

And so she said, "Go see can you find him."

I say, "Yes ma'am."

I put my mandolin down for a minute. Went out to the barn, stood in the barn. Hid from her to make her think I was looking for the pig. I come on back.

Say, "You see that pig anywhere, James?"

"Mama, I ain't see'd that pig nowhere."

Then I picked it up and went back again like I wasn't worried about the pig, which I wasn't, I was worried about that mandolin. I picked it up and went back. Then that got her attention.

She says, "What is that thing?"

I said, "Mandolin."

"Mandolin?"

I says, "Yeah."

"Where'd you get it?"

I said, "I got it from a man down the road."

"What man?"

Now if I had stole that mandolin, I wouldn't have been here today. The old folks kill you in them times if you steal. Better not steal nothing. I said, "I got it, mama, from the man there."

I didn't want to tell her I traded the pig off. You know, they give me the pig. In the yard near the bottom they had a willow tree sitting in the yard and she took four switches. She got every switch off that tree. The tree withered. She got all the switches. She come in there commenced,

"You gonna tell me something about that man and that thing there you got."

I said, "Oh mama, I got it."

She said, "I'm gonna whip you."

She said, "Pull them clothes off," say, "I ain't gonna whip them clothes. I bought them. I ain't gonna wear them out. But I'm gonna wear you out."

Uh, oh, I had to tell her. I said: "Mama I traded the pig for it."

She said, "Oh I ought to whip you to death."

She said, "No, I ain't gonna whip you son. You're crazy." Said, "This fall when we harvesting and have the meat, and eat the meat," said, "You eat that thing."

DON'T STEAL NOTHING
BYTHER SMITH

Byther Smith. Largo, Maryland, September 14, 1997. Photograph by Jay Boyar. Courtesy of the Bluebird Blues Festival.

I didn't have no money to buy a guitar with 'cause like I said my mother and father was dead by then. So I steal this corn out of the corncrib and go and trade it to this white boy to get a guitar. So he give it. His father came and took the guitar, but he didn't bring the corn back. This was the greatest part about it, he gets the guitar, but he didn't bring the corn back, which it wasn't very much. So later on my brother buys a twenty-two rifle and I steal the rifle out of the house and go and trade it to get me a guitar. My brother makes me get the rifle back. I had to take the guitar back to return the rifle. So after that I get mad and tell him, "I'm going to get me a guitar if its the last thing I do." I was gonna get me a guitar.

And so he says, "If you do you going to have to buy it. You don't steal nothing to go and trade."

So I worked for a white fellow fixing a fence, you know, something like a hog pasture or calf pasture. I work for him, I don't know how long. Seem like to me that it was a month, but I don't think it was more than about three weeks. But he finally just up and gives me an old guitar he had lying around there. Then I wouldn't help my brother around the house. My brother come in from work I wouldn't have gone out to the barn or taken care of none of the stock out in the barn. I wouldn't have done anything. I'm just sitting up there plucking along on the guitar. I wasn't playing nothing. So my brother, he got mad about that, and he just steps on the guitar and breaks the keyboard on that. And that really got next to me. So I get mad. One Sunday I go to church, then I get a fellow by the name of Charlie Sibley to take me to the bus line. And I caught the bus to Jackson, Mississippi, which was ninety-two miles from Monticello, Mississippi, which was my original home. I was born there. So I go up there to where one of my aunties was living in Jackson. I go up there and start out washing dishes in back of a little old restaurant there in back of a Greyhound bus station, and I buy me a guitar there from a pawnshop. And that's where I started learning to play a little bit.

I WAS STEALING THEIR GUITAR
JUNIOR KIMBROUGH

When I first started in music, I started when I was eight years old. I had three brothers outside of me, and a sister. My older brothers they were older than I was and they were already playing so they didn't want me to put my hands on their guitar. So me and my sister would be at the house so we used to get their guitars and play them. My sister was just as good a musician as I am right now.

So one Sunday morning; my daddy used to be a hair cutter, he used to play music too. He used to cut hair so there used to be a little guy they called Peg Leg Roosevelt, he had a guitar. So they come in that Sunday morning. They come in so I asked Roosevelt, I said: "Roosevelt, let me see your guitar."

My older brother told him "No, don't let him see it he ain't gonna do nothing but break the strings." But I surprised all of them. I got the guitar and played everything they played. That made me feel good. They just come out there and looked at me like this: "Where did he learn that from." But I was stealing their guitar. That's what it was.

WHO'S IN THERE PLAYING THAT GUITAR?
ARCHIE EDWARDS

I started playing when I was six or seven years old. See, when I was a kid, my father played and he had some friends that would come past the house on Saturday nights and play the guitar. In those days, people didn't have nothing to do but walk five or six miles and come by his house, you know, and eat dinner, drink whiskey, and play the guitar.

Boyd Maddox came by the house on a Saturday night back in the early thirties. On a cold Saturday night we were all sitting in the living room with daddy, and this fellow playing the guitar. So my mother fixed dinner for them and they went into the kitchen to eat dinner. So when they went to eat dinner, the fellow left the guitar on the bed there in the living room.

So there was one note that was ringing like crazy in my head. It pressed on my mind to go over there to the bed to where they laid that guitar down and make that certain note. In those days, you know, children were taught not to touch anything that belonged to anyone else. If you did you just got torn up. But this note that guy had made sounded so pretty that one mind told me, "Say, man, if you can just get over there to that bed and make that note just one time, real low, you'll have it made."

I finally got the courage to sneak over to the bed, and I picked up the guitar and I made the note. But I think I dropped down on it a little too heavy, and my daddy heard it. He says, "Who's in there playing the guitar?"

And the fellow said, "Uncle Roy, that's your boy playing the guitar."

Well, he was right I was; and Uncle Roy's boy been playing ever since. And I didn't get a whipping. That was the best part of it. It shocked my dad so much, I guess he figured he better leave me alone.

LEARN BY LYING
SAM CHATMON

Sam Chatmon. Washington, D.C., July 1976. Courtesy of the Smithsonian Center for Folklife and Cultural Heritage.

People ask places how I learned how to pick the guitar. They ask and I told the truth, told them I learned to play by lying. I would pull that guitar off the wall; see, there wasn't no cases in them days. I'd get that guitar off the wall, and I'd wind it until I broke a string and I'd slip back in and I'd put it back up there. They come in and say, "Who had my guitar?" And I'd say, "I didn't."

So you see I had lied and that's the way I learned to pick.

BUZZ ME BABY
MAMIE DAVIS

When I was four, we had just moved in to Greenville out of like the rural area of the country. And the first day we moved in to this house there was a little girl; I met a little girl about my age that stayed two or three doors down. She had lived there for a time so she asked my mom if I could walk around the corner with her, you know, that evening. Mom said, "Yes," and when we got around the corner there was this joint and I heard all this music going. So at first I was just standing there trying to peep up in there to see what was going on and that little girl kept saying, "Come on Mamie, we're gonna get in trouble. We gotta go."

But I was so involved in what they were doing, she went on and left me; and so when I looked around she was gone. So I went on up in the place because at home people would take their children to these kinds of places. So I figured it was all right to go in there, so I went up in there. The next thing I know I was standing around the jukebox singing along with it and dancing. People were throwing nickels and dimes up and I was enjoying myself.

Then it dawned on me that I had to get out of there. So when I come out, I didn't know which way to go because, like I said, we had just moved in to this house. I didn't know my way home. I was just right around the corner, but I didn't know that, and so I just started to walking. My mom, when I got home, my mom said that they had been looking for me all day; they'd had the police looking for me and everything. And she said I just stumbled upon my house. See, I was walking down the street heading toward my house and I was just walking and singing this song that they had been playing on the jukebox. It was a song that goes, "Buzz me, buzz me baby."[14] See, I was walking and just singing and I only knew one line, singing that one line over and over. And she said she realized then that I was musically inclined, you know, after she got through whipping me for being gone all day.

HE WOULD HAVE KILLED ME ABOUT THAT
BIG JOE DUSKIN

I don't know why I didn't get killed going out in the country; like I'd go through the woods one time I got chased by a wild bull. If you ever go in a ditch a bull will never come at you. I don't know why. He'll run up beside that ditch and he'll bellow like mad and run back and forth but he'll never go down in there. And I just stayed down in there until he finally got tired and he went on about his business. And I'd go on over to the church over there and jump behind the piano. Because they had a window like this and the piano was catty corner, so I just crawl over and jump behind there, and I'd sit down and listen to that. Just put my head next to it, almost on the sound board, and hear those old tunes like that. So I went to sleep behind there. And so what happened was one of the ladies heard me snoring she say, "Come here some of y'all. This boy over here laying by this piano asleep whose boy is this?"

My Uncle Bob, he come out and, "Oh Lord, this is Perry's boy." That's my dad's name.

Say, "I better take this boy back home. I bet the old man's having a fit about this boy."

And when we got almost to the house we hear him, "Hey, Joe." He's just hollering like a lion out in the woods.

[Uncle Bob] He said, "Boy, you hear your daddy calling you. Jump out of this wagon and run under the porch right quick. And I can tell him you're under there and maybe he won't bother you."

So Uncle Bob say, "Perry, what you looking for?"

"I'm trying to find that boy." He had his strap in his hand. "I'm trying to find that boy. I don't know where that devilish boy is."

Said: "Did you look under the house?" Because they had these houses built up.

The old man says, "No."

Says, "Look under the house. He might be there asleep."

And I'm laying there acting like I sleeping and he found me and he picked me up and hugged me and carried me in the house and put me to bed. I think it was John, Ed, Perry, and myself. It was four of us. Oh, man, those were the good old days. But I never did tell the old man I had been over there like that, no he would have killed me about that.

I GOT TO TAKE THIS BEATING
CHARLES BROWN

Chick Webb's band came to Galveston, Texas, to the auditorium. I wanted to go; so all the other kids were going. They wanted to hear this "Tisket a Tasket" by Ella Fitzgerald and Chick Webb.[15] So I told my grandmother, I say, "Mama, I want to go see Ella Fitzgerald and Chick Webb when they play there Friday night."

She says: "You can't go because I don't allow you to go to anything like that."

Because they church sisters, you know.

I say: "Mama, I am going to hear Ella Fitzgerald and Chick Webb."

So I went and I saw Chick Webb play his drums, and Ella Fitzgerald. So when I went home that night, my grandmother was waiting for me. She had plaited three cedar switches together and soaked them in this big old aluminum tub. She had soaked these three cedar switches that she put together. And when I walked in she said, "Take off your clothes. You think you grown, huh?"

I said, "Mama, what you gonna do?"

"Take off those clothes."

I mean, I'm sixteen years old and I was pretty big, but she was big, too. I knew not to fight her. I said, "I got to take this beating. I saw Ella Fitzgerald and Chick Webb." She whipped me until blood was on the top of those welts.

"I'm gonna teach you a lesson if you think you're grown."

But I didn't cry because I did what I wanted.

YOU HAD TO PLAY IT OUT
J. OTIS WILLIAMS

The first real musical experiences that I had that really hooked me to music were from the Rabbit Foot shows, the Silas Green from New Orleans.[16] See they had great blues bands. And when they came to town it was like if they were going to be in town for a couple nights, Friday or Saturday. They would have a parade around noon down through downtown, and they would have the big band marching drums and they would be playing all this good music. And little kids, dogs and cats and everything would be following them, and the best music that you ever wanted to hear. And they had some great blues singers, too, in these shows. Like a lot of people, I didn't know who they were when I heard them, but a lot of people played with the Rabbit Foot Minstrels or Silas Green.

These bands were all black, so after the shows they would play in the local jook joints. And I remember one in particular; the room where they played was right on the level of the street. So after the show instead of going on home we'd go on down there to the joint and stand outside the window and listen to them play and sing. And they had people like Roy Brown who sang that real classic blues. It was just, you couldn't go home, and you knew you were gonna get a whipping. But, it was just that, see, this was something that just never happened so you had to play it on out.

LEAVE THEM BOYS ALONE
CEDELL DAVIS

CeDell Davis. Clarksdale, Mississippi,
August 7, 1993. Photograph by Barry
Lee Pearson.

My momma didn't allow it. My momma used to run me out of the house
many a day because I was in there playing guitar. But my stepfather he'd
say, "Let that boy alone."

He never hit me a day in his life until I was grown. He never hit me.
The only thing he would do, "Boy come on and play. Go on and play
because someday you might make your living." Sure enough he was
right.

He said, "Don't pay momma no attention. She's old fashioned don't
pay her no attention." He was older than she was but he'd say, "Don't
pay her no attention, because some of these days you're gonna make you
living doing that."

I said, "You reckon?"

He say, "You don't never know. Do whatever you can, if you're
hired to make a living. Don't pay momma no attention"

Because you know what he'd do as soon as her back was turned
he'd say, "Hey boy you got a little money?"

I'd say: "Yeah I got forty or fifty cents."

"Give me fifty cents."

And he'd go get him a half pint with that you know. He liked to drink. My momma would jump on him and beat his ass. She'd come on and whip his butt. She was bad. But he wouldn't let her bother us, me and my brother. No, he wouldn't let her bother us. She'd get a switch or a strap or something and was gonna whip us. That would make him mad. "I want you to leave them boys alone. They ain't done nothing."

I RUN OFF TO CRENSHAW
ALBERT "SUNNYLAND SLIM" LUANDREW

My people didn't go for blues. My father was a Christian; Grandfather and Grandmother were Christian. They didn't go for that; called them "corn songs."[17] That was around 1912. Well, after my father married this stepmother, I must have been about six or seven. She was mean to me. My grandfather had another place about six miles out from Vance. Up there, that's where my father went, and that's where I started to catch the devil. Seven years old, eight years old, and at the same time these people that had the organ moved from Vance up to another little old place. A fellow called Blaines, he worked a lot of land; chopped cotton, picked cotton, people pay him. I was growing up, so my stepmother was mean. My cousin worked with my father, my father raised him and I. What I did, I could go around these girls and play one little piece on the organ that would stay in my head all night. And while the boys be around the girls, I'd be trying to put that to the organ, you know, until I got about eight or nine. I was scared. I was so scared of my father and people, my stepmother, until I couldn't concentrate on the organ too much. And what I did, I'd play, I tried to play when it would rain. You couldn't work. You go down and play.

So when I got about eleven years old I run off from home. My father kept on preaching. Now he got me that time, and I come back and they put me back out working. And when it would rain I'd go over to another lady's mother's church. My father was a pastor. She had a beautiful organ, and Jeff Morris would be over there. I can remember the first key I played in, F. And he tried to show me the way I do: I drawed the organ with my pencil the white keys and the black keys and where he had his hand, I'd put a print there. And when I seen it was the same thing, just below I'd make it get the sound; some of the sound would stay in my ear. I cut wood and stayed with a lady in Corton. Her husband gambled.

He didn't like to do nothing but gamble, sit around and drink all the time, go around where they gambled. That's the organ I first learned how to play, "Tramp, Tramp, the Boys are Marching." That's a song, a march in school. And I learned "If I Could Hear My Mother Pray Again." And it sounded pretty good.

And this next time I got to be about thirteen, I run off to Crenshaw. They found me again and me and her got into it again. I run off and went to a logging camp. That's where I losed him at. And I stayed there a while, and this fellow had an old piano and I'd stay around that. I wasn't doin' much. I used to play a little bit. And I got in love with a girl. This guy take her from me; mostly all the girls go with him. He had an old T-Model Ford. And that's where I changed, "If I Could Hear my Mother Pray," some of it, into the blues.

I COULD SEE STARS
STERLING "MR. SATAN" MAGEE

Sterling "Mr. Satan" Magee. Largo, Maryland, September 15, 1996. Photograph by Barry Lee Pearson.

My mother bought my sister a piano and by all means I learned to play it first; so I was very interested in music. But she was 100 percent Christian and the law was no boogie-woogie, no blues.

She says, "You can play Christian music, but no boogie-woogie and no blues in here."

"Yes ma'am, mama."

That was my reply.

But quite naturally at school, if the professor was out somewhere, I would play the piano. So when I get home I still had it in my mind to play this boogie-woogie; but I could only exercise the song on Saturday. On Saturday we'd take off and go to town, which is the big day for shopping and everything. Everybody here knows what I'm talking about. In the country you work all week, so the only free day you got to go to town is Saturday. But a lot of Saturdays I would choose to stay home because I could play me some boogie-woogie. So I'm in there playing that piano. Now mother and them's supposed to be over in town shopping, so I'm playing the boogie-woogie and I'm carried away, too. I'd be on it, my eyes closed, playing. I didn't know mother and father had come back the back way. The back door eased open. I'm steady playing boogie. All of a sudden I could see stars. "Pow!"

I just break right away from that into "Yes, Jesus Loves Me."

But I know what happened. Mama slipped in the back door and got me. "Whap!"

And I go right into my "Yes, Jesus Loves Me" and I'm crying, too.

I had it hard trying to play the blues and that is no joke. That is reality. If I could, I would have them put in jail now because I was totally abused.

I MADE THE BLUES INTO AMAZING GRACE
BIG JESSE YAWN

It's been a part of my life for as long as I can remember. Before the blues, the next thing to it, what's above it, is spirituals. I was into spirituals. I was brought up in a very strict household. I couldn't sing the blues, but I could go around the corner and do it. And that's what I did. But you could easily say that I'd get killed if I was caught in my mother's house singing what she called a reel. I never knew what a reel meant, but I knew it meant it was not a church song meaning you couldn't sing it in there. So I quickly learned how to change. I made the blues into "Amazing Grace" so I could save the butt whippings.

THE LORD'S GONNA STRIKE YOU DOWN
"H-BOMB" FERGUSON

Bobby "H-Bomb" Ferguson. Cuyahoga State Park, Ohio, September 21, 1985. Photograph by Dexter Hodges. Courtesy of the National Council for the Traditional Arts.

It started with my father being a small town minister. He sent me to music school to play the piano; church music, religious music. I played for the kids at Sunday school; and after Sunday school, everybody would go back upstairs and we would close the door, the kids and I. Then I got to playing the boogie-woogie until he caught me, and then he would crack me with whatever he put his hands on, belt, stick or what not. Tell me I'm gonna die and go to hell 'cause that's the Devil's music.

I say, "I'm sorry, daddy, I ain't gonna play it no more." And every chance I would get I would play it.

Now at that time I really wanted to play what I'm playing now, but naturally I had to go along with his program, you know, in his house.

And everybody in the neighborhood knew us and every time they see you, well, "That's Reverend Ferguson's kid. I'm gonna tell him he's been playing that dirty music." The neighbors tell on me. They hear you.

And everybody that had a piano, I would go to their house and play it. Sneak and do it. But it got back to him two and three days later, and he would walk in the door. And sometimes I forgot that I had did it.

"Ah, you was at Miss Clara's house the other day."

I said, "Yes, daddy"

He said, "You, was over there playing that boogie-woogie and that blues."

I said, "Yes, I was just fooling around."

He said, "What did I tell you? You want to go to hell son or what you want to do?"

I said, "No sir."

He said, "What do you think I'm paying that lady to teach you how to play for."

I said, "Play the music for the Lord and Sunday school."

"Well, why don't you do it?"

I said, "I do do it, daddy, but sometimes I want to play that blues."

"Well, I'm not going to pay my hard earned money for that. Now, you either gonna do what I tell you or you get out of my house."

I said, "I don't want to leave. I'm gonna stay here and I ain't gonna do it no more, I promise you."

"Now you suppose to go to Miss Clara's house." That's the school-teacher's name, I'll never forget it. An old lady, she teaches one hour at that time, I think it was a buck.

"I work hard for my dollar and I'm trying to make you be somebody. One day you'll play for a religious group and you'll appreciate what I did."

I said, "Yes sir, I realize that."

And every chance I get, I take and play the blues. My mother went along with me.

"Why don't you listen to your daddy and try to do what he says. You know he wants you to be in the church, and that stuff you're playing don't make no sense and gets you in a lot of trouble."

I said, "Momma, I know. But I don't know why I want to play the blues."

"Well, see, you listen to them old crazy records, and Buddy Johnson[18] and all these bands coming through there. You see them out there they jump up and be dancing. That happy music ain't nothing but trouble. You'll go to jail, son. So play what your daddy's paying you for and one day you'll thank him."

I said, "O.K. Momma, I'm gonna try that."

I still had hell in me. I went and played my way. Then when I got about fifteen or sixteen I really decided I don't want to play this church stuff.

Mama said, "You got something against the lord?"

I said, "No, ma'am, I don't have nothing against it."

"But what makes you want to play that kind of stuff? That's trash."

I say, "Well, to tell you the truth, mama, I might not be here. One day you'll hear about me, that's what you're gonna have. And that's all I got to say."

"But I'll tell you what; the Lord's gonna strike you down."

I said, "Well that's what he's gonna have to do 'cause I'm gonna play the blues."

HE'S LIVING OFF MY DAYS
BIG JOE DUSKIN

The old man wanted to bring a preacher out of the family, and he picked me out to do it. And I used to sit at his feet and go to sleep; he'd say: "Wake up boy."

And I'd wake up, and I was so sleepy. And I'd listen to him, and he'd say, "Do you know what Jesus said about so and so?"

And I'd answer him. And he'd know I was listening to him. Finally my mom came in there and said: "God, why don't you leave that kid alone. Let that boy rest sometime."

"Well, hell, I want that boy to be a good preacher one of these days."

At that time I didn't quite understand. So when we got up to Cincinnati here, that's what he wanted me to be. He said, "Joseph, now, I want you to be a minister."

I said, "Come on daddy, I can't do that." I said, "I got to go to school. I got to do this and the other and all that."

And he knew that I could play piano, and he told me, said, "If you ever let me catch you playing that devil's music I'm gonna skin you alive."

And that's what he did if he caught me playing what we called the devil's music. Everywhere he'd hear that piano he'd know it was me.

"That dirty scamp. I heard him."

He went around the back, and I'm trying to climb over the fence and, boy, he caught me and pulled me off that fence, took me back out on the street on Gorman Street, and just whipped the devil out of me. I mean he really got hold to me, too. And so when he did I run on ahead of him and I come to my mom she say, "What's the matter?"

I said, "Dad just knocked me down and, God, he liked to kill me with that bull whip, mom."

I said, "I wish to god he'd stop using that thing."

She said, "Lord, let me talk to Dus when he comes in." She called him Dus. She say, "Dus, what did you bother Joe for?"

"That dirty bear hugger."

He'd call you a bear hugger; and he called me that. Finally I went in the house, I said, "Dad, why don't you get with it."

At that time they were using a little slang. I said, "Why don't you get with it, dad. You read your bible every day and every time I look around you're whipping me because I'm playing this music."

I said, "God, I'll be playing that until I die and you'll have to be whipping me every time you turn around."

So he says, "Well, I don't want to be whipping me every time I turn around." He says, "Wait a minute, I'll tell you what. I'm eighty-nine years old, why don't you wait until I'm dead in the grave. Then you can play all you want to."

Well, I thought that was nice and I made the agreement to do it. So he'd take me to church, I'd play church songs and all that. So finally, when he got a hundred and one, I went straight to mama. I said, "Mom, look a here, you got to look at this. This old man is gonna live like Methuselah; look, he's never gonna go in the ground. He's living off my days; he's borrowing some of yours."

So she says, "You get out of here wanting your dad to die so you can play music."

I said, "No, I don't want him to die to play music. But I can't play none until he's in the ground. When's he gonna go in there? He's a hundred and one years old, and he promised that he'd be in the grave by this time. He made a promise and he's way over his due now."

He got a hundred and two, and a hundred and three, and a hundred and four. I just threw up both hands. I just never did touch the piano. I went in the army and I never broke that vow. I stuck to it when I come out. I never played. I just gave it up. And when he got a hundred and five, he died in my arms. That's the worst thing that ever happened to me in my life. I can feel the old man's head right now sometimes.

I WAS NEVER THERE
ERNESTINE "MISS TINA" JACKSON

Ernestine "Miss Tina" Jackson.
Washington, D.C., September 6, 1997.
Photograph by Barry Lee Pearson.

All of my younger years, my teenage years growing up, I was in a home church choir. I was in a church choir for about ten years, but I have never recorded gospel. But I sing a lot of it even now when I go home. This past month I went home and, of course, Mom had to have her thing. Mama's still in charge, so we have to do the thing with the choir; so we still sing gospel. My mother, she would do the Sunday programs for every event that there was and we had to sing on the program, so she had instant talent.

When I was in Mississippi, I was very young. We had the house parties and all that was great, and the jook joints. Well, Mama still don't know about that part. So maybe we shouldn't tell her. I left Mississippi when I was sixteen years old, so you see why I can't discuss the jook joints. I didn't go. I was never there. Not even the ones with the sawdust on the floor.

TURN AROUNDS

THIS IS SATAN'S MUSIC
JOHN CEPHAS

When I was growing up, and I grew up in a religious home, my father was a Baptist minister and all of my young years, even before I was attracted to the blues, I was always encouraged to play religious music. If I'm interested in music, this was the way to go. I can remember when I was about four or five years old my mother had my brother and myself in church singing spirituals as a duet at that early age. And as I grew up, and when they found out that I was kind of interested in blues, man, I used to get down, really get down in the country.

"This is the wrong way to go. Don't go to the houses of ill repute."

But whenever they would party, like on the weekends, Fridays or Saturdays when other people would come over, the first thing they would say was, "John, go get your guitar and come out and play a few numbers for some of the people here." In the house, you understand. And they would partake of the blues too. My father, he was an aspiring blues player. The first guitar I ever had in my life belonged to my father and I used to play his guitar. He wanted to learn to play blues. And when they would have those house parties, my father was right in the midst of them clapping his hands and having a good time. But they would always discourage me.

"No, no, don't do this, don't do this; please, don't do this."

But I didn't look at it like that. A lot of times they say, "Oh God, this is Satan's music, this is devil's music. Those people are getting drunk and they're down in there having a good time with women and they're doing all these things of ill repute. For God's sakes, don't do this."

But when the band struck up, they was right there.

I COULD COME OUT THE SIDE WINDOW
FONTELLA BASS

Every Friday, Saturday, I would leave my clothes; my uncle lived across the street with his wife, Aunt Edie, and I would leave clothes with them. My mother and them, Saturday night, nine o'clock, they would be in bed, you know, because of church. They'd have to get up at five o'clock in the morning get ready for Sunday school and so forth. Honey, I would be gone and get back in the window. See, I had a side window, like the way houses were made like a row house, you know. And I could come out the side window. I did it for years. The shows used to be in the levee, Red Top, Lakeside, you know, and they'd be singing the blues. I'd get right up there with them and sing the blues and they would be amazed.

And a lot of times it would get back to my mother, but they couldn't pronounce my name, you know, and I was real popular. But they said, "that girl," "that little young girl," but they couldn't pronounce my name, Fontella, so they would call me "Penelope," "Fonella," everything. And sometimes I'd get tickled because they would honestly be telling my mother but she wouldn't catch on because they'd have some other name you know. And I'd just play it right off.

But I guess I was close to forty before my mother let me know that she really knew, because I was with family, and the secret to that was with my grandfather. He say, "Hey, you can sing, you can dance, but no fellas, no alcohol, no smoking."

They were very strict. I had the freedom, but I had my limits.

WHY DON'T YOU PUT THAT THING DOWN
JOHNNIE BILLINGTON

Being a kid, growing up so to speak on a plantation, at twelve o'clock they had a fifteen-minute blues show on the radio station. And at twelve o'clock is when most of my people was at the house. We ate lunch at twelve. And being a kid, I'd listen to the radio because that's all we really had was the radio. So I listened to the radio, and I was just kind of interested in the sound that it had. And then during the day when they was working in the field, of course I was too small to work, but my parents were working and you'd be out there. I had noticed the birds, at that time there was a lot of birds in this part of the country, and they would be peeping late in the afternoon. And it was kind of like the guitar playing over there. They had a shuffle. This bird peeping and that one peeping, and they just kind of had a rhythm going and I would listen, "Jesus, that sounds great."

And it sounds almost like if he was playing an instrument. Then I might listen to the radio and, "Jesus, that's where those guys got that from." They kind of hear those different birds that was peeping late in the afternoon before it got dark, because after it got dark they all was quiet.

And so it made me very interested in trying to duplicate some of those sounds. And my father happened to get a hold of an old acoustic guitar and gave it to me. So I said, "Well, I'm gonna learn how to play it."

Having some sisters that was older, they used to say I'd be bumping on that thing around the house and not really doing a very good job. And they'd get mad and say, "You ain't going to play that guitar. Why don't you put that thing down?"

So I was determined to try to do it until I would go outside around the side of the house and keep on beating on it. My sisters would come outside and mess with me again. By this time my mother would take up for me, she'd say, "Now wait a minute. Now y'all leave him alone. You ran him out of the house because he was making noise and disturbing you as you say. But he went outside, went around the side of the house and was sitting around there on a bucket or something or other. He ain't playing, but he's entertaining himself. He's making some noise that he's satisfied with. Now don't bother him no more."

So then my sisters wouldn't never bother me anymore. Then later on, I finally got a tune kind of together that sounded worth something, and I was sitting there beating on it and I looked and saw my sisters and them patting their feet. And I said: "Wait a minute. What are you patting your foot for?"

"It sound pretty good."

"Oh, you the ones that said I ain't gonna do nothing with it."

SHE'S WORRYING ME
JOHN DEE HOLEMAN

I first started when I was a teenager about thirteen or fourteen years old. I had an uncle and a cousin that played guitar around those corn shuckings and wood cuttings and so forth. So at the time that I was a kid, I saw them do that, but at that time you couldn't touch what they had because they figure a kid, you'd knock it out of tune or whatever. So I just looked at them and watched different ones do it. So I picked my little get-up from looking at them; I stole some from just looking. So I go to the place that I was not playing, but just trying to learn, bang, banging on it, you know, and it was very noisy. It disturbed my mother and she say, "Boy I wish you would put that thing away. All that noise is worrying me to death."

So instead of disturbing her, I'd go out to the barn by myself and I would bang on it. The horses and the cows that were up there, they wouldn't say nothing. They didn't tell me to quit. So I wasn't getting anybody hurt. So I just kept tinking, tinking and messing with it until I could hit a little tune. So I finally learned to play a little bit. The first songs I remember playing were "Precious Lord Take My hand" and "Baby Please Don't Go."

And after that she come to like it. So then she told me, "Don't never come out to visit me unless you got that guitar and I can hear you play." Whilst I was learning, it worried her. But after I learned how to play she loved it. Instead of me worrying her about that, then she's worrying me.

YOU'RE GONNA TAKE IT BACK
LITTLE MILTON CAMPBELL

I loved the guitar so much. Always have and still do. I built, I guess, what every kid that likes music or whatever, the old thing up against the wall of the house. You take the two nails and the strings of haybailing wire, and you put these nails in the wall and you tie this wire around it. And you get a couple of bricks and put in on each end. And you use something to pick it with, and bottle. You get, you know, like a Hawaiian type sound. I call them guitars, other people call them other things, you know. But then I tried to make a guitar with boards. Naturally, it wouldn't stay; it wasn't stiff enough.

So after working and trying to save my little money doing odd things, and stealing a little money . . . when I say stealing I mean like not giving it all to my mom because that was a must. You make some money you got to go turn it in and then she give you what she wanted you to have. So I'd hold out. And I saved and saved until I saved up enough to pay for a little mail-order catalog guitar. And I think I ordered from a mail catalog which at that time was Walter Fields. And it cost fourteen dollars and I think about forty some cents. And when the notice came, I'd be the one to go and get the notice and what have you.

My mom said, "Maybe it's something you ordered for me or something I ordered, so go see what it is."

I knew what it was. I went and got the guitar and brought it back. I was all excited on the way back. I had took it from the box a few times, you know. And when she saw it she hit the ceiling. She hit the ceiling and told me, "You're gonna take it back! Where did you get the money from?"

And blah, blah, blah. We had a hell of a big go 'round.

So I was sitting outside sad, and my stepfather, whom I respect the utmost, he was the man of the house. He was the man. Whatever he said, that's what it was. So I was sitting out looking sad, sitting on the step waiting. When he came home he said, "What's wrong Milton?"

And I told him what had happened. He told me, he said, "Don't worry about it. I'll handle it."

And he went in and the voices raised a little bit then it was quiet, and after a while he came out and winked his eye at me. She never said anything else about the guitar. But through the years after I got to be successful I would tease her because I loved her dearly, and I always told her when I was a kid, I told her that one day she wouldn't have to worry about anything, that I would take good care of her. And I did do that. And I said, "Mom, you think maybe I should have took that guitar back?"

She said, "Hell, no, man. I'm glad you didn't."

She didn't use the words "Hell, no," but it meant the same thing. It's a true story.

GIVE ME SOME OF THAT OTHER STYLE
DOCTOR ROSS

When I first started off, I started by myself. But there was another friend; he was a good little bit older than I was. We called him G.P.; his name was George Jackson. So he would always stop in. And he heard me playing one day he decided, "Say, I'm gonna ask your father can you go out with me to play at birthday parties."

And so I said, "Oh, Papa might let you, take me out. I don't know, but I don't believe he will."

He said, "Mr. Jake Ross is an awful mean man, but I'm gonna try him. I'm gonna see if he'll let me take you out."

So he asked Papa one day. And Papa told him, "Well, this boy got quite a bit of work to do. He got to milk the cows and feed the hogs."

And he said, "Mr. Jake, I will bring him back; I guarantee it. I just want to keep him for about an hour. We're playing at a birthday party." And he said, "I'll help him do some of his work."

So Papa said, "O.K. if you help him. You feed the mules while he milks the cows, then he can go with you."

So we did that right quick and then we went off and I played at the birthday party. G.P. was playing the guitar and I was playing the harmonica; and another friend name Doc Tolbert, he was playing the bucket. You know, he could really play the bucket too. From that he eased me out into the jook houses where there is gambling going on and the people playing poker, blackjack, shooting dice, and everything.

So I could always tell my father I was going to the show in Tunica. See, I wouldn't have to come back. I'd tell him I was gonna stay all night with my brother tonight. So Papa said, "Go ahead. O.K."

So I would go to Tunica, stay there about forty minutes. Go in and peep at the show a little bit and then ease out, see. And the people was giving me nice money. And so I'd ease back to the jook house and play.

So it was some more men there. Some of them was older than my father, some of them just the same age he was. And they told him about it, say, "We never heard a young boy play like him."

Papa say, "Who's that?"

There was a man there name of Mr. Frank Williams; he told my father. They was strict, old people was strict in them days. He told my father, he says, "Mr. Jake?" He say, "Yeah, Frank," and he says, "Your little boy Isaiah say that man they call 'Sonny Boy' now he's great, but Sonny Boy won't touch him no where."

Papa say, "Oh Frank, oh no." Say, "Where did you hear him at?"

Say, "Mr. Jake, don't whip the boy." Say, "He plays at them house parties and birthday parties. I heard him up at Fred Danaworth's place."

"My son was up there playing after ten o'clock at night?"

He says, "Don't whip him, don't whip him, Mr. Jake. That boy, one of these days he's gonna make you a lot of money and you won't have to work no more."

And so now Papa knew about it. So about two weeks later he asks me about why I don't play him a piece. I'm ashamed of it you know.

I say, "Sir."

He said, "I want you to play me a piece."

I said, "Yes, sir," and I'm trying to think of something. I didn't know that he knew that I been out there playing the blues, and so I'm trying to think. And so, oh I played the "Old Freight Train."

He said, "Oh, that's good, but give me some of that other style. You play in a different style give me some of that style."

I said, "What style?"

He say, "I knows about it. I've heard about you. Go on and play like you did last Saturday night up at the jook house."

Oh, I thought he was gonna get me. I thought he was gonna whip me. He says, "I ain't gonna bother you, but if you don't play I'm gonna tear you up."

And lord have mercy, you talk about a little boy getting hell scared out of him! And I blowed, I blowed. I ain't never seen my father dance before, but he got out there and did he dance! Oh Lord! And then he sent my other uncle, Uncle Jody, to get a whole gallon of corn whiskey and Uncle Jody brought it back. And papa, that's the first time I ever saw him drink. And he drank and said, "I see what Frank and them was talking about." He say, "You is—nobody can touch you." He says, "You can play that harmonica better than anybody on the face of this earth I ever heard play."

And that's how I got started to playing.

YOU COULD HAVE BOUGHT ME FOR A PENNY
"H-BOMB" FERGUSON

Now here comes a band through town playing a dance; cost a dollar to go to the dance. I save up my little dollar and went to the dance. The band was playing the blues, Cat Anderson. When they took a break I walked backstage. They had a guard by the door, the manager.

I said, "Pardon me. Ah, you that guy that got this band playing the blues?"

He say, "Yeah, what you want?"

I said, "Well, I play a little blues on the piano and I'm from here. And I want to know could I, would he let me come up there and sing a song with him? I don't want to sing but one song and I want to find out what he thinks."

Well, he said, "You wait by this door and let me go and ask him." "Hey Cat, we got a little kid out here think he can sing and play the blues."

Cat said, "Tell him to come on in the dressing room." He says, "How long you been playing and singing."

I said, "About three years, now. I don't know a whole lot of songs but I know two or three of them real good."

"What key?"

I said, "B flat."

He said, "Wait a minute. Sit down." He went down the hall and brought the guitar player with him. He said, "Start singing." He told the guitar player, "Pick up behind him," and "I can tell what you know." I start singing.

He said, "Hey man, you don't sound too bad. Now you play almost as good as you sing?"

I said, "A little bit."

He said, "Well, we gonna let you play tonight. I'm gonna bring you up and let you sing behind the band." He had nine pieces.

I said, "I might be kind of nervous all them people out there."

He said, "Well, this is your home town. We gonna tell them it's a home town boy and let you do one. But I'll tell the band. We'll cue you on everything. We'll watch you. We gonna play about four songs and we gonna call you up. What's your name?"

I said, "Robert Ferguson, that's my real name."

"Well, what they call you?"

"Just say Bobby Ferguson."

He said, "That sounds like a stupid name for a singer."

I said, "Yes, but I'm just trying. I never did this before. Not in front of no public."

He said, "Well, O.K. When we get to it I'm gonna call you up."

I said, "Thank you very much, sir. I sure appreciate that."

I ran outside and told half of my friends that was there. I said, "I'm gonna go up on that stage and sing tonight."

They didn't believe me. "No you're not."

I said, "Yeah, honestly. Cat's gonna actually call me up there and I'm gonna sing the blues tonight in front of all these people."

I said, "You all think I ain't going up there. Watch me."

He called me. You could have bought me for a penny. I got nervous. Man, there was about two thousand people there. I got up on the stage. I was shaking. He had to pull me up there.

"Now, Ladies and Gentlemen, one of your own home town boys, said he's gonna sing the blues, Bobby Ferguson."

Everybody did like that [*applauds*]. Some of the people in that town didn't even know I was singing. But I got up there. It took me about five minutes to get myself together. They kicked off. I didn't know about that. Then he cut it off. He told me, "O.K. Start singing." So the band caught me. So later he say, "Man, about six months, you keep that up, you gonna be all right."

HE TURNED HIS BACK ON ME
JOHNNY SHINES

Robert [Johnson] was playing some of the stuff that I wanted to play and making chords that I was lacking, so I began to follow him around to hear him play. Not hear him play, but to watch him play. And he would catch me watching him and he'd get gone real quick.

Robert caught me looking at him watching his fingers and he turned his back on me and I didn't see him no more for about three months. So, I did meet him again and the same thing happened again. He walked off from me. Robert was doing some of the things that I wanted to do, things I never heard a guitar player do. And finally he said to me, one day he said, "Anything a person can do on a piano or a horn, I aim to do it on the guitar."

And he did. Robert was a man that could sit talking to you like I'm talking to you now, and listen to the radio at the same time. And whenever he got ready, he could play whatsoever he heard over the radio note for note, chord for chord. Whether he knew what chord he was making I don't think he did, but they just fell on his fingers. He did it. He played it and sang it whenever he got ready. He didn't have to go for it the second time. I had to go for it the third time, but he didn't. He could hear it one time and do it. In other words, I think he had a photographic memory.

So I ran into him again in Helena over at Robert Junior's mother's house. That's where Robert Johnson was staying and we set up a friendship. But it wasn't really too good of a friendship because that evening when I saw him playing, Robert turned and walked off. And I didn't see him no more for about three months. He caught me watching him play, you know. And that went on for close to a year. He'd catch me watching him and he'd walk away. He'd just disappear. Just get swallowed up in the crowd. So anyway I was staying in Hughes and I went into the restaurant where I lived. I lived in one of the apartments there. And the landlady says, "There's a fellow in your room up there."

I said: "Yeah, who is he?"

She say, "I don't know what his name is but he plays guitar and sings like a bird." I said: "That's Robert."

You know he had come where I was. All the time before he'd been shunning me. Now he had come where I was.

HONEY CAN PLAY NOW
DAVID "HONEYBOY" EDWARDS

Well, when I was young, after I quit playing with Big Joe,[19] I learned the ropes, so I went out by myself. So I learned from what he was doing and I played with different musicians then. See, I stayed with Big Joe about pretty close to a year and I was running around with him. See, at that time Joe was pretty rough. He liked to drink whiskey and get drunk and fight and so on. But I was young and I didn't want him to fight me and everything. We got along good as long as he wasn't drinking. He'd make money and he'd take care of me. He'd get a room for me to stay, he feed me, give me some change to put in my pocket.

So we'd play like little grocery stores, and we'd play little restaurants . . . on the streets, different places. But he'd collect the money because he was an old time hustler. He'd go to the hotel, count the money, give me some part, then he take some to pay for this and that you know. So he took care of me and learned me how to do.

And we went to the French Quarter in New Orleans. He met a French woman there and he was getting with her and she bought us some suits and things. Put suits on him and everything, clothes to straighten us up. And Joe got to clowning once again and want to fight, and so I slipped off and left him. I left Joe and I came down number 90 Highway right out of New Orleans. I walked. I had me a little harp rack in my pocket and a guitar. I had never played by myself so I said I got to try it. I come to Bay St. Louis and the people was on the river, on the bridge catching crabs with the nets, you know. Put the meat in the net and let them down and the crab go on in. Pull it up.

And say, "Boy can you play that guitar?"

Say, "I can do pretty good."

And I started to playing and racked my harmonica, and it was the first time. But I had been practicing good. They started chunking me nickels and dimes and things. I left then, went on to Pass Christian, Gulfport, and when I come to Gulfport I start playing on the streets. I was doing like Joe was doing. I got pretty good.

Two insurance guys picked me up, two white guys picked me up and carried me to Columbia and they carried me up to an old man's house who stayed by himself. They said, "This boy can play music good. Let him stay here with you and hustle around the city until he gets ready to leave."

"Yes, sir, he can stay here, yes, sir."

I stayed with the man then while I played. Well, I stayed about a week. I played around Columbia made a little money there and I left and come back to Greenwood where my family was. When I come home I was playing the guitar then and my sisters and them were standing around me just like they had never saw anybody play before.

"Honey can play now, Papa Honey can play."

THEY DIDN'T KNOW THE DIFFERENCE
JERRY MCCAIN

I just met Little Walter[20] one time when he came to Gadsden and he was a nice fellow. We rode around. I didn't drink. I just rode around in the back and played harmonica. And my brother and Little Walter was sitting up front. My brother knew where every bootlegger was so he just went from one to the other. Little Walter was crazy about that corn. He didn't care about no sealed liquor, but man, he drank that corn. And my brother knew where every damn bootlegger was. So we'd just go from one place to the other, you know, and he was drinking. And that's when

Little Walter had that thing out called "Juke" and the flip side was "I Can't Hold On Much Longer." His song went:

**YOU KNOW I'M CRAZY ABOUT YOU BABE
WONDER DO YOU EVER THINK OF ME.
YOU KNOW I'M JUST CRAZY ABOUT YOU BABY
I WONDER DO YOU EVER THINK OF ME?**

So they were up front and I'm sitting in the back and I started playing, singing: "Little Walter said he was crazy about you, baby."

He turned around and looked.

**HE SAID HE WONDERED IF YOU EVER THINK OF HIM.
OH, LITTLE WALTER SAID HE WAS CRAZY ABOUT YOU, GIRL.
HE OFTEN WONDERED DID YOU THINK OF HIM.
OH, BUT THE POOR BOY DIDN'T KNOW IT,
I WAS THE REASON HIS LIGHT WAS BURNING SO DIM.**

He said, "God damn man, that's all right, that's all right."

Boy, we rode around; shit, I play the harmonica, he sit up there, and he was high as a Georgia pine. And so when they had the gig that night, boy, the place was packed. And he had people jumping everywhere. And I don't know, hell, he wasn't older than I was, but he always— Sonny Boy Williamson was the same way—all of them, they want to call me "Junior." He say, "Hey Junior."

And he had them. Boy, they was rocking off that "Juke." I went up on the stage. He had one of those Marine band [harmonica]. He had done squeezed that motherfucker so until the back went down.

He just said, "Get your harmonica."

He had them going like that and they were jumping. I got up right there beside him, he handed the mike to me and I just kept going. And they were still dancing. Finally, an old guy looked up and said, "Hey y'all, that ain't Little Walter, that's Jerry."

And, shit, they didn't know the difference because during that time, I was playing just like him. He had them rocking; then when he switched over and give it to me it was still rocking. They didn't know the difference.

THAT'S WHAT THE WORLD NEEDS TODAY
KOKO TAYLOR

I went to Chicago with my boyfriend, which turned out to be my husband. His name is Robert Taylor, but everybody around Chicago knew him as Pop Taylor. After we got to Chicago—because I still loved the blues, singing the blues, listening to the blues—I realized a lot of people that I had been listening to on the radio in Memphis was right in Chicago. Howling Wolf, Jimmy Reed, Sonny Boy Williams, and all these folks, you know. The first thing we did when we got to Chicago was to find work. My husband was lucky enough to find a job at Wilson Packing Company, which was a slaughterhouse for cows and stuff like that. I was lucky. I got a job working for a rich family, a rich white family up on Chicago's North Shore, a suburb was called Wilmette, Winnetka, Glencoe, and all up there. I got a job working for these people. And things were going real good.

Weekends, when we both was off, we would go to these different clubs; and the guys got to where they'd know me from coming around on weekends, and my husband would tell them, "Well, my wife she sings, you know, she likes to sing." In the meantime my husband played guitar also. Pops would play his guitar at home sitting in the house and we'd make up songs you know, pretend they were songs. We just would sing them and he'd be playing, just me and him. So on weekends, he'd let them know, "My wife loves to sing."

And they say, "Come on up and you can do a song for us."

And it got to where it was a regular thing. Every weekend I would sit in with different bands. Muddy Waters, Howling Wolf, Jimmy Reed, J. B. Lenoir, and all those people. So it just kept up and up and on and on and on.

So they was having this big affair at a club in Chicago was called Sylvio's, and anyway, we attended that affair. So what the affair was, all the other bands and people and everybody came. It was like a jam session. It was like whoever wanted to go up and sing, play music, shoot marbles, or what ever; they would go up and do it. So I happened to be one of the people that went up to sing and when I finished, that particular day, this man walks up to me and introduced himself as Willie

Dixon.[21] And he says, "My God, I ain't heard a woman sing the blues like you sing the blues before." He says, "You know, we got a lot of men out here today that's singing the blues but not enough women. We don't have no women singing the blues." You know, he said, "That's what the world needs today, a woman like you singing the blues."

I LEFT ONE NIGHT WITH NOTHING
JOHN LEE HOOKER

John Lee Hooker. Washington, D.C., June 26, 1983. Photograph by Dave Penland. Courtesy of the Smithsonian Center for Folklife and Cultural Heritage.

My dad was a minister and he didn't want a guitar in his house. He said it was the devil's. And my mom, when I was twelve, got married again to a guitar player name of Willie Moore. I wanted to stay with my father, but he didn't want the guitar. And naturally that's what I wanted. That's why I went to my stepfather. He'd accept it. So I was about twelve years old then. I stayed around and he taught me what I am doing today. This style is my style, but I am playing today what I learned. So I took what he learned me and made something out of it, which I know he would be proud of what I did with it.

He had a big farm, horses and cows and things like that; but that wasn't my bag so I didn't want it. I didn't want to work in no fields. And I ran off from home and I came to Memphis and I stayed around there about a couple of months. My auntie saw me and she snitched on me, told on me where I was, and he come and got me and brought me back. But I said, "I'm not gonna stay," because I had a taste of the big city and the bright lights.

But I had to fool them. So I stayed about a couple months until they got it in their minds I wasn't going to leave no more. It got to the place that they thought I was going to stay. My first night back they watched me, but after so long they figured "Well, he ain't gonna run no more." So I left one night with nothing, maybe a couple of bucks in my pocket and a few clothes, and hit the road hitch-hiking.

I stopped in Memphis, said, "Well, they gonna get me here; my auntie's gonna tell on me again." So I went on to Cincinnati. So when I got there I run into this lady; she had a big house, a boarding house. I come in and she looked at me and said, "You look like a nice kid, you got some place to live?"

I said, "No."

She said, "You want to work around the house and help me and I'll put you up?"

I said, "Yes, ma'am."

And I stayed with her. She really taking a liking to me, like I was her son. And I would work around the house there and do things. I stayed there until I was about eighteen or nineteen and I went to Detroit. I heard things were really booming then, there was big money and you could do this and that. I had some money to take the Greyhound. I told my mama, said, "Look, I'm going to Detroit."

She said, "Be careful now, if you need me, you call me."

I said, "O.K."

She said, "You got any money?"

I said, "Yeah."

When I got there I got a little room. Things were cheap then, you got three or four, five dollars, you know, you could get a room for a month. I got there and in about two weeks I got a job and went to work. By that time I was old enough to get into bars. Used to play around for local bars and things like that for a long time. I was the hottest thing in

Detroit and still I had no name. Except in Detroit. Everybody would come around and say, "This kid"—I was just a boy—"has a different style." Everywhere I played, it was packed full of people. And I had a little small combo and I had a great long cord and I would walk the floor and play. And people would just, it would be all over town you'd hear it: "John Lee Hooker, John Lee Hooker."

WORKING THE BLUES

When I took up my guitar I just wanted
to play. And the first gig I went on, I wasn't
looking to make no money. But the band
leader handed me eleven dollars and my
eyes fell out of my head, and I said,
"Wow, that's nice."

BIG ED THOMPSON

MONEY

IT'S A JOB
NAPPY BROWN

I got in the music business about '51. I come out of gospel into music,
into the blues. I switched over and I been in blues ever since. And blues
is a great thing because it makes expression for the people just like the
gospel do. It teaches them a whole lot if they listen to it, you know.

When I was younger I was strictly in the gospel field. Well, I would
sing a little blues then, but I never would let my mother and them know
it; you know how that was, they didn't want it. You know all that, "You're
doing a bad thing. You're doing a bad thing."

That was at Charlotte, North Carolina, at my home. I don't know
why they felt that way. It's a tradition. Well, they felt like, well, if you do
the blues, you was doing the devil's work, you know. You didn't believe
in God. But they was highly mistaken because the blues is nothing but
a living. It's a job, like anything.

I'M PLAYING FOR THE MONEY
"LOVIE LEE" WATSON

When I was coming up, my folks were running a restaurant that had an old piano in it. I'd just bang on it every day until I found a little tune. Then I got into the church. I went to church after I went to banging on the old piano in our restaurant and I got to where I could play "Thou Has Not a Friend Like the Lordly Jesus." And then I just kept on it. In a little while the church wanted me. So I went to playing for the Baptist church, and they weren't paying me but a hundred dollars a month, twenty-five dollars a week. Well, then the Methodist people come up and said they'd give me two hundred dollars a month. I went to them. The Baptists, they said, "Don't leave us, little Watson." That's my name, Eddie L. Watson. They say, "You're not playing for the money, you're playing for God."

I said, "I'm playing for the money."

I AIN'T BEEN BACK TO CHURCH SINCE
WILLIAM "BOOGIE MAN" HUBBARD

William "Boogie-Man" Hubbard and the author. Jonesboro, Arkansas, April 20, 1996. Photograph by Joseph Donaghy. Courtesy of *Arkansas Review.*

I played in church for three dollars a Sunday; I was playing with Reverend Grady Johnson. I didn't know too many church songs, but whatever you play, if you play it in the right key back in them days, the choir would handle it. You ain't got to worry about it, just don't mess up the keys. I was playing out there and they gave me three dollars every Sunday and my mother wanted half of that. My mother wanted a dollar and a half out of that because she say, "You gonna have something for school, boy. You ain't gonna miss this money because you ain't gonna do nothing but buy candy and stuff." But anyway, I couldn't get no money. So I slipped in Johnny Caroll's one night. They needed a piano player and they know I could play a little bit. I had learned a little bit then. So a dude come and got me.

"Come on, Boogie, help me tonight. I'm gonna pay you twelve dollars." Man, twelve dollars a night! I say, "Come on."

It was on Saturday. I was about eighteen, seventeen or eighteen. I was almost grown. I wasn't grown but I was tall. And, man, I went and made them twelve dollars and I ain't been back to church since.

I THOUGHT I WAS RICH
BIG JOE DUSKIN

There used to be blues people going up and down the streets with guitars and all that; little organs sitting on the corner and play. That was right there in Cincinnati. Ah, you'd be surprised. Every day you could hear somebody play. There was a guy by the name of Blackjack; I learned a lot from him. He was a black fellow. Blackjack would go house to house; wherever there was a piano you'd hear him. And he'd see me, he'd say, "Come in here, Little Duskin, and play. I got to go another place."

I'd come in there and play. I'd make about, oh, a dollar and fifty cents. I thought I was rich. I'd change it up and go to rattle it in my pocket. I'd have about five or six gals following me. So, I'd go around and ask the guys at the clubs could I come and play in their beer garden. He says, "Well, you not old enough," guy says, "we can't let you come in."

So I don't know how I did it, but I got some glue and went and got a mustache from a horse's tail. I cut part of his tail off one night and about got kicked to death. And I'd cut it up in little pieces and stick it up there; that made me look grown up. Then I'd go in there and play. Police come in there they wouldn't say nothing because they didn't know. And then I got so I couldn't get it off my lip. So I just hung with it, you know and from that day I began to start playing professional.

THAT'S THE WAY I DID
LITTLE SAMMY DAVIS

You know I raised myself; I raised myself. Me and the harmonica, we raised ourselves. I left Mississippi and went to Florida. And I never did hang around the younger-age boys. I'd always be around where there was somebody playing checkers or what some of it was, the older folks that used to play them. And they'd get that checkerboard, and I'd get where they could hear that harp there. I wouldn't get up on them, I'd get where they could hear that harp.

"That little bastard can play the hell out of that thing. [*Laughs.*] Hey boy, come here. Come here, boy. Now you might as well tell me the truth because I know you done run away from home." Say, "Where's your dad and mama at?"

I say, "I ain't run away from no home. I'm out here playing and singing. Visiting some of my people out here."

"Who are your people?"

Sometimes I'd be looking at them, telling them who they is.

"I'm gonna ask so and so is they any relation to you."

"Hey, you know what I want you to do? I want you to play this song written by Sonny Boy Williams and I don't want you to miss nary a key neither."

And they give me a dollar, two or three dollars. Back then money was something then. You could take a nickel and buy you enough meat to last a week. And he'd, they'd treat you a dollar.

"Here, you take these two or three dollars. Now if you don't play it like I want you to play, I'm gonna take my money back."

I'd play it right. Wouldn't miss a note.

"You know boy, you play the hell out of that thing."

That's the way I did. That's what I'd be doing, but I would work too, you know, like in the yard or something like that.

PLAYING THE DOOR:
THE TRAVELING LOAFER BOARD
MOSES "HAYWIRE TOM" WILLIAMS

I started to make this door here from haywire. Mama had the haywire across the bed to pull it together keep the slats in there to keep the bed

Moses "Haywire Tom" Williams.
Vienna, Virginia, July 9, 1981.
Photograph by Margo
Rosenbaum. Courtesy of
the National Council for
the Traditional Arts.

from falling out. I decided I'd get me a bottle and I started chording across, but Mama decided she didn't want the bed put up in the house. So I string it upside the wall.

Well, I kept on going then and kept on chording it. By then I learned to play a little bit of something about, "I Roll and I Tumble and I Cried the Whole Night Long." I learned that. And when I learned that I just kept on trying, just kept on trying until I learned a little bit more. And that's why I got this here idea for playing the door. I used to have the door on the wall of the house, but I couldn't carry the house with me. I had to go to work and put it on the door, and after I put it on the door I could carry the door around.

But I think it helped me out a whole lot after I did that because I always did figure I wanted to be a big old boy all the time, regardless if I was young. I wanted to be the best son my Mama had so I could send my money home because I got tired of plowing that long-eared mule. So see, well, this here is really a traveling loafer board. When you're traveling and ain't got no money, ain't nobody gonna give you none unless you do something for it. And so, well, if you just do something for it they gonna give you the money to put in your pocket. Then probably you can eat and sleep right on. Now that's what they call a sure enough traveling board, the others call it a diddley-bow, and some of them call it a one-string piano, and some of them call it a broom wire slim, and all that kind of stuff, but I can't worry about what they call it. It did me good when I was in my traveling days. You see, the good Lord going to fix it so you can make it anyhow. Because, see, I didn't get no schooling, but this door schooled me a little bit to let me know that I could make some money. The way I started to making a little money, I started playing for the shoeshine boy at Itta Bena, Mississippi, and I had a whole lot of nickels and dimes to give Mama when I come home. And then she wanted to know where did I get so much money from because I wasn't making but fifty cents a day but I had over fifty cents when I got back home. That just let me know that I started making a little bit of something out of what I know.

WALKING LIKE A LOOSE MULE
EUGENE "SONNY BOY NELSON" POWELL

I went and left home with nothing but my guitar and went to Memphis. The first time I was ever in Memphis, I didn't run by Memphis, I was walking like a loose mule. I was going down the street playing a piece called "The Forty-Four Blues,"[1] and the women heard me playing that. When I passed their house they come to the door and say, "Mister, mister, come here."

Kept worrying me. I knew what they wanted. I went on back to the house. I didn't have but two bits I think, but I went back to the house, and they kept me all night, and throwed a ball that night. And the man that was courting the women, he liked it so good when he found out I was fixing to leave he said, "Don't you go. Stay here." And he give me seventeen dollars.

MONEY PUTS YOU IN THE MOOD
ALBERT "SUNNYLAND SLIM" LUANDREW

This fellow says, "Let's go out there to the sawmill. It's payday out there today."

So I had about a dollar or so and I didn't want to get broke. So I said, "I believe I'll go out there and sing the blues, play the blues real good."

So I seen Brother Montgomery,[2] he was playing out there. I didn't know him then; that's where I got to know him. I was broke and wanted some of that food I see. Hit around for my dollar; I never did want to spend my last dollar out there. So he was singing and he was drunk, said, "Hey now, can you sing? Go ahead and sing one."

I got started singing there and all the hustling women started coming down with their boots on . . . it's so muddy down there in 1923. Boy, them old gals started giving me quarters, you know. She had made some money off them people, the hustlers make some money they just give me some. And so we just started to have a little fun. So finally Brother got drunk and he got up and played "Rolling and Tumbling." I left there I had about seven or eight dollars myself. That puts you in the mood for doing something. Money puts you in the mood for doing something.

THAT'S YOUR QUARTER
JOHNNY SHINES

Robert Johnson told me, he'd say, "You stay down here on this corner, I'm going down on the other corner. And when I make a quarter, that's my quarter; when you make a quarter, that's your quarter. But if we stay down here together and we make a quarter, we only got twelve and one half cents apiece."

THIS IS FROM THE B. B. KING SIDE
STERLING "MR. SATAN" MAGEE

I used to play at the Echo Lounge in Tampa, Florida, and my mother and father were living in St. Petersburg, Florida. Every time we would get paid, usually on a Saturday night, quite naturally I would carry a certain amount of money home to my mother, and I would say, "This is from the B. B. King side, mama."[3] And she would smile with her blessed look. At the Echo Lounge there was plenty of liquor and everything, but she didn't care about that as long as the money got there. It's amazing but true. She wouldn't refuse the money because it came from the blues. They hate what makes it, but they love the money it made.

I GOT TO GO WHERE THE MONEY IS
PINETOP PERKINS

I went to, they call it, a barrelhouse over across the railroad tracks in Belzoni, Mississippi, where I was born. I used to be in a barrelhouse where people were gambling in the back, shooting dice and stuff. I'd go to banging on the piano, you know, trying to learn. But after a while they'd run me off, saying, "Boy, get off that thing."

And no sooner than they cool down, I'd go right back and bang on it again, you know, until one day I learned. So that one day I played an old tune that they played a long time ago about "I Ain't Got No Special Rider Here." And one of those cats heard it back there, say, "Hey, boy, what's that you're playing on that piano? Well, play it again. Here's fifty cents."

Oh, I played a right smart of stuff and I could sing, you know, sing like a bird. Then later on, I was playing out at a place in Vance, Mississippi, on the county line. A boy come through there, they called him Robert Nighthawk.[4] That's the first famous band I played with. So from there we went back to Helena, Arkansas. So we started advertising the band, the different places where we were going. So Mr. Max Moore, the Interstate Groceryman [who sponsored Sonny Boy's show], heard me over there playing and he liked the way I played, and he told Sonny Boy [Aleck Miller] to come over there and get me. Said he'd pay me to be on the air. So I had to give Robert two weeks' notice. I said, "Hey Boy, I got to go where the money is." So I started playing with Sonny Boy. Robert didn't like it, but I wasn't making no money over there. We were just advertising the band.

THAT'S WHAT'S KEEPING ME HERE
BYTHER SMITH

I used to work in a white club on a Tuesday, Wednesday, Thursday with some white boys. I mean, I was just playing guitar for them. Finally, one of the guys ask me, he says, "Smitty, I don't mean to be smart, but it's nobody here that's black but you. How do you feel working in here?"

I says, "It's just like I feel getting up and going to work in the morning. There're twenty-five whites there and three blacks. Here I feel the same way. I'm in here for one thing and one thing only, that means dollar. I'm not in here for no woman. I'm not in here to start no uproar with nobody. I'm just in here to make a dollar, get paid, be friendly with everybody in here, go out and get in my car go home."

He says, "I don't know how in the world you can feel like that. You don't drink. You don't smoke and here I offered you some pills and you won't take them." He says, "What's keeping you alive, keeping you in here?"

I says, "You know what's keeping me in here?"

He says, "What?"

I says, "When, my man who hired me, he pays me. That's what's keeping me in here."

I WOULDN'T COUNT PIES FOR YOU
ARCHIE EDWARDS

When I was eighteen years old, man, I was hitting the road, Jack. I left home to make it for myself. I left August 17, 1938, and I have not gone back to ask my mother and father for anything since. Never been broke since 1938 either. I left home with thirteen dollars in my pocket. They say that thirteen is an unlucky number but I don't believe it. I left home with thirteen dollars and today I got this shop. I got my home. I got cars, got property in New Jersey. But I got it the hard way, the old-fashioned way, as the man said: I earned it. So, when you get to be seventy years old, in my book if a person reached to be seventy-five years old if he wants to work give him every penny he makes because he earned it. But right now, if I went out and got me a job making fifty dollars a week, they'd have to get a percentage of it. And I'm past sixty-five you know, and I'm retired.

I worked fifty years almost and gave them part of my money. But now they don't want to give that back to me; they want to take that. If I went to work they'd still take my Social Security check. Every time I make a dollar they take so much out of the check. Next thing you know, all of it will be theirs if I was stupid enough to work.

But I told the lady the other day when I went down to file my personal property taxes. She says, "Has there been any change in your income over the last year?"

I say, "Nope. I'm not going to work anymore. Anybody who's worked as long as I have for nothing and reaches the retirement age and keeps on working has got to be a fool." I say, "Miss, I wouldn't count pies for you or the government if it was giving me every other pie. I wouldn't count them in order to make enough money to pay you people some more taxes." I said, "Daddy always said if you're twenty-one years old you ought to be able to look after yourself."

Uncle Sam's over twenty-one years old and if he can't look after himself he's going to suffer, because I'm not working for him anymore.

NAMES

YOU GOT TO GET A CATCHY NAME
"H-BOMB" FERGUSON

This dude, he was an old manager; his name was Chet Patterson. He said, "Uh, you know, you got a funny name to be in show business to be a singer. You got a pretty good voice, for blues singer, but 'Bobby Ferguson'? Most people don't even use their names. That's not catchy. You got to get a catchy name for show business."

I said, "Well, what do you got in mind? What do you think would sound good?"

"We gonna call you the Cobra Kid."

That's the first name I had. I said: "Do what! That's a snake."

He said, "You don't look at it that way. So that Bobby Ferguson don't mean shit; sounds like nothing."

That's exactly what he told me: "Anybody in show business, you don't use common names."

I said, "Why do you want to name me after a snake?"

"Man," he said, "see when you come out, you so damn skinny, but you got a big-ass mouth. So you strike people, you catch them off guard, see, when you walk on the stage. Bob, I'm gonna tell you, people think you gonna sing low 'cause of your size, and when you open your mouth, the god damn building falls out. So you strike people like a snake. So we gonna call you 'The Cobra Kid.' I think that's a nice name."

Now here's the catch. Lee Magid[5] said he didn't like the Cobra name. I said, "Here we go again."

I said, "That other guy I had that passed away, Mister Chet, now he named me."

He said, "I know it. I saw it on them little two record labels you were on." He call it penny ante stuff.

He said, "I got a name for you, gonna knock you out." At that time the H-bomb was hot. He said, "We're gonna keep your last name and I'm gonna call you H-Bomb Ferguson."

I said, "Man, you're talking about that bomb they're dropping. That's a bomb!"

He said, "Do you know that name means something. From years to come people will remember the H-Bomb."

I said, "Yeah, but that don't sound right. 'H-Bomb Ferguson,' that ain't human."

He said, "You're not, when you open your mouth, whether you believe it or not." He said, "I've sat in the audience many a night and I heard you. You don't weigh nothing, but when you open your mouth you sound like a cat that weighs three hundred pounds. You just explode. Your voice starts breaking out. So we're gonna call you H-Bomb Ferguson. And I already got the contract made up as such and that's what's gonna be on the record."

I said, "I don't know if I'll get used to that name. You all keep changin' my name."

BOOGIE CHILDREN
WILLIAM "BOOGIE MAN" HUBBARD

I'm gonna tell you the way I got to be named "Boogie." See, when I was going to school the police didn't allow us down on the corner by the school and those schoolgirls. I had got up around seventeen or eighteen; I didn't want to go to no school too much. I wanted to watch them girls and try to, well, anyway, so the police told us to stay off this corner. And I had about quit school. I was fixing to go in the Army. And we wouldn't stay off that corner because my girlfriend was going to that school. And finally, the police come up one day and he got me and another boy name Buck White, Skippy McDowell, and one they call "Chipmunk." He sang nice. Sang in those bands. He still plays, he sings now there down in Memphis. But the police told us to get in the car. So we was right in front of a house there on Carpenter Street; it was a lady had her window open. It was hot, man, wasn't no fans then back in them days. So she had the window open and had the radio in the window while she irons. She's got a little air come in the window and irons right at the window. So she had the radio sitting there and the radio was playing a number called "Boogie Children" by John Lee Hooker,[6] and I was standing up there after they done put all the rest of them in the car. See, I can tap dance, too, and when the police got ready for me to get in the car, I started to tap dance. And the police say, "No, no, come on." And when

I started tap dancing for the police, I backed way back and then I stretched out on him, you understand. I cut out. Everybody went to jail but me. So my name was "Boogie" when they come back. They named me "Boogie Children." That was my first name, all right; then they started calling me "Boogie Child" and then they kept on and then they called me just plain old "Boogie;" nothing else with it. And now they call me "Boogie Man." I'm sixty-five years old and I finally got to be a man.

THAT'S THE NAME
JERRY DANIELS

We were "King, Jack and the Jesters" when we were at Cincinnati. When we got to New York, a fellow that you know by the name of Bing Crosby, they were with Paul Whiteman and they were called "The Kingsmen" or "The Kings Jesters." Our name seemed to be a clash of interest with their office in New York and so they changed it. And as we were deciding on a name our manager there, Mr. Moe Gill, was signing a contract and some ink fell on the page. And he said, "Well, that's the name. The Ink Spots."

SUPER CHIKAN
JAMES "SUPER CHIKAN" JOHNSON

How I got my name "Super Chikan;" I was left at home with the chickens when everybody else had gone to the fields. I was too small to go and the chickens was always around the house talking and making noises and it was about all I could hear all day. So I started paying closer attention to them and it seemed to me like they knew what they were saying. And I would say something and they would look at me real curious like as if he wanted me to say it again. And I'd say it again and he would say something. I couldn't figure out what he said but I would imagine for myself what he was saying.

I had that one little rooster that I had, my pet rooster, he would always wake me up every morning, get up by my window and he'd call me. He said, "Mr. Johnson, get up, get up, time to get out of the bed and go to work." That's what it sound like he was saying.

So I used to go around telling everybody about my chickens and my chicken stories, and they called me "that old chicken boy." And as things went on they stopped calling me "old chicken boy" and they started calling me "chicken." And I got a job after a while driving a taxicab there in Clarksdale, and I drove so fast because I was always hyper-energetic; and I was such a fast driver until I could get there so quick when the old ladies called for me that they called me "super chicken." Said, "He's super fast;" say, "Send me that guy in the red car. Ooh, send the chicken over here, that 'super chicken.'"

And it caught on from there. So I used it for a CB handle when I was driving a truck, and they kept calling me that on the stage when I started playing the guitar because I'd tell a chicken story and I'd cackle like a chicken and I'd make my guitar cackle like a chicken. And sometimes I'd take the live chickens to the show with me, put them on the stage; that's when we really have a good time. A month ago I had two live game roosters on the stage there at the city auditorium in Clarksdale, and we went from the auditorium to the clubhouse for that night and played. And I took those chickens over there to the clubhouse and the crowd followed the chickens. They was watching the chickens more than they was me when I was performing. I get on the microphone and I'd cackle to the chickens and then they'd cackle right back to me. And when we started playing music, one chicken, his neck was going like that, right on time with the music.

I CHANGED MY NAME
SAM CHATMON

But you know I changed my name. My granddaddy was named Sam, and a lady in Bolton named me when I was born that made me miserable . . . names me Vivian. So I didn't like that. When I got up I told them, "That's a girl's name." I didn't want no Vivian. I changed my name, changed it to Sam. I been Sam ever since.

THAT AIN'T THE GUY
DOCTOR ROSS

Then I come on up and I went to Helena, Arkansas, and I loved to hear this guy name was Rice Miller, but he was going by the name of Sonny Boy Williamson. But he wasn't. Sonny Boy Williamson,[7] his home is in Jackson, Tennessee. But he left there in the early years and went to

Chicago, and he put out all them famous songs. And this other Sonny Boy, he called himself Sonny Boy, he got the spot over KFFA in Helena. And all the older people, he had them fooled. You know, back in them times they didn't have television; they just have radios. Hearing all those old folks, "Oh, that's him. That's the one put out 'Sugar Mama,' 'My Black Names Ringing,' 'Little School Girl' and all them songs."

A lot of people write in and sent him requests, you know, for him to play different numbers. He sung 'em and played them, but he couldn't. I says, "That ain't the guy." I say, "He never sounds like that record on that song there such as 'Sugar Mama' and that 'School Girl.' He can't play that."

And so then later some guy comes in from Chicago he says, "Oh no, the man Sonny Boy, he's in Chicago." He told his cousin, "He's a little black guy got two big teeth in the front and wears a hat." He says, "This one here can blow, but he's going wrong on that one's play, and using his name."

YOU'RE NOT JOHNNY SHINES
JOHNNY SHINES

Johnny Shines. Washington, D.C.
Photograph by Dave Penland. Courtesy
of the Smithsonian Center for Folklife
and Cultural Heritage.

Some people take another guy's name and try to make it on their name. But I just don't see why a person would do a thing like that. It don't make sense to me. I never wanted to be anybody but Johnny Shines. Lots of times place I go people say, "B. B. King."

I say, "No, I'm Johnny Shines."

I don't want to sell B.B.; I want to sell Johnny Shines. If I'm good, I want to be good as Johnny Shines. If I'm not good, I'm sorry; I just do the best I can. So me calling myself B. B. King don't make me good. People might say, "He calls himself Little B.B., but he sure don't play like Little B.B." You understand. So I just rather be myself.

It was a fellow on Forty-third Street, he played there; I don't know how long he played there. He had a big sign out there: "Johnny Shines appearing here nightly." And I had to go right by this sign going to work myself every night. I was playing at Forty-third and Lake Park at Tony's and I had to go by this sign. I'd look at it and laugh to myself. If he's gonna pass himself off as Johnny Shines, good.

And I've had people come in where I was playing and tell me "You're not Johnny Shines."

I say, "Well, you know, so O.K."

THE ROAD

YOU BEAT US PLAYING
EUGENE "SONNY BOY NELSON" POWELL

I was going to Louisiana and I stopped at a town called Columbia, Mississippi, below Jackson. I was going along playing my guitar and I got kind of lonesome feeling. I didn't know nobody. Then, a long time ago, you couldn't mess around no white folks' house because you were liable to get killed. If they didn't kill you, they catch you and beat you up, put you in the penitentiary for such a long length of time. It's hard on you.

When I was going that night they called me. It was three white boys. They had some guitars they call theyselves playing. I got there where they was, and I had my guitar and a jazz horn. And so they say, "Boy." That was them white boys:

"Boy."

I say, "What?"

"You can play that gitfiddle?"

"No, I'm trying to learn how." I just told them that.

"Well, let me hear you strike a tune. Strike something for us."

So, I went on to playing so good that they said, "The hell you can't play. You beat us playing. You play guitar better than any of us out here."

And directly the police did come by; they stopped me. Now he give me twenty cents. And when I got ready to go, them boys, the white boys, they gave me about three dollars. But I could beat every one of them playing guitar.

THE FIRST HIPPIES
JOHNNY SHINES

One of my cousins [Calvin Frazier][8] got in some serious trouble up in Arkansas and they told him in Memphis just get out of the United States and he would be out of trouble. So Robert [Johnson] and I took off with my cousin, out of the United States up to Canada. I wanted to go to

Canada anyway, because they told me, when I was a boy, that Canadians had one big eye in the middle of their head and I had never seen anyone with one big eye before. I couldn't believe that. I wanted to see for myself. And I did go and see. So we went up in Canada on a freight with my cousin; then we come back through Detroit and fooled around there for a while.

We'd play, sing, put the hat down and all that kind of stuff. We had a ball. We made money; we didn't starve to death, we made money.

Robert liked to travel. You could wake up anytime of night and say, "Let's go," and he was ready. He never asked you where or why or anything. He would get up and get dressed and get ready to go. And I often say, I guess him and I were the first hippies because we didn't care when, where, or how. If we wanted to go some place we went. We didn't care how we went. We'd ride, walk. If you asked us where we were going we didn't know, just anywhere. "Are you going North?"

"Yeah."

"Get in."

We'd get in and go.

HE WORKED HIS WAY ACROSS THE COUNTRY
EDDIE BURNS

When I first started paying attention to blues I met Sonny Boy Williamson Number Two [Aleck Miller]. I was walking with a man down the road. Sonny Boy Williamson Number Two used to travel from town to town and he walked a lot because he didn't have a car, I guess, and maybe he probably was low on cash, too, see. So I guess he probably just worked his way across the country, you know, with his harmonicas.

So this man was coming down the road, which happened to be Sonny Boy Williamson, and he had this belt around his waist and all these harmonicas on him. So he's just walking down old 49 Highway in Mississippi and we was walking. I was seven or eight, and that's going back a long ways, but I do remember what went on. So as they approached each other this man that I was with he said, asked Sonny Boy could he blow a little harmonica. And he said, "Yeah." He blowed harp. So then he asked him about a particular tune which was Peetie

Wheatstraw made it, a thing called "I'll Be So Glad When Good Whiskey Comes Back in Style Again."[9] So he gave him a dime; well this was back around 1936 or '37, and Sonny Boy blowed it. And we were off on our way.

WHICH ONE WAS ROBERT JOHNSON
ROBERT LOCKWOOD JUNIOR

I played on the streets. That's the only place to play sixty years ago. People were playing on street corners and at people's houses like house parties. People would be gambling a little bit, drinking liquor, frying, cook fish. I seen Robert make so much money sitting on the street corner playing the blues until, man, I mean, I couldn't imagine playing nothing else. When I played with Robert, I was playing his records, "Kind Hearted Woman," "Sweet Home Chicago," "Dust My Broom." I was playing all that. After I had learned to play pretty good, Robert put me on one end a bridge and he went on the other end and we both played. People were confused. They didn't know which one was Robert Johnson.

I'M GONNA LOCK YOU UP
DAVID "HONEYBOY" EDWARDS

I used to play on the street corner. Sometimes, some towns I play on the streets, I block the streets so much the police run me off the corner, say, "You can't block the streets; now go on back home. Don't come around here a runaway again." Say, "If I catch you here I'm gonna lock you up."

But I was trying to make those nickels and dimes and quarters. I'd slip and play a piece right quick. Sometimes I'd get to a vacant lot. They run me off the streets, so I go out there in a vacant lot and play and I could get a big crowd. Sometimes I'd hang out there a couple hours make me three or four dollars in nickels and dimes. After I make enough that I think I can make that day, then I go to the little room, put my guitar up, go eat, sit around and laugh and talk with some of them friends I meet, and we drink. Next day I get back out go to another town.

WE HAD THE HIGHWAY BLOCKED UP
JOHNNY SHINES

We were staying in this hotel; called it a hotel, it wasn't nothing but a pasteboard house. We had a room there, Robert [Johnson] and I did. And we went to get breakfast in the morning and I happened to look as we started back. I look up I saw this blaze and this smoke.

"Robert, that looks like the hotel we're staying in."

He said, "Yeah, it is."

We struck out running, and when we got there to where it was burning it was too late for us to try to get in there and get our guitars. So they burned up.

So I had never heard Robert try to play a harp. I didn't even know he had a harp. I didn't know he knew anything about a harp. So we lit out up Highway 61 and got a good piece up the road near about Turrell, Arkansas. Robert reached into his pocket and got his harmonica out and started blowing that harmonica and dancing in the highway. And I started singing. And in a few minutes we had the highway blocked up. And the police was the closest ones to us, the highway patrol. So when people call in complaining about the highways blocked up, they had to call the people that we were playing to. We had a heck of a time. We got to Steele, Missouri; Robert and I both bought new guitars.

WE HAD STOPPED TRAFFIC
JERRY DANIELS

We started in Indianapolis as a coffeepot band on the street around here. Some of the members of it were a fellow they used to call Slim Green and Taps Miller. A coffeepot band is, fellows used to get kazoos, a little tin jazz horn. You put some tissue paper together in it and improvise on it and it sounds like an instrument, and that's the part the guys would play in the coffeepot. And the rhythm section was the washboards. And so that's the way that went about.

And we were playing on the circle, I'll never forget it; it seems like yesterday. We were on the circle playing and gathered quite a crowd. And along came the gendarmes and locked us all up because we had stopped traffic. And a reporter, Mr. Williams, was nice enough to write it up in *The Star,* and with that headline we skyrocketed.

THAT WAS REAL FUNNY
LAVESTER "BIG LUCKY" CARTER

We played in jook joints. A joint it had beer selling and sandwiches and all that kind of stuff, just a common joint. We used to play in Arkansas quite a bit, here in Arkansas. Carruthersville, Missouri. Oh yeah, we played all over in the South here. Carruthersville was as far as we would go. That was about our range. There was one funny thing happened here in Arkansas. We were on our way to a gig. A highway patrolman stopped us and made us go to his house and play for his family. [*Laughs.*] He didn't give us any reason really. He just wanted us to play, and he carried us to his house and we played. And when we got through playing, we went on back home. I don't remember if he paid us nothing. That was real funny, in a way. Real funny.

HOW MUCH YOU'ALL MAKE
MELVIN LEE

You know a whole lot of things go down. I can remember one time we were getting ready to leave town and we were all sitting on the sidewalk running our mouths. We was going to Arkansas. I laid my bass on the sidewalk with the rest of the equipment and everybody loaded up. We got over in Arkansas, we just going down the highway, and I asked, I said, "Man, did you put my bass on the truck?"

He said, "No, I thought you did."

I said, "No."

We were in the car sitting arguing over that and turned around and went back and the thing was still laying on the side of the street! Nobody didn't want it. [*Laughs.*] And on the way back the police stopped us and carried us to jail and we all ended all locked up. And the police said, "How much you'all make?"

That was years ago. And the whole band didn't get but four hundred dollars for the whole gig. And we said, "Well we didn't make but four hundred dollars."

He said, "Well you'all just about barely got enough to get out."
Said, "How much it cost?"
He said, "Four hundred. All the money."
But we were glad to get out. A lot of strange things happened to you, but that was true.

HE WON'T WORK
DAVID "HONEYBOY" EDWARDS

Well, I'm gonna tell you, the white people down south really didn't care much for the blues back in that time. The old-time white people, way back in the eighteen-hundreds there, on the farm, used to have the Negro for their slave, work for nothing. What happened, the white man found out that if the Negro learned how to play blues good enough to make him a quarter, he wouldn't work for fifty cents a day. Would you? So when he see one coming with a guitar on his shoulder, he get madder than hell. He get mad. That's them old farmers then.

And there have always been two types of people. You take some white boys coming up, they had cars and girlfriends, give country dances. They'd take me out and I'd play for them and they'd take care of me. But them old farmers, they'd rather see a dog than to see you coming down the street with a guitar. You got that machine on your back, "He won't work." Sometimes they pick you up and try to put you on a county farm, anything. You had to dodge that bullshit. And later they just throwed that out of their mind, you know what I mean. Music got kind of proper and then they started playing in the theaters, on the streets in town, picture shows, anything. But when I first started playing, on a Monday morning, you better not be out there with no guitar, on the plantation, staying all day, all night long. You better get away from there or stay in all day long. That night you leave out when everybody come out of the fields.

PRETTY UNHEALTHY TO BE A MUSICIAN
JOHNNY SHINES

It was pretty unhealthy in Arkansas at the time. If you were a musician walking down the highway or walking the railroad and the sheriff run down on you and you didn't have a certain amount of money in your pocket, you went to the county farm. As a matter of fact, you were taken up as an animal or something like that and leased out to these prison farms run by big plantation owners. I don't know what contributions they gave to the state, but they put these people out on these farms and things working as lease labor. During the time back then, it was pretty unhealthy to be a musician because you were not one that was known to work. And if you weren't known to be a work ox or slave, it was open season on you. Police could come and shoot you down and there was nothing said about it. There was people I've known for them to be killed in different places in the area for just being there. That was all they did is be there. They were just there at the time and they were killed.

A good friend of mine, a piano player, he got put on a farm in 1937 during the high water. Something broke loose in the river and they made him go after it and he couldn't swim. But he went after it and he drowned. His name was Robert Parnell. A damned good piano player, but he didn't have a certain amount of money in his pocket, which was five dollars, and they put him on this farm. Something broke loose during the high water and that water was rushing like thirty miles an hour. They made him go out there after this object and he never did make it to it. He drowned. That's how times were back in those days.

SHIP IT
MOSES RASCOE

I got picked up one time with my guitar and that was down in Georgia. So I didn't know whether the guitar did it or I was just out there hitchhiking. But after that, I just didn't walk with no guitar, I always had a town picked out I wanted to go and I'd just ship it there.

GO ON HOME
"H-BOMB" FERGUSON

I ran in to B. B. King several years ago in Memphis, Tennessee. I had played a job down there, Friday, Saturday, and Sunday. I played Friday night, Saturday night; Sunday night, when I came in to play, to get my money, the guy closed it up and left town. I was stuck with twenty dollars. That's all I had. And I owed a hotel bill of forty-six dollars. By coincidence, he was passing through. He stopped at this restaurant; I was sitting there drinking coffee and I didn't know what I was gonna do. And he had a mobile home. He pulled in there and came in. I saw him and I told him. He said, "What!" I said, "Yeah man." I told him they messed me up and I got to pay this hotel bill or they'll put my ass in jail. And I don't have enough money. He said, "How much you need, H?" I said, "I owe about sixty-seven dollars." He say, "Here's one hundred and fifty. Now go on home." He gave me three fifty-dollar bills. "Will that take care of everything, get you back home?" I said, "Yeah, more than enough." He said, "I'll see you later . . . and quit fooling with them two-cent ass clubs."

A BLIND MAN SHOWED YOU
MELVIN LEE

Since Rufus Thomas[10] is coming to town, I'll tell one that happened when I was with him. We was down in El Dorado and when we got ready to leave there Rufus told me, say, "You got the first drive."

I say, "Yeah, yes, well, just tell me which way to go." You know, when I get to the highway which way do I go right or left?

And they said, "Go right."

Well, we had a blind trumpet player in the band, and when I got to the highway I went right like they said. Everybody went to sleep except the trumpet player, who was sitting up there with me. And we drove. . . . I guess I drove about three or four hours and the trumpet player told me, say, "Hey man?"

I said, "What?"

He said, "You going the wrong way."

Man, this cat's blind and he says, "Hey you going the wrong way."

"Man, you don't know what's happening here, you know, You can't see nothing."

He said, "We didn't come this way."

I said, "Oh man, don't give me that stuff."

And I just kept driving. Man, I guess day started to breaking and sure enough I was going the wrong way. Rufus woke up and said, "Where we going at?" [*Laughs.*]

I said, "I don't know. I see the wrong license plates. Man, I don't know where we are." I said, "You take it. I'm tired."

And we talk about this now. That was back in the 1960s. Every time we see each other we talk about that now; me and Rufus. Well, that was really comical.

"A blind man showed you was going wrong and you couldn't even see that."

DO THE HOUDINI
HOWARD ARMSTRONG

The first musicians who played at a jook were guys like myself, so to speak, street musicians; a guy who had gotten down from a carnival or something. They would come there and the doors were open to them. Well, it wasn't very long until they went in hock to the boss. They were in worse condition than they were before they came there because a lot of them would try to keep up with those crooked dice tables and what not that they had there; the little fast girls, the little bar flies and things. Well, they were in hock to the boss first thing you know. And I've seen, when they would be closing, during the last number on the stage, you know, fixing to close down the dance thing for the night, they'd have a flunky come by with a croaker sack. You might have called it a burlap bag or feed sack. Come around the edge of the platform where we be playing, "Hey man, give me your axe. Drop your instrument in this sack."

I don't care if it's a sax or trumpet or whatever it is; you in hock to the boss, put your instrument in there. They'd put that under lock and key until the next performance the next night. Now if you wanted to cut out, you know, do the Houdini, disappear in the greenwood like Robin Hood, O.K.; you do it without your instrument. I remember one night a guy threw his instrument out the window when nobody was looking, in the snow. So he pretends like he's going to the men's room or somewhere and took on out the back door and they never saw him. See, he was one of the few that got away with his instrument.

THE ROPE BROKE
"H-BOMB" FERGUSON

They had a tour called the Weinburger Tour. This is the tour that B. B. King, Tiny Bradshaw,[11] and me made. This guy's name was Weinburger; he was a promoter. He start you out in West Virginia. It was Charleston, Wheeling, I'll never forget it because that was the first tour we made when we start making big money. We went from there to Jacksonville, Miami, Savannah, Georgia, Mobile, Alabama. Man, this cat had them lined up. Just like every other night we was at different places.

When I was doing this, they used to rope off the dance hall; the white was over here and the black was over here. I ain't gonna never forget none of it. And sometimes when we played, we had a half-hour to get the hell out of there 'cause the sheriff came up and told us, "You all get the hell out of here when you get through." And they'd be dancing. But you know one thing; people are funny. I don't care if it was prejudiced then. Do you know a lot of white people would cross the line and come on the colored side of the dance. I used to be able to tell in a second just looking at them. The sheriff would grab them and push them back but they'd still do it. The blacks wouldn't do it because they know they'd go to jail if they broke the rope line. So they had police lined up. You dance on your side, everybody dance on their side. And they would come over.

I didn't forget none of it. I remember we went to a restaurant; I'd be hungry. Like most of the dances at that time was over like one o'clock. We used to stop by to get us something to eat.

"Oh, you was the band that played tonight."

"Yeah."

"Well, I'll tell you what, we ain't gonna give you a goddamn thing, nigger."

I said, "Now lady, can I get me a hamburger or a sandwich to go?" 'Cause you can't get nothing until next morning. Everything closed.

"Yeah well" she says, "you wait a minute, let me see if I can go back here and scrape up something."

"Hamburgers fifty cents," she said, "cost you a dollar."

I said, "A dollar? The sign says fifty cents."

She say, "That's for whites."

"Oh," I say, "Well, I didn't know that."

The cats in the band say, "Be cool, man, we from out of town you don't want to get in no trouble down here."

So we just go along with the program. I could write a book on that shit.

WHERE DID YOU LEARN TO SPEAK SPANISH?
JOHN "SO BLUE" WESTON

I was going out in Johnson, Tennessee, and I wanted some hot food. I didn't want no bologna, cheese, and crackers. And I went in this restaurant that said "White Only" above the door. And the guy says to me, "Say Boy, can't you read?"

And I ignored the question. He asked it again. I said, "Well, I reads a leetle bit but I no read-a too much in English; it very difficult for me."

"Well, where are you from?"

"I from South America."

"I know you certainly didn't sound like you was from around here."

And then this guy in there, I believe he was from out in Texas, he spoke good Spanish and he asked, said, "Donde aprendiste Español?"

I said, "Mi papa, mi papa aprendio Español." Said, "Well, I learned from my dad." Who really did speak Spanish.

I sit there and had a beef rib tip dinner with all the vegetables and everything that goes with it. And this man wouldn't even let me pay for it. And the guy says, "Well, if you're ever back through these parts be sure and stop and holler at me."

I said, "Well, I'd do that because you got-a here good food. I like good food. You see how much fat I am now. I like your food."

"All right."

Well, I got about, I guess it was about two miles, and I think I really did cry after I got down the highway because he wouldn't accept me without this dialect. And that hurt me.

THEY WALKED THE STREET
WILLIAM LEE "DOCTOR FEELGOOD," "PIANO RED" PERRYMAN

I got into music from a boy on up just banging around house parties, house rent parties, going from house to house playing. That's how I started out playing when I was about seventeen. I played with Willie McTell, Buddy Moss, Curly Weaver, Charlie Hicks; course I didn't know too much about Barbecue Bob, but he used to know my brother, Rufus "Speckled Red." But I knew the rest of those guys 'cause they walked the streets with their guitars on their back. And during the day they would have them daytime parties, house to house where they had that White Lightning at; and they made a little money doing that. They'd try this side of town this morning, the other side the next morning. They go in a different territory every day. Just start walking, people call 'em in with their guitars say, "How about playing us a number?" About twenty or thirty minutes they'd have a house full or porch full so they could get a little money out of it. And then some of them drank and they got all the free drinks they wanted. People rather buy you a drink than to give you the money, you know.[12]

MAXWELL STREET
DAVID "HONEYBOY" EDWARDS

I and Little Walter come here together. Come to Chicago in 1945 and played all the summer of 1945 on the streets. Me, Little Walter, Jimmy Rogers, Earl Hooker—he was real young then—Floyd Jones, John Henry Barbee, Stovepipe, we were all playing right there on the streets. Every day, we were playing everyday. Robert Nighthawk would come and sit in sometimes. Well, he didn't want to sit in too much because he was playing a little club at night. But he'd come by and we'd be playing so good out there that he'd have to pick up a guitar and play some.

It wasn't as many clubs as there are now, but we made more money in the streets because a club will pay you a certain amount, price about ten or twelve dollars a night, sometimes eight or ten dollars a night at that time, but we were making more than that on the streets. We'd make fifteen or twenty dollars apiece in the streets sometime because, at that time, all the steel mills was open in Chicago. There was so many people. People came from the South, everywhere, to get a job. That's right after wartime. And all the stockyards was open, you know, slaughter pens, all that was open and people was working. And people didn't have no where to stay then. All they had was like I rent this room here, sometimes two or three shifts would sleep in this bed. I'd get up and go to work, a shift would be getting off, and the landlady would change linens again. There was just so many people there in Chicago.

And when they'd come off from work, they wouldn't go right to bed, they'd come on out there and get them some breakfast or get them a good drink, walk the street and listen at us play the blues.

Them guys, all them people, was working all them jobs. They stay up until along about eleven, twelve, go lay down until about two-thirty, four o' clock, get up and go to work. And Friday and Saturday nights, we had a good night. Friday, Saturday, Sunday, oh, it's just like all the people that live out of town would be down on Maxwell Street.[13] There were just so many people you couldn't walk the streets; you had to turn sideways.

THE POOR SUPPORTED THE POOR
HENRY TOWNSEND

I worked rent parties in St. Louis in the Depression times. The musicians had a little access to nickels and dimes rather than the other guy that was looking for a job 'cause there wasn't any such thing. And we would get together after the landlords threaten to put them out and the musicians would kind of put their little money together and buy some kind of commodities, some drinks, to sell at the party. Then we'd put the party on. That was the way we had to aid the people that were more unfortunate than we were.

The thing went on month after month. It'd be here this month, some place else next month. But the musicians was some kind of, what they say, "a relief agency" for the people that was in total distress. It was done more or less not only for house rent, sometimes it was done for collections of food.

It started out in one little segment of town down around a street called Biddle Street, and it continued and spread all over the city. So we kind of, in later years, we kind of entitled that "the poor taking care of the poor" which was the facts. That's the way it was done. And this continued, on through until the WPA days give some kind of relief.

We used to get some old piano or something or other, put it on somebody's truck and ride up and down the street to advertise where this thing was gonna be. The musicians wasn't getting anything out of it. I guess we felt it was a duty for us to do. So, saying again, the poor supported the poor.

RENT PARTIES
FONTELLA BASS

I gave a few rent parties myself. I lived in the project, and to get that forty dollars a month I used to give Paree parties. That was Paree wine. What I would do is take five dollars and buy up some Parees, and you could get a fifth of Paree for twenty-five cents, and some Robin Hood wine. Forty, they used to call it. "Thirty-nine and One, Robin Hood Wine." And you could serve your party. And my uncle worked at the Holiday Drive-In so we would have little boxes of hot dogs, buns, and popcorn.

And I used to take the kitchen table and I had a ping-pong table that would turn around and I would put it on top of there and it would make a casino table. And then I'd put a blanket over it. So that was the gambling house.

Then on some Friday evenings I would buy a large buffalo fish. You could get a large buffalo fish at that time for about five dollars. I'd have them slice that buffalo and I'd fry fish and make a pot of spaghetti and make some homemade slaw. Dinner, a dollar twenty-five; laughs and plenty of beer, and that time the beer that was going really strong was Falstaff and Griesedieck. So we had nice times, nice times. And anytime after twelve o'clock midnight that's when the tables would start. See everything else closed up at one o'clock so people couldn't get in the door till after twelve.

It was getting pretty big. At first it started with just a few people and then we would have maybe up to twenty, twenty-five persons would come. The fellows that would gamble maybe would bring their ladies and they would sit in the living room and I would serenade them with records and food and, you know, and everything.

One night I came home and it was almost a hundred people waiting to get in my house. I lived on the sixth floor so you had to get off on the fifth floor to get up to the sixth floor, and all these people were standing in the stairwells waiting for me to get home.

I said, "Wow!"

So everybody heard about the set and wanted to join in. So it was like an after-hours place so I kind of didn't want the police, so I kind of busted it up after that. But the house made money. Now that's what we call rent parties. And since I was a starving musician at the time, you know, working sometimes on the weekend or two or three gigs a week; that's what I did when I ran short.

SMITTY'S WORKING HERE
BYTHER SMITH

We were out here in Cicero playing, and that's when they didn't even want blacks out there. Union sent us there. We carried our equipment out there. I guess they thought they hired me to help bring it out there. And the fellows in the club treated me well, you know, said, "Have a drink, come on take a drink."

I said, "I don't drink."

They gave me a couple of orange juices. So we went out there in the van and carried all the equipment out there, and I had two white boys with me at that particular time. Everything was so lovely that evening. So that night we come back, I drove my car out there. Well, everybody came in their own car. So I go out there by myself, just me, you know. I didn't take my wife with me. I just went out there by myself and go by and pick up the organ player. So him and I, we rode on out there together. So when I pull up, I get there before they did, so we just sit there in the car and we just talking. So about 8:30, I get out. I go on in. The guy meets me at the door and asks me where I was going. I says, "I'm working here."

He says, "Naw. Smitty's working here, a fellow by the name of Smitty."

I says, "Well, I am Smitty."

And I had to wait until the owner came down there. Then they call Mr. Samuels, president of the union. They call him. He says, "I sent you a man out there. Isn't he there?"

So this fellow here says, "You got a colored dude out here."

He says, "That's who I sent."

And that night when we got off of work, them boys had to fight for me to get out of there.

COULDN'T GET IN THE JOINT
JOHNNY SHINES

Some guys asked me to go out to the Apex one Sunday night with them. So I went out there with a fellow they call Spoons, I guess you heard of him, "Pork Chop,"[14] and another boy that played guitar; he had a metal thing on his chording hand, I can't think of his name. But anyway, we all went out there. They asked me to go out there with them, so, you know the "Apex Chateau" was a big place and it wasn't over ten or fifteen people in there. And it looked real silly playing in there to me. Anyway, when we got through playing everybody was going and getting their money you know, so they told me said, "Mr. Richardson says come in here."

So I went in where Mr. Richardson was. So he says, "O.K. here's your money." And he hands me three dollars.

I said: "This is my money?"

He said, "Yes."

I said, "How much does a case of that Global Beer cost?"

He said, "Two dollars and something."

I said, "Why don't you take the whole three and buy you a case of beer. Maybe it would help you along."

He said, "Well, that's what I paid the rest of the guys."

I said, "Well, good. Well, why don't you split that up and give it to them, then they'll have four dollars."

He looked at me and laughed. He said, "Look sir, before you go I want to talk with you." So he asked me how much would I charge him to put a band in there.

I said, "I don't know, it depends on what kind of band you want."

He said: "I want the best."

I said, "Well the best will cost you scale." At that time I didn't belong to no union; I didn't know what scales was, see.

He said, "Well, if you put me a band in here I'll pay them what you charge."

So I said, "Well, I'll have to have eighteen dollars as the leader and the rest of the guys will have to have twelve."

At the time the scale was ten dollars a man on the side and the leader, I think, as twelve-fifty. I really didn't know what the scales was. I was just playing in different places, you know, I'd set my own price. If I liked the looks of the place, I'd set my price depending on how the place looked to me.

So he said, "It don't make any difference about that."

So on our way back I was telling Pork Chop, I said, "This guy asked me about putting a band there."

Pork Chop say: "Sure enough."

I said, "Yeah."

So Friday night we all loaded up and went out there; we played that Friday night. These same little fifteen or twenty people were there that Friday night. So we got started to playing good and people began to come in from around the area. So I guess it added up to about sixty or seventy people before we got done playing. So Saturday night the word had got around that a good band was there, and the place was, I guess about twice that many as was there Friday. Sunday night, it was pretty good Sunday night, so he asked me would I come in Thursday night next week. I said, "Yeah." So Thursday night the place was filled up. The word had got around. This was out in Robbins [Illinois], so we was out there about two weeks and by then you couldn't get in the place. We played out there for more than two years.

LIKE A VAMPIRE
ROOSEVELT BARNES

I have my own club in Greenville, Mississippi. It's kind of rough but we have a lot of good times there. There's a lot of shooting on the outside, but once you make it inside, you're safe. My club's a little different than a jook joint on account of I'm in the city. Jook joints is mostly in the country. People do what they want in the country, you know. There's no laws or nothing that would be out there. I used to play all night. Sometimes I wouldn't even stop for no intermission. Ninety-minute sets just straight on through three or four hours without stopping, and it ain't been no long time ago since we did it either. I remember one night I was playing to a man sitting up in my club, he was sitting there sleeping, I was still playing. The next day I slept all day that day. I mostly stay up all night every night and sleep in the daytime like a vampire.

I'M NOT DEAD, I'M HERE

HE WAS JEALOUS
PRECIOUS BRYANT

Precious Bryant. Helena, Arkansas, October 11, 2003. Photograph by Barry Lee Pearson.

I got a group, a show with my sisters, named the Bussey Sisters, and they wanted to come. But see, they ain't like me. I ain't got no husband. They got husbands, somebody to make them sit down. I ain't got nobody to tell me nothing. I'm by myself. I can go when I get ready. Oh, yes, if my husband didn't die, I wouldn't be doing what I'm doing. No, because he was just crazy jealous. If my husband didn't die I wouldn't be where I am today. I remember one time when I was playing the guitar, he come and snatched the guitar out of my hand and me and him got into fighting. But you see, he didn't understand. I ain't trying to tempt nobody, I just love playing music. But he couldn't understand that.

HE'S ALREADY ANGRY
DAVID "HONEYBOY" EDWARDS

In later years, most women music lovers; down south, they love the blues. And the men would think the women love the musicians. Most of the time that's the reason the musicians didn't get along with some of the men. Some of the men thought that he wanted his women. But all the time he wouldn't be at a woman, that woman would be at him. Woman come buy you a drink, sit down by you, laugh and talk. Why it's nothing to you all, but the man's sitting rolling his eyes and he thinks that it might be something. So after I found all of that was happening, a woman come up say, "Honeyboy, play me such and such a thing." I'd get the request, tell them go sit down and don't bother me 'cause I don't want no trouble. After the request tell 'em, "Well, sit down."

Every once in awhile guy come up be drinking, say, that's my woman, or that's my old lady, leave her alone. I'd say, "Man, I'm not talking." You know that's always happening. At times like that I found it's better to play it for them. You play them a couple of numbers, tell them go ahead and sit down leave me alone; you got an old man. I'll play it for you when you go back over yonder and I'm gonna stay over here. Go back there. And at that time a man got a good job, got a good-looking woman; he die about that woman. He knows there's not another one out there like that for him, and he don't want to lose that woman. At that time he'd kill you about her 'cause he don't want to lose that woman. You know he got a nice little woman and he feels, "I won't get nothing like this no more." He'd kill you about her. It's true. It really is.

I used to sit down at night, lay down and think about these things and map it out and I say, "That's true. Leave those women alone if you want to live." So if they sit down I say, "Are you married?"

They say, "No, but I got an old man but we is on the bust."

I say, "I'll see you later when you got yourself straightened out."

He's already angry 'cause of me talking to her.

PERSONA NON GRATA
J. OTIS WILLIAMS

There is always a certain group of women who would run after musicians. They were just like camp followers, so my uncle would joke about it when some musician would be in there. He would say, "I tell you, musicians, in Grenada, don't take nothing with you that you didn't bring here." He was talking about the women because they like the musicians because they were dressed slick and had their hair gassed, conked, you know what I mean. It would just be laying there shining.

But a lot of time, people just call them, say, "Hey, he ain't nothing but an old tramp. He won't work, he just messin' around with that old guitar." But the guys didn't like them because these guys would be around home all day and they had to go to work. So this meant that they had a chance to sneak in their house and, you know, be with their ladies. So a guy who always had a guitar was never popular with men. When they refer to him, they never just refer to him my his name; they call him "Old So and So." That meant that he was *persona non grata*.

ONE OF THEM GET JEALOUS
JESSIE MAE HEMPHILL

I never like to play at no house parties. I don't want to do that or play at no jook. It's too dangerous. You'll get killed for nothing. You get up there and you start to playing and sometimes you'd be at these places where women are jealous of their man. And because one of the men maybe say, "Play, Miss Hemphill," they get jealous of it and could hurt me. And I wouldn't be meaning nothing. So I don't play at them kind. I play where I have protection for myself, places I know somebody there's gonna help watch over me. But at a jook and a house party, I don't play for them. I'll play a big club, but there's gonna be cops there. And I go to all these blues festivals and play, but there'd be more people there than me and there ain't nobody jealous of nobody because everybody laughs and talks with people. That's what I like. I don't like to be in a place that's a private something; you say something to the wrong man, you got a fight somebody. Because, see, I ain't going to fight with nobody. I ain't gonna fight with nobody because I ain't got no one to fight but me and I don't know how many there be of them. You go to a place like that, they'll try to gang you up, you know. Their friends, and somebody else, they try to gang on me.

THAT WILL MAKE THEM THROW A BRICK
GEORGE WASHINGTON JR.

Well, they'll get jealous of you over their women getting out there and go to cutting up over your music, dancing, and going on; then the men going to get mad with you. Then the men are gonna want to do something, or throw a brick in there, or shoot in there or something. You know that's what it's all about. So you got to be careful about that. Their old lady or maybe their girlfriends get to dancing out there on the floor and you know how they do over musicians playing the songs that they like. They'll go to cutting up, "Hey baby, play it a long time." And all like this, see. That will make them throw a brick in there or either shoot a bullet in there. So that's the way that kind of stuff come up. You didn't get around to do nothing. You didn't have to do nothing. They'll do that. Women go to cutting up like that over you, it will make the men mad. And then they'll want to do something to you. I had to watch out for all that. Through all my playing I had to watch for all that because it was dangerous that way.

I AIN'T DOCTOR ROSS
DOCTOR ROSS

I always laugh and talk, smile with everybody, but I'm kind of like the little boy from the West; I'm different from the rest. Lot of them musicians, they get their head bad and they go out after a woman. Some of them tell them, "No, I'm not married."

It happened to me. These women came up said, "We heard you on that program." "Oh, that's Dr. Ross." And then one of the guys [in the band] say, "I'm Dr. Ross."

"No you don't sound like him, your voice ain't like that."

Now who is Dr. Ross? Wait a minute. Just say, "Good morning." That guy say, "Good morning." You say, "Good morning." Now she said, "That's him now. I know by the way he. . . ."

I say: "No, I ain't Dr. Ross."

She say: "Oh, yes you are. You're the one. We thought you was a great big old man weighed about two hundred and sixty pounds."

And then them guys come in there and say, "Yeah, that's him there."

Oh, Lord, she'd be all over me then. I wished I would die because I was tired of that.

They would say, "Dr. Ross, why don't you say something to these women?"

I said, "Man, I ain't gonna let these women get me killed." I said, "I'm gonna laugh and talk with them but I'm gonna be just like school teacher."

CONQUERED THE BULLY OF THE TOWN
TED BOGAN

We were staying with a lady she had three daughters and one son. And they had a guy, a common-in-law guy, really. So, he was a heavy drinker; and he was a bully too, just to keep them afraid of him. But I didn't know anything about it. So Sunday morning I had a brand new shirt. I was putting it on and standing by the dresser, had a mirror on the dresser. And he accused me of going with her. And I ain't never give her a thought at all. So I told him I wasn't. He told me I was a liar. I said, "You're two of them." When I said that, he lunged at me. But I could see him coming through the mirror. When he come to me, I whirled around so fast and so strong. He had a grip on that brand new shirt, he got a grip and when I whirled it snagged all the way down to there. And when I turned around I hit him with my fist, knocked him down. I was so angry when I hit him; I hit him on the floor. See, the first time I hit him was enough. The next time I hit him was on that floor.

And then the people started telling me, say, "You better watch yourself because you done conquered the bully of the town." Said, "They out to get you." So that was just all right for me to get away. I didn't know who was who.

I WANT IT BACK
JOHN JACKSON

I used to dance a lot when I was growing up, but I ain't danced since I quit playing music back there in 1946. I haven't done any dancing. I don't reckon I will now. I'm too old for that. I quit in 1946. There wasn't no command for this kind of music and all you was playing for was parties or dances; and people used to fight so bad. And I hadn't long got married then and went to play for a dance. Well, I went there that night to play for this party. And I always get back in one little corner of the house and was sitting back there playing, and I guess these people had danced one set. And finally here come this fellow in and sat down where I was playing, beside of me, and I didn't pay too much attention to him. And finally I looked around at him like that, he was crying, great big drops of water falling out his eyes. And I commenced to feeling kind of funny because I didn't know what was going on there with him. And

John and Cora Jackson,
Fairfax Station, Virginia,
1978. Photograph by
Kathy James. Courtesy
of the National Council
for the Traditional Arts.

all at once he looked around at me like this and he said, "I want you to play that guitar, goddamn you, or put it down."

I knew the fellow but I didn't know him well. I said, "Nokes, I'm gonna play a little bit and you play some." I said, "Nokes, the people here want everybody to have a good time."

And he had a pair of these striped coveralls on and great big pair of shoes with iron on the heel and toe. He raised his feet up and he struck them down on the floor, sparks flew out from around them. He said, "I done told you to play that guitar, goddamn you, or put it down."

And he jumped up to hit me and it was a couple of my friends standing there, Richard May and I don't remember who the other fellow was, but any way they grabbed him and got into a tussle and they taken him out and quieted him down. And I kept sitting there playing. Finally in about ten minutes he come back and sat down again. And I didn't say nothing to him. He sat there with his arms folded like this. All at once he told me, said, "You stole my guitar and goddamn you, I'm gonna have to kill you."

I said, "Nokes, you didn't even have a guitar when you come in here."

"Oh yes I did."

He opened up a switchblade knife. And that's when my friend grabbed him and that's what started the fight. You ain't never saw such a fight as that in all your days; it must have been two hundred people there. Man, they tore that man's house up, knocked the windows out, was beating up the furniture. You know, hitting one another and falling all over the tables and chairs. So I grabbed my wife by one hand, the guitar in the other one and we started out the back door. This old big house was built on the side of the hill and it must have been thirty or forty steps from the back all the way to the ground. And we got about half way down we heard a terrible noise and looked, somebody hit somebody over the head with a table leg or something. And this man come rolling down them steps, like that, we stepped aside and he shot by us and hit the ground and I'll be dogged, after all that falling he jumped up from there and went out in the dark running we didn't know where he went. By the time we got down to the ground somebody threw a gallon jug and it come right over our head—"wama, wama, wama"—you know how something's blowing in the wind like a jug, and it hit a locust tree in front of us and busted.

Moments later we got in the car and I got that started and I got out of there. And my cousin got trapped behind. He couldn't leave. And he said the fellow that started the fight, somebody bit off the end of his finger. Now whether it's true, I don't know. And said the man done went home and got an old shot gun or something and hid behind the fence where everybody comes out. He said when my cousin started through he started on him and said, "Look, hold on there. Somebody got half of my finger and I want it back."

And I never went to any more dances. That was enough.

BUCKET OF BLOOD
BIG JOE DUSKIN

There was a joint up on Freeman Avenue a guy got punched in his puss there one night and he bled pretty bad, and they called it "The Bucket of Blood." But it was a nice place. It just so happened this guy just got a little too much to drink and he was messing with people and they punched him in the mouth. So that's why they called it "The Bucket of Blood." Then they had another place, it was called Gorman and Army Cafe. That's the way they named them, right after the street corner, so anybody could know where to go. Then they had another place on Lynn Street I played called "Five by Fives." This guy was a great big man. He's bigger than Joe Turner. And they called him "Five by Five" because he was five feel tall and five feet wide or whatever. I played in his place for a while. Then they had another place called "Gut Cut Inn" and that was up on Davis Street. These was nice places, but they were just a little rough. If a guy got cut, that's what they named it after. This guy got cut in the stomach, they named it "The Gut Cut Inn."

EXIT STAGE RIGHT
JAMES "STRAWBOSS" WHEELER

We was playing a show down in Waycross, Georgia. This is when I was with Otis Clay.[15] We was on the stage, and I don't know what brought all this on. Maybe it started before we got there, but there was this kind of ugly lady. She was there, just having a good time; she was dancing and going on and I guess somebody had ruffled her feathers. Anyway she left and she came back. And we was on stage, we was hard into our show, you know, just dancing and singing and going on. And she came back in. She came back in dancing and all of a sudden she reached in her purse and pulled this big thirty-eight out.

And I say, "Otis. Otis."

And he asks me, says, "What's the matter?"

I say, "It's time to go."

He says, "What do you mean it's time to go?"

I said, "Look this woman's got a god damn gun."

And he said, "That's right. Exit stage right."

PLAY BETTER WITH ONE ARM
PINETOP PERKINS

I went over in Helena, Arkansas, and one of those bad ladies got hold
to it and stabbed me in the arm and I couldn't play guitar no more then.
I could pound down but I couldn't chord the guitar. I would call it a
freak accident. I was back in a café; we call it "Dreamland Cafe." Me and
the boys was back there, you know, drinking beer and a little whiskey
once in a while. A lady come back there and went to the bathroom. So
after she went into the bathroom, I just shut the door behind her, you
know, to keep people from looking at her. So her used-to-be husband
come on in and put two or three barrels of ashes up against the door
and she couldn't get out for 'round about an hour, an hour and a half.
So I'm the last somebody she saw shut the door. So she didn't ask no
hard questions when she did see me, she just lit on in to me. So I played
one-armed for a pretty good while. People say, "Hey, you play better
with one arm than you did two."

RAZOR-TOTING WOMEN
CEDELL DAVIS

There was razor-toting women, razor-toting women. I'm gonna tell you
about a woman I know, an auntie of mine. She believed in toting a knife
and she sure would kill you. I know she killed three people. She killed
one lady with a meat cleaver and then she killed two other people with
a knife. But she never went to prison nary a time because she'd always
run away.

And you know, they didn't do too much about people killing a
woman back in them days, no ways. You're on your farm or whatever or
work for somebody, they say, "Oh, no, don't bother them, he works with
me or she works with me." That's about all to it. That's the way she did.

Some of them women, man, they wear stockings back in them days,
you know when they didn't have garters; they put on that, twist them
up, you know, and then have a razor sticking in there. And you mess
with them or something, look like you're bothering somebody, you better run. Because when you see her snatch that dress up on the side and
reach in there, you better be getting out of the way. She cut your throat.
I ain't joking. Yes, indeed she would.

THE STABBINGEST WOMAN I EVER SEEN
"UNCLE JESSIE" WHITE

Johnnie Jones,[16] he's the one that learned me how to play a piano. Anyway, me and him was supposed to play at the Crystal Palace. We were out all that day and then when I went home, I had this other girl. That was before I got married. I come home and when me and him walked in, my old lady stabbed me all the way through this arm. I sure am glad my arm caught that knife. That knife went in this side and come out the other side. She cut me, almost cut me and tried to run me down to finish me, but I ran. [*Laughs.*] She was going after me with that big knife and I sure had to get out of the way. And that's the awfullest woman.

I went to the doctor and they said, "We gonna have to call the police."

The police told me, said, "Look, you didn't get cut accidentally, somebody cut you. You just won't tell us."

But I couldn't tell them because that was my old lady that stabbed me. Anyway, she dreaded it though because she had to get out and work then, because I wasn't able to work. She say, told me, "I sure hate I did that." [*Laughs.*]

I laid around there, but she sure had to get out and work because I couldn't do nothing for four or five months.

That was Frances, that mean woman I had. She'd cut people. And she had scars. You could cut her and she looked like she didn't [care]. You know, I ain't messing with a person look like they don't care about their hide getting cut up. You know she was fighting a girl, and that girl was cutting and she was licking that blood and cutting back. She was the stabbingest woman I ever seen.

ELMORE, YOU WON'T PLAY NO MORE
BIG BILL HILL

I spent years with the late Elmore James. I sent for him, I think I have it framed in my office, May the something, 1963. I don't know the exact year; don't hold me to this. But anyway, he came from Mississippi to play for me. He came on a Sunday. He was residing temporarily on the North Side of Chicago, so he called me up. I had a religious program from eight to ten. After I went off my eight-to-ten religious program he called me up and said, "I'm in Chicago."

So I went over to his house and we talked. He played that Monday night for me. I only had one day of advertising and the house was loaded. At this time I had the largest nightspot in Chicago by the name of The Copacabana Club. My seating capacity was one thousand and fifty, and this night with one day of advertising, we must have had over five hundred people.

That Friday night just dressing to come for his final or last gig the big boss man says, "Elmore, you won't play anymore." And the whole of Chicago went into tears. I had reinstated him in the union because he was out temporarily. He died. It was shockingest thing that I ever witnessed in my life. It was on a Friday night. He was dressing and someone said they heard something hit the floor. And they went to his room and there he was on his knees and he keeled over and died. So we called the fire department and they couldn't save him. It was the most terrifying thing that I have ever witnessed. One of the great artists. I still am a great admirer of the late Elmore James. No one touched me more than this here, I mean blues-wise, because he did it from here [his heart]. No imitation; originality, from here. An old timer, he played the blues because he felt the blues and he lived them.

I'M NOT DEAD, I'M HERE
JOHNNY SHINES

Some things you just don't believe. Just like me, a lot of folks said I was dead. Several times they'd have me dead. Oh, I remember one night a fellow got killed. The people, you know, were looking at him laying out there in the streets. His name was Johnny, you know, and he was a musician. So the people who went there and looked at him just agreed it was Johnny Shines. And I walked into work that night and everybody says, "No this can't be."

I'm wondering what's wrong with these folks.

"Man, we just come over from looking at you."

I said, "So what."

"You supposed to be dead."

"Oh what? Me?"

You see what had happened, the guy that killed the boy, him and I had got into it, I guess, about two months before this, see. I had knocked the guy all upside the head. He pulled a knife there and he was bad about killing me. Well, he had killed six or seven guys; so they all told me say, "You got to watch him because he'll sure get you. He'll get you after he slips up on you. He sure gonna get you."

And when this boy got killed, his name was Johnny, and he was a musician, a tenor guitar player, and he was kind of heavy like myself at that time. So this guy come up and stabbed him and everybody just took it for granted that it was me. So I walked in that night and everybody looked so silly, it made me feel silly. Then they went on and told me what had happened. This was in Chicago.

Well, you see, I'm not dead; I'm here.

WINNERS AND LOSERS

I DON'T NEED NO HELP
JAMES "SON" THOMAS

James Thomas. Washington, D.C., July 1976. Photograph by Carl Fleischhauer. Courtesy of the Smithsonian Center for Folklife and Cultural Heritage.

My uncle, he played music. Also, my granddaddy, he played some, too. Didn't have no electric then. They'd sit around home and play a lot. People would come around Sundays and Saturday nights; sometimes they would give a party. Well, that's a big gang coming in there Saturday night. They spend their money there. Next time someone else give one and they all would go down there to the next house. So after I got large enough to play, I wasn't able to buy no guitar at that time, but I had learned how to play two songs. So my uncle, he wouldn't let me play his when I got ready. I had to give him fifty cents, a dollars, to play his guitar. And I couldn't keep it too long. So I got a chance to pay him back when I bought me a brand new Gene Autry guitar. And he didn't have a guitar then, you know. I started playing for the teenagers and he be running up and down the road looking for me to borrow the guitar to play for some of the grown people. I said, "Well, we busy now."

Well, he went and got him some kind of little guitar, but it wasn't electric. By then I had done got an electric and I was playing at one place. We got a job and the crowd had to come by his place for to get to where I was playing at. But he didn't have an amplifier. So he was down there just playing; I put my amplifier in the window and started playing, after a while the house was packed!! Jam packed!! I had to get up on the counter and play they was so many people there. After a while, here come my uncle, with his guitar on his shoulder. He come in there says, "You need any help?" I said, "No! I don't need no help."

IF I BEAT YOU PLAYING
YOU GOT TO LEAVE FLORENCE
CLARENCE BUTLER

It was a young boy I will never forget, a young boy named Carter Bodie. He was nineteen years old. And everywhere he went to play, well, they say, "Well, Butch Butler plays that. . . . I heard Butch Butler play that." He never met my daddy but every where he went to those fish fries and played, somebody always tell him, "Man, you playing the same thing I heard Butch play." Now he's got to find this Butch; he been hearing about Daddy all the time.

So one Sunday morning, he knocked up on the door. I let him in. He say, "Butch Butler stay here?"

I say, "Yeah, he stays here."

"Is he in? You wake him." Said, "You tell him Carter Bodie wants to see him."

So Daddy came to the door and moved me out of the way. I was about seven years old.

He said, "I'm Butch. What you want?"

"My name is Carter."

"Oh yeah. I heard about you. Tell me you play a pretty good guitar." He said, "I play the best guitar."

He say, "Oh yeah?"

He say, "I come to challenge you, old man, today." He said, "If I beat you playing you got to leave Florence. But if you beat me then I'll leave Florence."

And my dad say, "Okay. Alright." He said, "You hungry?"

Mama, she was in there fixing breakfast. So my daddy went out and washed up and everything. And she called us all in for breakfast. After breakfast, it was an old tree sitting out in front of the house, a big old shade tree. And it was hot. It was August and way down south it didn't get ninety degrees, it got a hundred degrees down there in the shade. But it was early that Sunday morning. It wasn't even nine o'clock, but it was just getting up there, so he went out and brought two chairs up under that tree.

I don't know where those people come from but before they got set and went to playing, it was a yard full of people. So the duel went on. I have to say, for a while there was this young guy, he wasn't but nineteen, he was doing a pretty good job on my dad.

So my dad say, "Well, it's time to pull out the stops on you," and my daddy started playing something that I never heard him play before. And I know Carter never heard him play it before because he started playing stuff like "John Henry the Steel Driving Man" and all them type of stuff. And Carter didn't know what he was doing. He didn't know the chords he was playing. That was something new to him.

But that's the only reason he really beat him. He pulled out the stops on him. He told him, he said, "Don't never learn nobody all you know. Don't ever show anybody all you know." He say, "I got things I learned when I was nine years old." He says, "The things I learned when I was nine years old, I don't play anymore. That was my learning period."

He says, "This is what I'm putting on you."

And sure enough, Carter Bodie was true to his word. He left and went to the next county.

YOU'RE GONNA PUT YOUR GUITAR DOWN
JOHN JACKSON

This fellow name was Tom Terrell; we had known him 'round there for about a year. And shortly after that, we met this convict from a chain gang. Tom Terrell said there wasn't no man ever was born could pick no guitar with him. So my father knew this convict. Nobody around that we had ever seen pick any guitar could do anything with him with no guitar. So he told Tom Terrell, "When you meet this man you gonna put your guitar down."

He said: "That I got to see."

So Tom Terrell come over to where this convict named Happy was at. Tom played two or three songs said, "Now I want to see somebody match that."

So my father says to Happy, "Now Happy, get a hold of that guitar and show Tom how its done now." And I'm telling you, he played very much like Lonnie Johnson in drop key and open tuning and he started picking blues, "Midnight Blues." And Tom Terrell got so upset he cried. When he got through with the guitar and handed it back to him he busted it all to pieces over top of a rock.

He really did.

I GOT MY HEAD CUT
JOHNNY SHINES

I ran up on Robert Johnson in 1934 or the early part of 1935. I ran up on him in Helena, Arkansas. I had turned pro just about then; I was playing in clubs and things. I wasn't exactly making my living doing it, but I was living at it. Anyway, I was playing in Hughes in a place called Doc Pickens. An old piano player called "M and O," he was playing there, and I was playing under him, and he was telling me about this guy in Helena. He was supposed to be tough. But you know the guys had an act of cutting heads. You know, you hit up on a guy that's supposed to be good, you supposed to beat him playing, well this is what "M and O" expected. Evidently he had some kind of bone to pick with Robert as a musician. At that time I was young, strong, playing hard, singing loud, and he thought I could outdo Robert Johnson. He wanted me to go to Helena and cut Robert's head, outdo him and steal his crowd away from him; pull his crowd away from him. In other words, I make all the money; he makes nothing. That's what they call "head cutting." So finally one day we hopped a freight train and went to Helena and I ran into a buzz saw. I got my head cut. It wasn't like "M and O" thought it would be. I thought I was raising a lot of Cain, but I found out I wasn't doing nothing. I had just been making noise. He took my crowd.

BLACK ELVIS
WILLIE COBBS

Willie Cobbs. At home in Arkansas, 2002. Photograph by Brett Bonner. Courtesy of Living Blues.

When I grew up a little I started playing with Eddie Boyd and playing around a lot with the Howling Wolf and them, all those cats back in those days. So, like I was on a show, Howling Wolf used me for an opening up singer with his group once in awhile. And they used to call me, like, "Black Elvis Presley." I had just got out the service. I was physically in good shape, could do a lot of dancin'. You know, I was raised up in the jook house, and I never could dance with nobody, but I could get me one of those chairs and get in the corner with that chair and I could cut some steps that you ain't never seen. So at that time Elvis Presley was making all that shaking, so everybody called me "Black Elvis" because I was so active on the stage. And so one day Wolf caught my coattail and told me [*in Wolf's voice*], "Say boy, listen here, now I want to let you understand you're not the star of this show. You better get your ass and set it down. You jump around here, twist around here and break my microphone cord, I'm gonna break these fourteens off in your you know what."

PLAY B. B. KING
YANK RACHELL

I'm Yank Rachell. I don't go around trying to play like Muddy Waters and B.B. Everybody you see trying to play like B. B. King or Muddy Waters. I'm not them; I'm me. I went to play one night and sat down and played. They came out there and say, "Can you play B. B. King?"

I said, "Yeah, put some strings on him. I'll play him."

THEY DON'T KNOW WHO I AM
JACOB DAWSON

There were adventures, arguments with James Brown,[17] fights with Little Milton, arguments with Albert King. They were all good ones, but nothing like nobody hurting each other. We were here in Washington, D.C., right here in this city at the Howard Theater. We opened at the Howard Theater when I was working with James Brown. It had just re-opened, and the show hadn't started and something came up about the money thing, you know. And James and I was at each other's throat behind the curtain. We got the mayor and all his family and everybody sitting at the front of the stage, because the lights was on but the curtain was drawn, you know. And they hear these two voices back there just cussing and raising all kinds of sand. They don't know who I am. I'm just the guitar player. But they know who James Brown's voice was [*laughs*]; so I think they kept him out of there for a while.

PLAYED THE WHOLE GIG BY HIMSELF
EDDIE BURNS

He [Sonny Boy Williamson Number Two] had a live broadcast on KFFA Delta Network Interstate Groceries, coming out of Helena, Arkansas. So when I saw him again, he was coming to Clarksdale and played in a place, a jook joint really, called the Green Spot. He made a big impression on me right there because I was fooling around with the harmonica at that time. And so they had this gambling house on the back of the jook joint, see, and when the time come to hit, Sonny Boy went on stage but the band was still back there gambling. So when they came out from back there, they was fired. Sonny Boy played the whole gig by himself.

Didn't let them play. But the next day they were on the air with him again. But he didn't let them play that gig that night.

He did numbers like, "I Love You For Sentimental Reasons," and "Tanya" by Joe Liggins,[18] and "Honeydripper" by Joe Liggins, "Kidney Stew" by Eddie Cleanhead Vinson, and I was really impressed by that. I didn't know the harmonica could really sound so good. He was a whole lot different than John Lee Williamson Number One. The man was very talented; I mean, I have to take my hat off to him even though he's dead now.

I ASKED FOR WHAT I GOT
WILLIAM "BOOGIE MAN" HUBBARD

I left here with Roscoe Gordon.[19] Me and him went to Tallulah, Louisiana, and we got into it about that money because I was a long way from home, and he caused me to come away from home. And we made, he made about thirteen or fourteen hundred dollars that night and he's gonna give me a hundred fifty dollars. And we got into it about that. We had a little scuffle about it.

But I asked for what I got. See, I'm riding in *his* car and *I'm* in Tallulah, Louisiana, and I *live* in Memphis. But I met a girl that night. Man, I knew I wasn't riding back with him because I had just jumped on him and we just got to fighting. Well, he paid me after we got to fighting. So she said, "I will get you home. I'm gonna take you to the airport and get you a ticket now." So she took me to the airport, and bought me a ticket from Tallulah to Memphis, Tennessee. The ticket was good until the next night. I had to spend a day and a night over there with her, but I didn't care. I mean, Roscoe and them was gone and left me in that town. They left me in Tallulah and they was going to New Orleans.

YOU START KICKING
BIG JOE DUSKIN

The funniest thing happened up around New York City. Ella Fitzgerald was just a young kid at that time; I don't think she was sixteen years old. And she was singing this song "Tisket-a-Tasket." Fletcher Henderson was in there gambling, and I come in to tell Fletcher that there was a girl out singing. He should come out and hear it. He cussed me and run me out, "You come in here and make me lose my money in a crap game! Get out of here with this stuff."

So I left and when I did, he come out. But Chick Webb caught her and signed her up. Got permission from her mom to use her. Fletcher Henderson come out and heard her singing. He say, "Who is that?"

I told him, I said, "Ella Fitzgerald."

He said, "Listen, take this note up there and give it her."

I said: "It's too late now, Henderson."

"What do you mean?"

"Chick Webb already got her. That's him playing drums. That's his band."

"What?" he said, "Why didn't you tell me?"

I said, "I tried to tell you that when you was gambling, and Fletch, you almost kicked my tail and run me out. So therefore I just thought you didn't want to be bothered."

And Fletcher Henderson told me, says, "I'm gonna bend over and you start kicking. I'll tell you when to stop."[20]

GIVE ME SMITTY'S MONEY
BYTHER SMITH

I was out there working with Junior Wells[21] one night. Junior called me up; I had just got home. He called me, say, "Man, I need a guitar player. Can you come help?" I said, "Yeah, Junior." He says, "What time you get there?" I say, "I'll be there by the time you get started to work."

So I get dressed and goes on out there. I get there about five minutes before work time, Sammy Lawhorn was sittin' up there. When I walked in Sammy says, uh, "Hot Dog. Here comes my baby. Everybody gotta bring it in for my baby." I was bringing my guitar and amplifier in. Sammy says, "Queen Bee, give me Smitty's money now. I'm gonna drink it up." And that woman paid Sammy! See, he's just sitting at the bar, he's not working, he's just sitting at the bar. So she goes and pays him. Now, when I get off work, I'm standing there, I say, "O.K. Queen Bee, come on and give Smitty his money so I can go." Just like that you know. She says, "Uh, Smitty I done paid you. I gave your money to

Sammy Lawhorn." Honest to God, and I thought she was kidding. So I go and put my stuff in the car and come back in there said, "Woman, you better pay me:"

"You ain't getting nothing; I done paid Sammy Lawhorn and Sammy done drink that money up." Sammy got drunk and gone home. So Junior Wells said, "Queen, I hired that man to come out here. Now you pay that man 'cause I told him what you were paying. Now you pay that man and you get your money from Sammy because you give Sammy the money. Sammy wasn't working. I hired that man," he says. "I called that man up here from home, out off his bed to come out there to help me."

I HAVE WORKED FOR LESS THAN THAT
LITTLE MILTON CAMPBELL

My oldest brother and I were uptown, we lived right on the outskirts of the city, and we heard this music across the street at a little jook joint and went in there. And it was Eddie Cusic, one Sunday evening, you know. And I had been trying to play the guitar a few years. Couldn't play worth a damn, but I knew nothing about electric guitar. His guitar had the hole in it with the pick up; it fit across the hole. And he let me play it, and I thought that was the most beautifulest sound. And I could sing, so he let me sing a few tunes. I could always sing because I started singing from a little boy, a little bitty thing in church. My mom had me participating in church programs and what have you.

So then he said, "Listen man, if you gonna be in town Saturday, Friday or Saturday, won't you come by." He was playing a club, just little clubs around there in the city. He said, "Maybe you can sit in with me and do a few tunes."

So I said I'd love that. So that Friday and Saturday, man, I was uptown. And he let me sit in and people started applauding and hollering and what have you, you know, that young strong voice. Couldn't play worth a damn, but I could sing. And pretty soon he invited me back the next week. Went back and the same thing, same reaction of the crowd. So Eddie said, "Listen, do you want to work with me? Or work for me, whatever you want to call it?"

I said, "Sure."

So he was paying me a dollar and fifty cents a night. I thought that was good. So if we work three nights you know how much I was making? Four dollars and fifty cents; and I have worked for less than that. I have gone with some big bands and some bands over in Greenville after I moved from Leland to Greenville. We call him King Mack Simmons and his Aces of Swing or something like that. And a bunch of us young guys, he would promise us ten or twelve dollars and that was big money then. But then once we got out there, some time I have worked for thirty, thirty-five cents. When the gig was over, I got thirty-five cents. [*Laughs.*]

And we would always swear that we were not gonna go back out there with him anymore, you know. He had a gimmick; that he would go by and talk to us individually, and he would come to me and say, "Listen, I talked to the rest of them and they're gonna go."

So, I wouldn't want my buddies to go and I not go so, "Will you go?" I said, "Yeah, O.K."

Then he'd go do the same thing. And when he got through going around one on one each time, he'd have the whole band back together again.

WHERE'S MY MONEY
CEDELL DAVIS

Rice Miller, the one who called himself Sonny Boy, he gambled a lot, drink plenty whiskey, liked plenty ladies. He sure would gamble all the money, and if you lay down there asleep with the money, he gonna get that too. Boy, he used to do that. We used to have a time about that. He'd say, "You ain't nothing but a babe under me."

I say, "I can play just as good as you can."

"Yeah, I know you can play come and go along with me."

I said, "Man, I ain't going nowhere with you. That's because you, shucks, you pay me alright, but you get up and steal the money."

I'd go to sleep, you know, he'd ease up there steal my money, you know. When I wake up, I said, "Look here, man, where's my money?"

"What?" Acting like he don't know nothing about it.

I say, "Man, where's my money?" I say, "I know you got it."

"No baby, no, no. Wait a minute, wait a minute, I ain't got it."

Well, I cussed back in them days, but they weren't going to fight me or nothing because they knew I was right, see. They wouldn't fight. Man, we'd raise sand.

"We'll pay you. We'll pay you. It's no question; I'm gonna pay you."

Robert Nighthawk would do the same thing, but he wouldn't steal it out of my pocket or steal it, just like I say. I go to bed, lay my money on the table, see; all right, he wouldn't steal it or nothing like that, but what he'd do he'd borrow it from you. And then tell a lie say he didn't borrow none.

I say, "Man, you a so and so liar, you did borrow my money and you know you did."

"I don't remember."

I said, "Now, you didn't forget it because you remember coming borrowing it didn't you?"

"Oh well maybe I did."

I said, "Maybe nothing, you pay me my money."

I THOUGHT HE MIGHT LIKE IT
MELVIN LEE

Furry Lewis,[22] he had to have his liquor. He was gonna drink that whiskey. He drank . . . he used to drink the cheapest liquor you get. He couldn't drink no good whiskey; good whiskey would make him sick. He would drink Ten High. And anyway, we were on the bus, they had rented us a bus, we were traveling but we had to stop in this little town to get Furry Lewis some whiskey. And they didn't have no Ten High, so I just got him a bottle of Old Granddad. I thought he might like it. And he took a couple swallows of that and it like to killed him. He was sick for two weeks off of drinking that. He couldn't stand any good whiskey; he had to have Ten High. But he was gonna drink. He was going to make a movie, the guy told him said, "We ain't gonna have no drinking on the set."

He said, "Well, it ain't gonna be no set. If I can't drink it won't be no set."

He told that guy, "When I go to church on Sunday the preacher have me a pint of whiskey."

I SAW A BEAR
FRUTELAND JACKSON

I got a story. I had the pleasure of touring with David "Honeyboy" Edwards, class of 1915. And he's eighty-two, I think, or eighty-three. And we were in Duluth, Minnesota, at the Duluth Minnesota Blues Festival. And so we pulled up at this store, this convenience store, I went in there to buy some items and when I came back Honeyboy said, "Fruteland! Fruteland! I just saw a bear!"

I said, "You didn't see no bear."

He say, "I did. I saw a bear."

I said, "Honeyboy, where's your half pint? You didn't see no bear."

"No, I saw it."

I said, "You're from Mississippi. That was a big dog. You didn't see a bear."

"I know what I saw."

I said, "You didn't see no bear; now let's go."

I get in the car and we take off. The very next day we pull up at the same convenience store and I go in the store to pick up some items. When I come out, the car was blocking the front part, so I went around the back. I saw a bear! And it was in the garbage cans. So it scared me because I'm thinking, "Bear! It's gonna eat me!" I'm not afraid of snakes or spiders, but bears! So then I run. I get around front to the car I say, "Honeyboy, I saw a bear."

He said, "You didn't see no bear."

I said, "Yes, I did."

He said, "No, you didn't see no bear."

He said, "Where's your half pint?"

I said, "I ain't got no half pint. I saw a bear."

He said, "You're from Mississippi, that was a big dog."

I said, "O.K. Honeyboy, you saw a bear and I saw a bear."

And then when I started asking around they said bears did come out and eat garbage, so I figured they probably got high cholesterol and high blood pressure like we do. And unless they're pregnant or something they don't really bother you, but don't grab one.

He just came back at me, "That was a big dog." So whenever we would see each other, I say, "How about that big dog, Honeyboy." And we'd laugh.

PLEASE DON'T HOLLER
HOWARD ARMSTRONG

One night we had played on the North Side. We had a guy called Washboard Sam.[23] Washboard, he claimed that good whiskey would make him sick so he drank all this garbage liquor. He made it out of swill from the garbage can. And Washboard got mightily high that night. We had been playing in a big white night club, and we were coming through the residential part out near Gamble and Diversey or somewhere on the North Side. And they didn't want us out there to tell the truth. But Washboard decided he was gonna "whoop."

They said, "Washboard, please don't holler."

"Oh, I'm gonna holler, oh hell, yeah. I'm gonna holler; I just got to holler. I feel too good to keep my mouth shut."

Said, "Please, don't holler, Washboard."

I said, "Let the fool go ahead and holler."

"Go ahead and holler!"

And he hollered just about this loud [*real soft*], "Ooh whee."

JUST RELAXING
JOE WILLIE WILKINS

We were working this job outside and they got this stage with stone steps up to it and then it drops off. Roosevelt Sykes was there. We were all high. And he's dressed in this suit, real nice suit. So he had to go to the bathroom and he is going to just step off the back stage, you know, take a leak off of the stage. But he don't know how far the ground is. So down he falls. We run over and he's lying on his back in the mud and water. We say, "Roosevelt, what you doing there?" So he's lying on his back and he looks up and says, "Just relaxing."

Club Jabot. Photograph by Barry Lee Pearson.

THE LAST WORD

Now when the wolf leaves a place,
he lifts both feet like a rabbit.
Nobody can see where he goes.

HOWLIN' WOLF

BRIGHT LIGHTS, BIG CITY
J. OTIS WILLIAMS

Well, surprisingly, the blues never made me sad. Listening to the blues
gave me hope. It made me anticipate going to big cities, and made me
anticipate travel because they talked about trains, you know, and traveling out on the highway. Bright lights, big city, all these things made me
want to go see these things because I had never been on a train. I had
never been to a big city.

You can imagine going to the train station. We would go to the train
station and just look at the trains. People would just be sitting in the club
car under the bright lights, just eating, and that whistle would blow and
it would just start easing off. Man! And you with your little raggedy self
would just be standing there, just saying, "Damn. If I could just catch that
train and go to Chicago or Memphis." Just listening to the music, it would
give you a feeling of elation, like this anticipation that these things were
going to happen.

I GOT A RIGHT TO JUMP
ALGIA MAE HINTON

My husband was so jealous I couldn't even do nothing. When I had the
old man I had to sit still. I couldn't hardly give my mama a piece of candy.
He was so jealous he couldn't even stand me to talk. That ain't good.
He used to keep his eyes on me. I liked to play guitar, but he didn't like
to see me play. I say, "Man, I'm used to playing guitar." He cussed
though. I ain't gonna tell you what he said. I said, "Well, one of these

days I will be playing my guitar." So I didn't play until after he died. It was about six years before I went out playing a guitar to the house parties. So that's why I'm playing now. I can jump up now. Ain't got no man telling me to make no biscuits. So I got a right to jump.

SHE MIGHT DO ME LIKE GRANDMA DID YOU
ARCHIE EDWARDS

When I was going with my wife before we got married she got a chance to hear me play the guitar one night. So I played that Blind Boy Fuller song about "She's So Sweet."[1] She said to herself, "He will never get away from me." So about ten years later we were married and living out where we are. So one day my little grandson was sitting out on the porch with me and I played that song.

And he said, "Granddaddy, I like that song."

"Yeah, you do?"

"Yeah, I like that song, Granddaddy!!"

So in the meantime my next-door neighbor had a little granddaughter that was two or three years old. They had gotten to be very close you know. And I said, "Grandson, are you gonna sing this song to that little girl?" Well, I sang this song to grandma way before we got married and grandma said, "You will never get away from me." "Now remember, son, that's been over thirty-six years ago. You still gonna sing that song to your little girl?"

"Yeah, I'm gonna sing that song to my little girl."

Three days later I came home from work one evening he's sitting on the stairs with his little head in his hand. I parked the car, opened the gate, come on in. He just say there. I said, "Hi, grandson."

"Hi, Granddaddy."

"Are you sick?"

"No."

"What's wrong?" I said: "Aw come on, come on you can't jive Granddaddy. Something's wrong boy you can tell Granddaddy anything."

He straightened up took a deep breath. "Granddaddy, I ain't gonna play that song to that little girl."

I said, "Oh you're not?" I said, "Why?"

"Because, Granddaddy, she just might do me like grandma did you."

I'M GONNA HELP YOU PACK
"UNCLE JESSIE" WHITE

But I was so glad when she told me she was gonna leave. Honestly, I was. We were up in the Delta, you know, in the Delta, pulling all that cotton. We was up there; me and her. And it was getting kind of late, and we was sitting there in the camp. I wasn't saying nothing.

She say, "I'm going to leave."

I said, "What you say, what? I misunderstood you?"

She said, "I'm gonna leave."

I say, "Well, I'm gonna help you pack." [*Laughs.*]

I did. And got up and helped her pack her things and walked her to the bus line.

I said, "I sure hope the bus don't break down."

I walked her to the bus line and sure enough she got on that bus. I didn't see her no more. In about six months, I was at this Rhumboogie, that nightclub out there. And she walked in there. And I hadn't seen her in about six months. She happened to walk in there.

She say, "Hello, Jessie."

I say, "Hi."

She say, "I'm going home with you tonight."

I said, "Is you?" I was scared to tell her no. Sure enough that's the truth.

She said, "I'll be down there."

I went home and got in the bed. About two-thirty that night somebody knocked on my door. I didn't believe it was her; but I'm gonna tell y'all the truth, I wouldn't tell you a story. She come in there and stayed all night with me and she ain't never bothered me no more. She never said nothing else to me.

BIG SARAH
CLARENCE BUTLER

There was this kind in every town. We had the same thing in our town, Florence, Alabama. I live in Alabama, he [Uncle Jessie White] lived in Mississippi, right up the road from each other. We had one gal called Big Sarah. Big Sarah was some kind of woman, boy, I'm telling you. She had six babies and a husband. And she could hit harder than any Joe Louis I seen. And she was married; her husband couldn't do nothing with her. He tried to chastise her and she had to knock him out. I mean out.

So when she get ready for a beau, she go in one of them jook joints and she look in there, see you. Well, she'd tell him, "You going home with me tonight."

He say, "I ain't going nowhere."

She say, "You watch. You wait a minute when the show is over, you're going home with me."

So the dude's about half drunk an still be messing with all them women in there. The time she get ready go, she go over there and tell him, "Let's go."

Now you know how you is when you half drunk now, "I ain't going nowhere."

She say, "Well, you going. Either you have to go or whup me. Now which one is it? Which one is easier to do?" She said, "The best thing is come and go. Because you whup me, I'll go on about my business, But it's gonna look bad for you to get a whupping and go." [*Laughs.*] "It's better to go without the whupping."

And he would say something stupid, like, you know, the "F" word you and all that, and she'd knock him down and the fight's on. He'd get up, or try to. This dude named Billy, he was what's called the "tush hog" down there, you understand. He was a knockout artist. Other words, them guys could be in the ring because they could one point you and you're out. Gone. He hit that lady with all he had. And I done seen Billy knock out a many guys, big and small. He hit that woman.

She shook her head and said, "That's all you got?" And knocked him down. She got through whupping him, he got up, they left, they stayed together for about two months, him and her, Big Sarah and Billy. But he wasn't going, but after he got the whupping, he went. She told him so. She said, "It was bad for you to get the whupping and still go. Better to go without the whupping. You gonna look bad before your friends." We was all down there. Everybody knew him was in there. He went with her.

But the woman was good looking. She was a little on the heavy side but she wasn't gawky big, you know what I'm saying. She had a neat waistline, big, you know, and a big butt. And she had a nice-looking face, but I don't know where that woman got her strength from.

And a guy come in. . . . We was over in Scipio one night, guy come in, he wanted her, she didn't want him. And then, vice-versa, the guy cracked her with a chair. I thought he hurt her. He knocked her down and she just shook it off and turned around and knocked him out the door. Plumb out the door, from that man's glass door. And he cracked a chair, tore it all to pieces and it didn't break the skin on her.

I told myself, "If you ever walk over to me and say let's go, I'm going."

Club Champagne. Clarksdale, Mississippi. Photograph by Barry Lee Pearson.

CONTRIBUTORS

Because of the large number of artists involved, these portraits are quite brief, with names, instruments played, birth date, place of birth, major accomplishments, and supplementary references when available. Nor is quality and quantity of information uniform, partly because the contributors are not uniformly documented in other research sources and partly because I asked different questions over the past three decades. Furthermore, almost half of the contributors are now deceased. I will supply death dates when available, but I will not speculate where the date is not confirmed. Premature obituaries hurt business. Furthermore, many artists have changed their names over the course of their career for professional or personal reasons. I will list them here by their given name but also supply professional names. Finally, I will also note the interview date or place.

ADAMS, JOHN TYLER "J. T." (17 February 1911–) Guitar. Born in Morganfield, Kentucky. His father played banjo in a string band. He also worked in a family string band performing for black and white dances. Moving to Indianapolis, Indiana, in 1941, he worked outside of music, playing informally with Yank Rachell, Guitar Pete Franklin, and Shirley Griffith, with whom he recorded in the 1960s. Interviewed Indianapolis, 16 April 1976.

ARMSTRONG, WILLIAM HOWARD "LOUIE BLUIE." (4 March 1909–27 July 2003) Violin, Mandolin, Guitar. Born in Dayton, Tennessee. His parents were musicians, and he worked in a family string band playing for both black and white audiences. He worked radio and medicine shows with various string bands, worked and recorded in Chicago, and later moved to Michigan. In the 1960s, he reunited with former partners Carl Martin and Ted Bogan, forming successful string band Martin, Bogan, and Armstrong. Following the death of Martin and Bogan, he continued to perform. In 1990 he was named a National Heritage Fellow. See film, *Louie Bluie,* produced and directed by Terry Zwigoff (1985); and John Brisbin: "Howard Armstrong: The Interview," *Living Blues* 169 (September–October 2003): 42–47; Part II, vol. 170 (November–December 2003): 44–49; Part III, vol. 171 (January–February 2004): 32–39. Interviewed in Washington, D.C., 28 June 1988 and 24 August 1990.

BAKER, ETTA. (31 March 1913–) Guitar, Banjo. Born in Caldwell, North Carolina. Both parents were musicians; her father played banjo and guitar, and danced. She learned guitar from her father and played for dances at house parties and cornshuckings. She also plays piano, banjo, and fiddle. Around 1973 she became active on the folk and blues festival circuit and was named a National Heritage Fellow in 1991. See Ted Olson, "Etta Baker: What My Daddy Gave Me," *Living Blues* 107 (February 1993): 28–30. Interviewed in Largo, Maryland, 19 September 1993.

BARNES, BRADY "DOC." (1 May 1908–c. 1986) Guitar. Born in Arnoldsville, Georgia. First learned to play quills and organ; learned guitar in his twenties. Played suppers and dances until he joined the church. Played guitar with gospel quartet, Gospel Pilgrims, then sang religious songs with wife in church and at several folk festivals. See also Art Rosenbaum, *Folk Visions and Folk Voices: Traditional Music and Song in North Georgia* (Athens, University of Georgia Press, 1983), 23–54. Interviewed in Vienna, Virginia, 17 July 1982.

BARNES, ROOSEVELT "BOOBA." (25 September 1936–3 April 1996) Guitar, Harmonica. Born in Longwood, Mississippi. He learned harmonica as a youngster, then guitar. Primarily a Delta jook musician, he worked in various bands in both Chicago and Greenville, Mississippi, where he ran his own Playboy Club from 1985. In 1990 he recorded *The Heartbroken Man* for Jim O'Neal's Rooster label, and was featured in Robert Mugge's film *Deep Blues*. See "The Heartbroken Man: Roosevelt 'Booba' Barnes," *Living Blues* 100 (November–December 1991): 10–15. Interviewed in Largo, Maryland, 19 September 1993.

BASS, FONTELLA. (3 July 1940–) Piano. Born in St. Louis, Missouri. Her family, particularly her mother and grandmother, were professional gospel artists. A child prodigy, she learned piano as a youngster and in her teens began to slip out to local blues clubs. Switching to rhythm and blues in the late 1950s, she worked with Oliver Sain and Little Milton. In the 1960s she was in Chicago recording for Chess Records, scoring such hits as "Rescue Me" and "Recovery." She later returned to gospel. Interviewed Johnstown, Pennsylvania, 5 September 1992.

BILLINGTON, JOHNNIE. (1935–) Guitar. Born in Crowder, Mississippi. He taught himself to play guitar as a youngster. Left the Delta to work and play in Chicago, then returned to the Delta around 1977 and became involved in teaching blues to Delta children. His band, J. B and the Midnighters, is composed of his blues students. Interviewed in Clarksdale, Mississippi, 1 August 1997.

BOGAN, THEODORE. (10 May 1910–29 January 1990) Guitar. Born in Spartanburg, South Carolina. He learned guitar as a youngster from local songster Pink Anderson. He played on radio and in medicine shows. He first teamed with string-band musician Howard Armstrong and Carl Martin in a group called the Four Keys. Recorded in Chicago in the 1930s and played local taverns. The group was reunited as the Martin, Bogan, and Armstrong string band in the 1960s. See film *Louie Bluie* (1985). Interviewed Washington, D.C., 3 July 1986.

BOYCE, R. L. (c. 1955–) Drums and Guitar. Born near Senetobia, Mississippi. Inspired by his uncle, fife and drum master Otha Turner, he learned drums in the early 1970s and has been playing with his uncle ever since in the Rising Star Fife and Drum Band. He also currently plays guitar in the Mississippi hill-country style and is looking to record. Interviewed in Clarksdale, Mississippi, 2 August 1997.

BROWN, CHARLES. (13 September 1922–21 January 1999) Piano. Born in Texas City, Texas. Encouraged by his grandmother, he learned piano and played for her church group. During high school and college, where he eventually received a degree in chemistry, he began to work with jazz and rhythm-and-blues groups. Settling in Los Angeles in 1944, he joined Johnny Moore's Three Blazers, recording for several labels. His song "Drifting Blues" was the top R&B record of 1946. He had a number of hits in the late 1940s and early 1950s and eventually worked as the headliner. Continuing to work through the 1980s, he again became popular and in 1997 was named a National Heritage Fellow. See John Anthony Brisbin, "Charles Brown: Living Blues Interview," *Living Blues* 118 (December 1994): 10–29. Interviewed Washington, D.C., 4 July 1993.

BROWN, NAPOLEON "NAPPY." (12 October 1929–) Born in Charlotte, North Carolina. He showed an early interest in gospel working with the Golden Bells, Selah Jubilee Singers, and Heavenly Lights. In 1955 he switched to rhythm and blues, signing with Savoy Records. After several hits in the late 1950s, he returned to North Carolina and gospel. In the 1980s he returned to blues recording for various labels. Interviewed Chicago, 9 June 1990.

BRYANT, PRECIOUS. (4 January 1942–) Guitar. Born in Talbot County, Georgia. Her father played guitar and banjo. She learned to play blues and religious songs. She and her sisters formed a gospel group, the Bussey Sisters, and in 1993 she was teamed up with harmonica player Neal Pattman. Currently lives in Waverly Hall, Georgia. Interviewed in Chattanooga, Tennessee, 9 October 1993.

BURNETT, CHESTER "HOWLIN' WOLF." (10 June 1910–10 January 1976) Guitar, Harmonica. Born in West Point, Mississippi. Influenced by Delta legends Charley Patton and Willie Brown, he learned guitar and harmonica. Working as a farmer, he played local jooks and suppers with other Delta notables. Moving to West Memphis, Arkansas, in 1948, he formed a band and played over local radio. In the early 1950s he recorded for Memphis-based Sam Phillips, who alternately leased his material to Chess and RPM.

Moving to Chicago in 1953, he recorded for Chess the rest of his life. A major figure in the golden age of Chicago Blues, he was a highly influential vocalist and band leader. See James Segrest and Mark Hoffman, *Moanin' at Midnight: The Life and Times of Howlin' Wolf* (New York: Pantheon 2004), 120–36. Interviewed in Ann Arbor, Michigan, August 1969.

BURNS, EDDIE. (8 February 1928–) Guitar, Harmonica. Born in Belzoni, Mississippi. Father played guitar, harmonica, and piano. He first learned harmonica at age ten. Moved north in 1946, settling in Detroit in 1948, where he learned guitar, and where he recorded with John Lee Hooker. Recorded on his own for several labels from 1948 through mid-1960s, including "Orange Driver" for Harvey label. In the mid-1970s he resumed touring and recording. See Jas Obrecht, "Eddie Guitar Burns: Inside Detroit Blues" *Living Blues* 32 (March–April 2001), 28–39. Interviewed Washington, D.C., 16 June 1987 and 28 June 1987.

BURRISS, JOHN "J. C." (1928–15 May 1988) Harmonica. Born in Kings Mountain, North Carolina. He grew up in North Carolina, moving to New York City in 1949, where he learned harmonica from his uncle Sonny Terry. He moved to California in 1959 and recorded for Arhoolie in 1975. A favorite on the festival circuit, he was a fine traditional entertainer who played bones and harmonica, and demonstrated his family of dancing dolls that he referred to as Mr. Jack and family. Interviewed in Vienna, Virginia, 8 August 1981.

BUTLER, CLARENCE. (21 January 1942–22 December 2003) Guitar. Born in Florence, Alabama. Along with his twin brother, Curtis, he learned from his father. Through his teens he played jooks and clubs throughout the South, moving to Detroit in the early 1960s. Performs with his brother as the Butler Twins. Interviewed 14 September 1999.

BUTLER, GEORGE "WILD CHILD." (1 October 1936–March 2005) Harmonica. Born in Autaugaville, Alabama, where he learned harmonica as a youngster. He played local jooks and suppers and eventually moved to Chicago in the mid-1960s. Since then he has toured and recorded for various labels, moving to Canada in 1985. Interviewed Chicago, July 1974.

CAMPBELL, MILTON "LITTLE MILTON." (7 September 1934–) Guitar. Born in Inverness, Mississippi. He learned guitar as a youngster, and first performed with Delta artist Eddie Cusic. After working Delta jooks he recorded for Sam Phillips in the early 1950s. Moving to St. Louis, he recorded for Bobbin and became a successful bandleader. In 1961 he began an eight-year stint with Chess Records, scoring several hits including "We're Gonna Make It," number one in 1965. He has recorded for Stax, Glades, and Malaco and remains one of the most successful blues artists of all time. See Jim O'Neal and Patty Johnson, "Little Milton: Living Blues Interview," *Living Blues* 114 (April 1994): 18–39. Interviewed Dayton, Ohio, 22 June 1996.

CAMPBELL, WILL "FRENCHY." (c. 1930s) Born in Marianna, Arkansas. He learned to sing from listening to records. He moved to Waterloo, Iowa, where he sometimes works with Louis McTizic's Blues Machine. Interviewed in Clarksdale, Mississippi, 5 August 1995.

CARTER, LAVESTER "BIG LUCKY." (10 February 1920–24 December 2001) Guitar. Born in Weir, Mississippi. He made a guitar as a youngster. Sang with a gospel quartet around 1946. Worked with a blues band in jooks and clubs around Memphis and Arkansas. Lives in Memphis today. See Scott Barretta, "Big Lucky Carter," *Living Blues* 34 (September–October 2003): 116–17. Interviewed Jonesboro, Arkansas, 20 April 1996.

CEPHAS, JOHN "BOWLING GREEN." (4 September 1930–) Guitar. Born in Washington, D.C. He grew up in a musical family and began singing in church as a youngster. His grandfather, father, and aunt all played guitar, and he was especially influenced by his cousin David Tallia Ferro. After years playing house parties in Virginia, he quit music, returning to it in the 1970s after meeting pianist Chief Ellis. In the mid-1970s he formed a duet with harmonica player Phil Wiggins. Since then he has toured the world, recorded prolifically and was named a National Heritage Fellow in 1989. He currently records for Alligator records. See Barry Lee Pearson, *Virginia-Piedmont Blues* (Philadelphia: University of Pennsylvania Press, 1990).

CHATMON, VIVIAN "SAM." (10 January 1897–2 February 1983) Guitar. Born in Bolton, Mississippi. He grew up in a musical family in which nine brothers played music, as did his father, a noted fiddler. Along with brothers Bo Carter and Lonnie Chatmon, and neighbor Walter Vincson, he was part of the Mississippi Sheiks, a prolific string band who recorded in the 1920s and 1930s. Rediscovered during the blues revival of the 1960s, he played the festival circuit and recorded up to his death. Interviewed Washington, D.C., September 1976.

COBBS, WILLIE. (15 July 1932–) Guitar, Harmonica. Born in Smale, Arkansas. He began to sing in church and worked with a gospel quartet. Moving to Chicago in 1951, he worked the local club scene. In 1961 he recorded a blues hit, "You Don't Love Me." He worked in Chicago and Memphis, settling in Dewitt, Arkansas, in 1969. He continues to tour and has recently recorded for the Rooster label. See Brett Bonner, "Willie Cobbs: I Want to do Some Music We Can Shake Our Ass To," *Living Blues* 154 (November–December 2000): 14–23. Interviewed in Chicago, 9 June 1990.

CONTRIBUTORS

Cusic, Eddie. (4 January 1926–) Guitar. Born in Leland/Wilmot, Mississippi. Inspired by local jook-joint musicians, he made a homemade guitar. Later he learned guitar and played local Delta jooks. In the 1950s he worked with the Rhythm Aces. In the 1990s he began to play festivals. Interviewed in Washington, D.C., 30 June 1991.

Daniels, Jerry. (1912–1995) Guitar. From Indianapolis, Indiana. One of the original Ink Spots, Daniels began playing in a group he described as a "coffee pot band;" a washboard band that played the streets of Indianapolis. The group formed in 1931 and performed on radio out of Cincinnati and was originally called King, Jack and Jesters. According to Daniels, manager Moe Gill in New York changed the name. Daniels sang tenor and played guitar and in 1936 Bill Kenny replaced him. At the time of the interview, he was a bank executive and a guest of my student John Vardeman. Interviewed Indianapolis, 18 April 1974.

Davis, CeDell. (1926–) Guitar, Harmonica. Born and raised in Helena, Arkansas. He played one-string guitar, then learned guitar and harmonica, and claims to have played on the radio by age fourteen. Lived briefly in Clarksdale, Mississippi, in 1932 and 1936. In the 1940s he briefly lived in St. Louis. Worked with Robert Nighthawk on station KFFA and with Sonny Boy Williamson Number Two. Currently lives in Arkansas. See Louis Guida and William Black, "CeDell Davis," *Living Blues* 32 (May–June 1977): 19–24; Barry Lee Pearson, "Pine Bluff Blues: CeDell Davis," *Living Blues* 166 (November–December 2002): 28–37. Interviewed in Clarksdale, Mississippi, 7 August 1993.

Davis, Mamie "Mamie Galore." (24 September 1940–6 October 2001) Vocalist. Born in Erwin, Mississippi. She later moved to Greenville, where she sang religious songs as a youngster and started in rhythm and blues in high school. Later worked as an Ikette with Ike and Tina Turner and sang with Little Milton. Recorded for several labels in the 1960s and lived in Chicago and Louisiana. She returned to Greenville, Mississippi, in 1972. Interviewed Washington, D.C., 5 July 1991.

Davis, Samuel "Little Sammy." (1929–) Harmonica. Born in Winona, Mississippi. He began to play harmonica at age twelve. He ran away from home at age fourteen and played on the streets in Florida from 1946. Played with Albert King, Boyd Gilmore, and Earl Hooker. Played in Chicago and Florida. First recorded in Miami in 1953. Currently signed with Delmark and works out of Poughkeepsie, New York. Interviewed Washington, D.C., 7 September 1996.

Dawson, Jacob. (7 May 1930–) Guitar. Born in Starkville, Mississippi. His mother and father were musicians who played and sang church music.

He worked with a vocal group, the Moonlighters. Moved to St. Louis and Chicago in the 1960s. Worked with Little Milton. In the 1970s played guitar with Albert King and James Brown. In the 1990s he worked with Magic Slim. Currently living in Chicago. Interviewed Washington, D.C., 7 September 1996.

DORSEY, HENRY. (c. 1928–) Guitar. Born in Rayville, Louisiana. He grew up on a farm on the Louisiana side of the Mississippi River, where his family worked cotton. He made a one-string guitar; then his father, a harmonica player and buck dancer, bought him a guitar when he was nine. He played informally with harmonica player Wayne Tookie Collum until he started on the blues festival circuit in 1985. Interviewed in Washington, D.C., 2 July 1997.

DUSKIN, JOSEPH L. "BIG JOE." (10 February 1921–) Piano. Born in Birmingham, Alabama. He learned piano as a child and listened to local Birmingham pianists. As a youngster he moved to Cincinnati, where he played in local clubs. He quit music, worked as a policeman and now tours as a boogie-woogie pianist. Recorded for Arhoolie and other European labels. See Steven C. Tracy, *Going to Cincinnati: A History of the Blues in the Queen City* (Urbana: University of Illinois Press, 1993). Interviewed Johnstown, Pennsylvania, 4 September 1992, and Largo, Maryland, 2 October 1993.

EARLY, HEZIKIAH. Drums, Harmonica. Born outside Natchez, Mississippi. Influenced by Papa George Lightfoot, he learned drums and harmonica as a youngster. He put together a band to play for local house parties, Hezikiah and the Houserockers. He plays for local clubs in Mississippi and Louisiana. Recorded for High Water label and played on the festival circuit. Interviewed in Washington, D.C., 29 June 1985.

EDWARDS, ARCHIE. (4 September 1918–18 June 1998) Guitar. Born in Union Hall, Virginia. His father played banjo, guitar, and harmonica, and several brothers also played guitar. Edwards first learned banjo but switched to guitar. Played for country house parties in Virginia. Moved to Seat Pleasant, Maryland, in the 1950s, where he worked as a truck driver, policeman, barber, and cab driver. He began to play in public after meeting Mississippi John Hurt and Skip James in the 1960s. Recorded for L and R and Maple-shade. Founded the D.C. Blues Society. Interviewed off and on from 1976. See Barry Lee Pearson, *Virginia-Piedmont Blues* (Philadelphia: University of Pennsylvania Press, 1990).

EDWARDS, DAVID "HONEYBOY." (28 June 1915–) Guitar. Born in Shaw, Mississippi. Edwards learned guitar as a youngster and was a protégé of Big Joe Williams. He was an itinerant musician down south, then moved to Chicago in the mid-1940s. He worked with Big Walter Horton,

Little Walter Jacobs, and others in Memphis and Chicago and continues to record and tour. Currently records for Earwig. See Edwards as told to Janis Martinson and Michael Frank, *The World Don't Owe Me Nothing* (Chicago, Chicago Review Press, 1997); Barry Lee Pearson, *Sounds So Good to Me: The Bluesman's Story* (Philadelphia: University of Tennessee Press). Interviewed in Vienna, Virginia, 25 July 1979; Baltimore, 13 January 1991; Washington, D.C., June 1992; and Chicago, 2 June 1995.

ELLIS, WILBERT "BIG CHIEF." (10 November 1914 – 20 December 1977) Piano. Born in Birmingham, Alabama. He learned piano as a youngster from local piano players. During the Depression, he hoboed to Knoxville, Tennessee, playing cafes and jooks. In 1936, he moved to New York and in the 1950s recorded for the Continental label. In 1972 he moved to Washington, D.C., where he ran a liquor store. In the mid-1970s, he met guitarist John Cephas and teamed up with him and harmonica player Phil Wiggins and bassist James Bellamy to form the Barrel House Rockers. He moved back to Birmingham shortly before his death. See "Wilbert 'Big Chief' Ellis," *Living Blues* 63 (January–February, 1985): 28–35.

FERGUSON, BOBBY "H-BOMB." (1930 or 1931–) Piano. Born in Charleston, South Carolina. He learned piano as a youngster; as a teenager, he formed a band in North Carolina and went on tour. He played around New York City, recording from the early 1950s for Derby, Atlas, Savoy, Specialty, and others and played with Big Ed Thompson's band. He moved to Cincinnati, where he currently lives, and continues to record and perform. Noted for his costumes and wigs, Ferguson is an outstanding vocalist and showman. See Steven C. Tracy, *Going to Cincinnati: A History of the Blues in the Queen City* (Urbana: University of Illinois Press, 1993); Barry Lee Pearson, "One Day You're Gonna Hear About Me: The H-Bomb Ferguson Story," *Living Blues* 69 (1986): 15–25. Interviewed Peninsula, Ohio, 21 September 1985.

FLUKER, CORA. (c. 1930s–) Guitar. Born in Livingston, Alabama. Inspired by Uncle Rich Amerson, she sang work songs in the field. She made a guitar as a youngster and was active in church work. She moved to Mississippi and plays both blues and gospel and is a prolific songwriter. Interviewed in Clarksdale, Mississippi, 7 August 1993.

FORD, JAMES "T-MODEL." "TAIL DRAGGER." (1924–) Guitar. From Greenville/ Forest, Mississippi. He began to play guitar when he was fifty-eight years old. Today he plays with a drummer, working house parties and small clubs. Interviewed in Clarksdale, Mississippi, 7 August 1993.

HALL, SANDRA. (5 September c 1947–) Vocalist. Born in Atlanta. Growing up in a musical family, she began singing professionally with her sister at age twelve as the Soul Sisters. During the 1960s, she worked with a trio called the Exotics. After working as a go-go dancer and a nurse, she turned to the blues full time in the late 1980s and has been working festivals and the Atlanta clubs since then. See Steve Cheeseborough, "Atlanta's Empress of the Blues," *Living Blues* 143 (January–February 1999): 28–33. Interviewed in Largo, Maryland, 19 September 1999.

HARRIS, BILL. (1925–1988) Guitar. Born in Nashville, North Carolina. He first played organ in his family's church. After moving to Washington, D.C., he studied jazz and classical guitar. He worked with R&B legends the Clovers through the 1950s. In 1975 he hosted a local radio show called "Hootie Blues," and opened a blues club called Pigfoot. In the late 1980s he lost the club to the IRS. Interviewed in Washington, D.C., 1978.

HEMPHILL, JESSIE MAE "SHE WOLF." (6 October 1934–) Guitar, Drums. Born in Sonatobia, Mississippi, she was inspired by her grandfather, Sid Hemphill, a respected songster and fiddler. She taught herself to play guitar when still a child; her mother and her aunt Rosa Lee Hill also taught her. Although she has played in groups, she now works solo and has recorded for Vogue and High Water. See George Mitchell, *Blow My Blues Away* (Baton Rouge: Louisiana University Press, 1971) 77–99, and "Ain't Got Tears to Cry With: Jessie Mae Hemphill," *Living Blues* 100 (November–December 1991): 16–21.

HILL, WILLIAM "BIG BILL." (1914–17 April 1983) Born in Arkansas, he later moved to Chicago, where he was active as a blues promoter and radio personality on WOPA. He often broadcast live blues from his club, the Copacabana, and was one of the city's best-known blues emcees. He emceed the first Ann Arbor Blues Festivals as well. See Big Bill Hill, "Chicago Blues Radio," *Living Blues* 7 (Winter 1971–72): 13–14. Interviewed in Ann Arbor, Michigan, August 1969.

HINTON, ALGIA MAE. (29 August 1929–) Guitar. Born in Selma, O'Neal Township, of Johnston County, North Carolina. Her mother, Ollie O'Neal, played five instruments, including guitar, and her sister played guitar and banjo. Algia Mae played for house parties and country dances and is herself a fine buck dancer. See Mary Anne McDonald, "Algia Mae Hinton: Keep Us Dancing and Kept Us Singing," *Living Blues* 107 (April 1993): 25–26. Interviewed in Largo, Maryland, 18 September 1994.

HOGAN, SILAS. (15 September 1911–9 January 1994) Guitar. Born in Westover, Louisiana. His father was a musician, and his two uncles played guitar and taught him to play when he was sixteen. He worked with his uncles as a youngster playing house parties. In 1940 he moved to Scotlandville, Louisiana, and met Slim Harpo, Lightning Slim, and Guitar Kelly, with whom he would work for years. He formed the Rhythm Ramblers in

1956, playing around Baton Rouge, and recorded for the Excello label in the 1960s. Interviewed in Washington, D.C., 27 June 1985.

HOLEMAN, JOHN DEE. (1929–) Guitar. Born in Orange County, North Carolina. Inspired by an uncle, Holman learned to play guitar at age fourteen. Drawing repertory from radio and records, he began to play house parties and cornshuckings. A mid–1970s encounter with folklorist Glenn Hinson led to festival work. During the 1980s he worked with piano player Friz Holloway. A fine dancer as well as a guitarist and singer, he was named a National Heritage Fellow in 1990. See Barry Lee Pearson, "John Dee Holeman: Bull City Blues," *Living Blues* 107 (February 1993): 31–32. Interviewed in Washington, D.C., August 1983.

HOOKER, JOHN LEE. (22 August 1917–21 June 2001) Guitar. Born in Clarksdale, Mississippi. He learned guitar from stepfather William Moore and sang in church. He moved to Memphis at age fifteen and played on streets, then moved to Cincinnati and worked with the Fairfield Four and the Big Six gospel quartets. In 1948 he moved to Detroit, where he played local clubs and parties. He began his prolific recording career in 1948 with the hit "Boogie Chillen'." Recording under various names and for many labels, he had several hits for VeeJay. He moved to California in 1970 and continued to record until his death in 2001. One of the blues' major stars, he was named a National Heritage Fellow in 1983 and was inducted into the Rock and Roll Hall of Fame in 1990. See Jim and Amy O'Neal, "Living Blues Interview: John Lee Hooker," *Living Blues* 44 (Autumn 1979): 14–221 *Blues Guitar: The Men Who Made the Music,* edited by Jas Obrecht (San Francisco: GPI Books/Miller Freeman, 1990); and Jas Obrecht, "John Lee Hooker Boogie All the Time," *Living Blues* 133 (May–June 1997): 12–21. Interviewed in Washington, D.C., 26 June 1983.

HUBBARD, WILLIAM "BOOGIE MAN." (c. 1931–) Piano. Born in Memphis. Hubbard learned piano from Willie Winston while still in school. He played in church as a youngster but switched to blues at age eighteen. He worked with various bands, including Roscoe Gordon and the Fieldstone, and was working with Lavester "Big Lucky" Carter in 1996. Interviewed in Jonesboro, Arkansas, 20 April 1996.

HURT, JOHN "JUNIOR," "MAN." (22 January 1932–) Guitar. Born near Avalon, Mississippi, in Carroll County. He was inspired by his Mississippi guitarist father, John Hurt, and learned guitar as a youngster. Never very active as a musician, he played parties and festivals in the 1980s and 1990s. See Lawrence Hoffman, "John William Hurt: And Daddy Would Play All Night Long," *Living Blues* 109 (May June 1993): 38–42.

HYPOLITE, HARRY. (c. 1938–) Guitar. Born in St. Martinsville, Louisiana, he learned guitar at age thirteen and played blues and later zydeco at local house parties and clubs. He worked outside of music until he teamed up with Clifton Chenier, and after Chenier's death he worked with Clifton's son C. J. Chenier as lead guitarist. Interviewed in Dayton, Ohio, 22 June 1996.

JACKSON, ERNESTINE "MISS TINA." (c 1955–) Vocalist. Born in Poplarsville, Mississippi. Her mother was active in church music and Ernestine first learned to sing in church and at home. She moved to the Washington, D.C. area in the early 1970s. Interviewed in Washington, D.C., 6 September 1968.

JACKSON, FRUTELAND. (1953–) Guitar. Born in Doddsville, Mississippi, and raised in Mississippi and Chicago, he returned to Mississippi in the mid–1980s. After studying acting, he became a dedicated blues musician and now teaches and performs a history in blues in schools. See David Nelson, "Fruteland Jackson: We Don't Have to Sing About Cows, Corn and Plantations," *Living Blues* 117, September–October 1994, 54–59. Interviewed in Jonesboro, Arkansas, 18 April 1998.

JACKSON, JOHN. (25 February 1924–20 January 2002) Guitar, Banjo. Born in the F T Valley near Woodville, Virginia. Jackson was inspired as a youngster to learn guitar by a convict named Happy. He picked up songs from recordings and from his father, who was also a musician. He played primarily at house parties or mountain hoedowns. In 1950 he moved to Fairfax, Virginia, near Washington, where he was "discovered" by folklorist Chuck Perdue. He then became active on the coffeehouse circuit and played festivals around the world. He recorded for Rounder and Arhoolie and was named a National Heritage Fellow in 1986. See Cheryl Brauner and Barry Lee Pearson, "John Jackson's East Virginia Blues," *Living Blues* 63 (January–February 1985): 10–13; Barry Lee Pearson, "John Jackson: I Used to Walk Thirty Miles with a Guitar on My Back," *Living Blues* 163 (May–June 2002): 28–37. Interviewed in Vienna, Virginia, 14 July 1999.

JEFFERSON, MARY. (10 August 1926–August 2002) Vocalist. A lifelong resident of Washington, D.C., she grew up next door to the Howard Theater in the heart of D.C.'s African American entertainment district. Her mother ran a "bootlegger's house" that attracted show business clientele. At age fifteen she began singing at the Republic Gardens. From the 1950s to the 1990s, she remained a vital part of D.C.'s blues and jazz scene, often working with Nap Turner. She appeared in several feature films and was on several episodes of "Homicide." Interviewed in Largo, Maryland, 22 September 2001.

CONTRIBUTORS

JOHNSON, JACK "BIG JACK." (30 July 1940–) Guitar. Born in Lambert, Mississippi. His father played violin, and he learned guitar as a youngster and accompanied his father at country dances. He teamed up with Frank Frost and Sam Carr in St. Louis in the early 1960s, the group later taking the name the Jelly Roll Kings. Working as a truck driver, he played southern jooks and clubs. In 1987 he recorded for Earwig and continues to record and play, fronting his own band, currently based out of Pennsylvania. See Brett Bonner, "Big Jack Johnson: The Oil Man," *Living Blues* 100 (November–December 1991): 22–26. Interviewed in Chicago, 3 June 1999.

JOHNSON, JAMES "SUPER CHIKAN." (16 February 1951) Guitar. Born in Darling, Mississippi. Johnson grew up on a farm and was inspired to be a musician by his uncle, Big Jack Johnson, and by his grandfather who played violin. He taught himself to play guitar, worked as a cab driver in Clarksdale, and began to play at local jooks. Recorded for the Rooster label in 1996. See John Ruskey, "Good Day From Super Chikan," *Living Blues* 132 (March–April 1997): 38–39. Interviewed in Jonesboro, Arkansas, 11 April 1997.

KIMBROUGH, DAVID "JUNIOR." (28 June 1930–17 January 1998) Guitar. Born in Hudsonville, Mississippi, he learned guitar as a youngster, as did his brothers and sister. Later he came under the influence of Fred McDowell. He first played house parties and picnics and then country jooks. He began to hold his own fish fries and then bought his own jook joint, where he and R. L. Burnside played. In the early 1990s he recorded for Fat Possum and is featured in the film *Deep Blues*. See David Nelson, "The Beginning and the End of Music: Junior Kimbrough," *Living Blues* 100 (November–December 1991): 27–29. Interviewed in Clarksdale, Mississippi, 6 August 1993.

LEE, MELVIN. (c. 1930s–) Bass. Born in Memphis. Lee played guitar in church as a youngster, then switched to bass in the 1950s and worked with Rufus Thomas and Piano Red. He traveled with the Memphis Blues Caravan in the early 1970s. Currently working with Big Lucky Carter in and around Memphis. Interviewed in Washington, D.C., 6 July 1997.

LOCKWOOD JUNIOR, ROBERT. (27 March 1915–) Guitar. Born in Marvel, Arkansas. He first began learning organ but switched to guitar. Inspired by Robert Johnson, who helped make him a "homemade" instrument, he was an adept student and began to play the streets at age fifteen. He later teamed up with Sonny Boy Williamson Number Two (Aleck Miller) to play local jooks. Testing his skill in Memphis, St. Louis, and Chicago, he recorded for Bluebird in 1941, then reunited with Williamson as a member of the King Biscuit radio group. In the 1950s he moved to Chicago, eventually working with various groups, and as a studio guitarist in 1961. He continued to record as a featured artist for various labels. In 1995 he was named a National Heritage Fellow. See Larry Hoffman, "Robert Lockwood, Jr.: Living Blues Interview," *Living Blues* 121 (June 1995): 12–29. Interviewed in Washington, D.C., 1 July 1991.

LOWERY, ROBERT. (1932–) Guitar. Born in Shuler, Arkansas. His father and several uncles played guitar and, by age seventeen, he was proficient enough to play on the streets. He played in local roadhouses until he moved to California in 1956. He continued to play informally, eventually working the festival circuit. See Gregory Isola, "Robert Lowery and Virgil Thrasher: Going Up the Country," *Blues Revue* 19 (September–October 1995): 52–53. Interviewed in Washington, D.C., 21 August 1976.

LUANDREW, ALBERT "SUNNYLAND SLIM." (5 September 1907– 17 March 1995) Piano. Born in Vance, Mississippi, he learned piano as a youngster. After running away from home several times, he got a job playing for a local theater. He began to play parties and local work-camp jooks around Lambert, Mississippi, then moved to Memphis in the mid–1920s to play Beale Street clubs. He moved to Chicago in the 1940s, where he worked with major artists like Muddy Water and recorded for dozens of labels as featured artist or sideman. A fixture on the Chicago club scene, he continued to record and tour through the mid-1990s. An influential stylist and elder statesman of Chicago blues piano, he was named a National Heritage Fellow in 1988. See David Whiteis, "A Tender Heart and a Hustler's Soul: Sunnyland Slim's Long Life in the Blues," *Living Blues* 90 (March–April 1990): 14–23. Interviewed in Washington, D.C., February 1978.

MAGEE, STERLING "MR. SATAN." (20 May 1936–) Guitar. Born in Mount Olive, Mississippi. He first learned piano, then guitar; made a one-string guitar. He left home to play at the Echo Lounge in Tampa, Florida. He worked with various bands, including Noble Watts, King Curtis, James Brown, Etta James. He settled in New York to play on the streets of Harlem, and in 1986 he paired up with harmonica player Adam Gussow. The duo recorded together and now play taverns and festivals as well as on the street. A true mystic, he is also a gifted visual artist. See Margey Peters, "Satan and Adam," *Living Blues* 129 (September–October 1996): 14–25. Interviewed in Largo, Maryland, 15 September 1996.

MCCAIN, JERRY. (19 June 1930–) Harmonica. Born in Gadsden, Alabama. His mother played guitar and sang religious songs; he began to play harmonica from age five. McCain later worked the streets and formed a group, the Upstarts, in the 1950s. He recorded for Trumpet, Excello, Okeh, Jewel, and others through the 1950s, 1960s, and 1970s and worked the festival circuit through the 1980s and 1990s. See David Nelson, "Jerry McCain: I Got to Sing the Blues," *Living Blues* 113 (January–February 1994): 8–19. Interviewed in Chicago, 9 June 1990, and Chattanooga, Tennessee, 20 October 1995.

CONTRIBUTORS

McGEE, "BIG BO." (9 October 1928–3 March 2002) Harmonica. Born in Emelle, Alabama, and Portersville, Mississippi. His grandmother played harmonica in local jooks and taught him to play when he was a child. He played local jook joints, then supported himself by driving an explosives truck for forty years. Later teamed up with guitarist Little Whit Wells, playing the Tuscaloosa, Alabama, area. Interviewed in Largo, Maryland, 14 September 1997.

MOLTON, FLORA. (1908–31 May 1991) Guitar. Born in Louisa County, Virginia. She first learned organ and accordion and later switched to guitar. Although she once played blues, she later switched exclusively to religious material. Moving to Washington, D.C., in 1937, she became a familiar figure as a street singer. Despite her religious repertory, she actively worked with D.C. blues artists, playing with Phil Wiggins and others. See Eleanor Ellis, "Flora Molton: From a Little Girl I've Been Singing, Singing, Singing," *Living Blues* 86 (May–June 1989): 22–32. Interviewed in Washington, D.C. 23 April 1983.

OWENS, JACK. (17 November 1904–9 February 1997) Guitar. Born in Bentonia, Mississippi, he grew up in the country with his grandfather whose name he took. Inspired by his father and uncle, he learned to play guitar and played for local house parties with Skip James. He ran his own jook joint. "Discovered" by folklorist David Evans in 1966, he recorded for Testament and Wolf. He was named a National Heritage Fellow in 1993. See Alan Lomax, *The Land Where the Blues Began* (New York: Pantheon, 1993); Ted Olson, "I Feel Like It Is Part of Me," Bentonia Blues Part II, *Living Blues* 104 (July–August 1992): 25–39. Interviewed in Clarksdale, Mississippi, 6 August 1993.

PERKINS, JOE WILLIE "PINETOP." (7 July 1913–) Piano. Born in Belzoni, Mississippi. Perkins first played guitar, then switched to piano; he played in jooks and cafes around Belzoni. In the 1940s, he worked with guitarist Robert Nighthawk, then left him to work with Sonny Boy Williamson's King Biscuit Time group that broadcast on KFFA in Helena. He relocated in Chicago and East St. Louis, Illinois, and worked with various artists. Recorded extensively for various labels. Today he tours with his own band. See "Pinetop's Boogie," *Living Blues* 97 (May–June 1991): 10–16. Interviewed in Vienna, Virginia, 12 March 1994.

PERRYMAN, WILLIAM LEE "DOCTOR FEELGOOD," "PIANO RED." (19 October 1911–25 July 1985) Guitar. Born in Hampton, Georgia, he learned piano as a teenager and began to work for house parties. His older brother was Rufus "Speckled Red" Perryman, also a noted piano player. As a youngster he played with Atlanta-based artists Willie McTell and Buddy Moss. He recorded extensively from the 1950s for Victor and Groove; in the

1960s recorded as Dr. Feelgood and the Interns for Okeh. He recorded, toured, and performed on radio through the 1970s and early 1980s. Interviewed in Vienna, Virginia, 17 July 1982.

PITCHFORD, LONNIE. (8 October 1955–8 November 1998) Guitar, Bass, Keyboards. Born in Lexington, Mississippi. He made a one-string guitar as a youngster, graduating to real guitar soon afterward. He worked Delta jooks and became involved in the festival circuit while still a young man. Equally at ease with gospel or blues, in an electric band format or as a solo acoustic act, he continues to record and play festivals. He is featured in both Alan Lomax's film, Robert Mugge's *Deep Blues* (1991). See also David Nelson and Lauri Lawson, "It's Best to Let the Cake Stay Cake: Lonnie Pitchford," *Living Blues* 94 (November–December 1990): 44–47. Interviewed in Clarksdale, Mississippi, 9 June 1990.

POWELL, EUGENE "SONNY BOY NELSON." (8 December 1908—November 1998) Guitar. Born in Utica, Mississippi. He learned to play guitar in three days when he was eight years old. He moved to Lombardy, near Parchman Prison, and then ran away to work as street musician. Powell worked local parties, and he went to Memphis at age fourteen. He recorded for Bluebird in 1936 with his wife Mississippi Matilda and eventually ran his own jook joint. He returned to music in the 1970s and has recorded. He worked the festival circuit through 1996. See Simon Bronner, "Living Blues Interview: Eugene Powell, Sonny Boy Nelson," *Living Blues* 43 (Summer 1979): 14–25. Interviewed in Clarksdale, Mississippi, 6 August 1993.

QUIMBY, DOUG. (1936–) Singer, Percussionist, Storyteller. Born in Baconton, Georgia, he grew up on a farm and has been singing since age five. As a youngster, he sang blues as he worked in the fields but later switched to religious music. In 1963 he worked with a gospel quartet, the Sensational Friendly Stars. In 1969 he joined Bessie Jones and the Georgia Sea Island Singers. He and his wife Frankie have been active on the festival and school circuit for the past twenty years as musicians and educators. Interviewed in Chattanooga, Tennessee, 8 October 1994.

QUIMBY, FRANKIE SULLIVAN. (1937–) Vocalist, Storyteller. Born in Brunswick, Georgia, she grew up on St. Simon Island and heard blues at house parties and jooks. In 1969 she joined Bessie Jones and the Georgia Sea Island Singers. Inspired by Jones, she began to perform older traditional ring games, songs, and spirituals. She and her husband Doug tour, perform, and educate. Interviewed in Chattanooga, Tennessee, 8 October 1994.

RACHELL, JAMES "YANK." (16 March 1910–9 April 1997) Guitar and Mandolin. Born in Brownsville, Tennessee. Rachell grew up on a farm and learned mandolin at age eight. Beginning in 1919, he worked country house parties with Hambone Willie Newburn and Sleepy John Estes. He first recorded for Victor with Estes in 1929, worked and recorded with John Lee "Sonny Boy" Williamson in the 1930s, and recorded for Bluebird. He worked in St. Louis with Peetie Wheatstraw, then moved to Indianapolis in 1958. Reunited with Estes in the 1960s, he worked the festival circuit, recording for Delmark and other labels. Throughout his life he worked outside music and never left his family. See "The Man Behind the Mandolin," *Living Blues* 79 (March–April 1988): 10–21; Richard Congress, *Blues Mandolin Man: The Life and Music of Yank Rachell* (Jackson: University of Mississippi Press, 2001). Interviewed in Indianapolis, Indiana, Winter 1974, and Largo, Maryland, 2 October 1993.

RASCOE, MOSES. (1917–6 March 1994) Guitar. Born in Windsor, North Carolina. His father played harmonica and his mother, piano, and he began to learn guitar at age thirteen, first playing the streets and then jook joints. He hoboed around the South, then moved to York, Pennsylvania, in 1940. During the 1980s he began to play on the festival circuit, recording for Flying Fish in 1987. See Jack Roberts, "Moses Rascoe," *Living Blues* 87 (August 1989): 23–25. Interviewed in Johnstown, Pennsylvania, 2 September 1990.

ROSS, ISAIAH "DOCTOR ROSS." (21 October 1925–28 May 1993) Harmonica. Born in Tunica, Mississippi. His father played harmonica, and Ross began to play at age six. As a youngster he played for house parties, then graduated to jook joints. In the late 1940s, he worked on several radio shows, including WDIA in Memphis with his band, the Jump and Jive Boys. In the early 1950s he recorded for the Sun label. Fed up with Sun, he left Memphis for Flint, Michigan, where he worked for General Motors for over thirty years. He recorded for several labels and began touring as a one-man band in the 1970s and 1980s. See Barry Lee Pearson, "Doctor Ross: One Man Boogie," *Living Blues* 99 (September–October 1991): 10–17. Interviewed in Washington, D.C., 24 June 1983, and Peninsula, Ohio, 25 September 1983.

SAVAGE, DAVID. (c. 1940s–23 June 1992) Born in Rosedale, Mississippi, younger brother of Joseph. He learned to sing working in the fields and sang in local Mississippi jooks around Greenville. A friend of Eddie Boyd, he went to Chicago in the 1960s. Savage spent several stretches in Parchman Prison. Interviewed in Washington, D.C., 29 June 1991.

SAVAGE, JOSEPH. (c. late 1930s–23 June 1992) Born in Rosedale, Mississippi, older brother of David. He also served time in Parchman Farm but escaped. Featured in Alan Lomax's film and book, *The Land Where the Blues Began* (New York: Pantheon, 1993). Both brothers were killed in a house fire. Interviewed in Washington, D.C., 29 June 1991.

SHINES, CANDY. Born in Tuscaloosa, Alabama. Her father died when she was three, and her mother ran a jook joint. She learned to sing and dance in the jook, listening to musicians such as Blind Bud Bailey. She married blues artist Johnny Shines and began to perform with him. She continues to perform, generally working with guitarist Kent duChaine. Interviewed in Washington, D.C., June 1991.

SHINES, JOHNNY "NED." (15 April 1915–20 April 1992) Guitar. Born in Frayser, Tennessee. His mother and brother played guitar, and he taught himself to play and then worked the streets, house parties, and fish fries. Teaming up with Robert Johnson, they traveled to Detroit together. After a stay in Memphis, he went to Chicago in 1941, where he played Maxwell Street and various clubs. In the 1950s he recorded for Chess and J.O.B. In the late 1950s he retired from music but returned to it in the 1960s, recording for several labels. In 1969 he moved to Holt, Alabama. Through the 1970s and 1980s he continued to tour the festival circuit and record for Rounder and other labels. A stroke in the 1980s curtailed his fine guitar technique, but he continued to sing and play through 1991, when he performed at the Smithsonian Folklife Festival. See Jas Obrecht, "Johnny Shines: Whupped Around and Screwed Around But Still Hanging On," *Living Blues* 90 (March–April 1990): 24–31. Interviewed in Washington, D.C., February 1978 and June 1991.

SMITH, BYTHER. (17 April 1932) Guitar. Born in Monticello, Mississippi. As a youngster he learned to play guitar and harmonica in Mississippi. He briefly played bass with a country-and-western group in Arizona. Moving to Chicago in 1956, he picked up pointers from his cousin J. B. Lenoir and neighbor Robert Junior Lockwood. In the 1960s he worked in Chicago clubs, becoming head of the house band at Theresa's. He recorded from the 1960s to the present and continues to tour with various bands. See Mark Lipscomb and Barbara Anderson, "Byther Smith: Come to Me Overnight Something Like a Dream," *Living Blues* (May–June 1991): 25–30. Interviewed Chicago, May 1974.

SMOTHERS, OTIS "BIG SMOKEY." (21 March 1924–23 July 1993) Guitar. Born in Lexington, Mississippi. Inspired by an aunt who bought him his first guitar and taught him to play, he began to play house parties and school events. He moved to Chicago in 1947 and played with Arthur "Big Boy" Spires. In the 1960s, guided by Willie Dixon, he began to record for the King Federal label in Cincinnati, Ohio. A stalwart on the Chicago club scene, he worked with many artists, generally as a sideman. See Steve Wisner, "Chicago Blues Yesterday and Today: Smokey Smothers, Big Otis and Little Abe," *Living Blues* 37 (March–April 1978): 18–21. Interviewed in Chicago, 8 June 1990.

CONTRIBUTORS

SYKES, ROOSEVELT. (31 January 1906–11 July 1983) Piano. Born in Elmar, Arkansas, he grew up with his grandfather and learned organ and piano as a youngster. He ran away from home at age fifteen and studied under various jook-joint piano players in Helena, Arkansas, and St. Louis, Missouri. In the mid–1920s he teamed up with Lee Green and then returned to St. Louis. In 1929 he began a prolific recording career that would span seven decades. Recording under various names, he settled in Chicago in 1941, putting together a big touring band, the Honey-drippers. He worked in a trio with Memphis Minnie in the late 1940s and continued to record. In the early 1950s he teamed up with Lonnie Johnson. During the 1960s he worked in New Orleans. A highly influen-tial stylist, he was also an excellent songwriter. See John Bentley, "The Honeydripper: Roosevelt Sykes," *Living Blues* 9 (Summer 1972): 21–23. Interviewed in Ann Arbor, Michigan, August 1969.

TAYLOR, CORA WALTON "KOKO." (28 September 1935–) She was born in Memphis but grew up in the town of Bartlett just outside Memphis. Taylor first sang gospel but began to listen to blues on the radio. In 1953 she and her husband-to-be moved to Chicago, where she broke into the club scene sitting in with various bands on the weekends. "Discovered" by promoter Willie Dixon, she recorded for Chess, scoring a hit, "Wang Dang Doodle," in 1966. In the 1970s she joined Alligator Records and during the 1980s and 1990s dominated the Chicago-style blues scene, appearing in several films and winning numerous awards. She continues to be a major star. See Mary Katherine Aldin, "Koko Taylor: Down in the Bottom of that Chitlin' Bucket," *Living Blues* 110 (July–August 1993): 10–21. Interviewed in Baltimore, Maryland, 29 April 1993.

TAYLOR, EDDIE. (29 January 1923–25 December 1985) Guitar. Born in Benoit, Mississippi. His mother bought him a guitar when he was thirteen and, by the late 1930s, he was playing on the streets in the company of Robert Johnson. In 1943 he moved to Memphis, working the streets and clubs with various artists. In 1949 he moved to Chicago, where he reunited with old friend Jimmy Reed. In the 1950s, he recorded on his own and with Reed for VeeJay. Through the 1960s, 1970s, and into the 1980s he worked the Chicago club scene and was a well-respected session man who recorded with Elmore James and John Lee Hooker. See Justin O'Brien, "Eddie Taylor 1923–1985," *Living Blues* 72 (1986): 31–33; John Anthony Brisbin, "Tribute to Eddie Taylor," *Living Blues* 151 (May–June 2002): 32–51. Interviewed in Chicago, 1974.

THOMAS, JAMES "SON." (14 October 1926–26 June 1993) Guitar. Born in Eden, Mississippi; settled in Leland, Mississippi. His uncle owned a guitar that he would borrow. He played local house parties and jooks in Mississippi through the 1960s. Filmed by folklorist William Ferris, he began to play festivals and universities. Performing through the 1970s and 1980s, Thomas appeared in numerous films and documentaries. He was a fine sculptor as well as a good blues player. See William Ferris, *Blues From the Delta* (Garden City N.Y.: Anchor Press, 1984) and *Blues Guitar: The Men Who Made the Music*, ed. Jas Obrecht (San Francisco: GPI Books/Miller Freeman, 1990) 40–43. Interviewed in Bloomington, Indiana, March 1973, and Washington, D.C., July 1976.

THOMPSON, EDWARD "BIG ED." (22 January 1935–22–April 1993) Guitar. Born in Bethlehem, Georgia. He moved to Cincinnati at age ten. He listened to blues and country on the radio and bought a mail-order guitar and instruction book. He learned to read music in high school and at that time formed a band to play around the Cincinnati area. About 1955 he teamed up with H-Bomb Ferguson and worked as a sideman through the 1960s. He recorded with various artists for King Records and worked festival and live gigs through the 1980s. Interviewed in Peninsula, Ohio, 22 September 1985.

THORNTON, WILLIE MAE "BIG MAMA." (11 December 1926–25 July 1984) Drums, Harmonica. Born in Montgomery, Alabama. Thornton first sang in the church but ran away with the Hot Harlem Revue at age fourteen. She moved to Houston, Texas, in 1948, recorded for the Peacock label in 1951, and scored a number-one hit, "Hound Dog," in 1953. In 1957 she moved to California, working Bay Area clubs. Through the 1960s and 1970s she recorded and toured working clubs and the festival circuit. See Bill Carpenter, "Big Mama Thornton: 200 Pounds of Boogaloo," *Living Blues* 106 (November–December): 26–32. Interviewed in Ann Arbor, Michigan, August 1969.

TOWNSEND, HENRY "MULE." (27 October 1909–) Piano, Guitar. Born in Shelby, Mississippi. Early on he moved to Cairo, Illinois, then to St. Louis, Missouri. His father was a musician, Henry taught himself to play guitar, harmonica, and piano. Townsend worked rent parties and played clubs with various artists, including Walter Davis, Robert Nighthawk, and Roosevelt Sykes. He recorded from the late 1920s for Paramount, Columbia, Bluebird, and others and continued to play through the 1940s and 1950s at clubs and dances. Through the 1960s and 1970s, Townsend continued to reside in St. Louis, recording for documentary labels and touring the festival circuit. Active up through the 1990s as a musician and blues historian, he was named a National Heritage Fellow in 1985. See Henry Townsend as told to Bill Green Smith, *Henry Townsend: A Blues Life* (Urbana, University of Illinois Press, 1999). Interviewed in Vienna, Virginia, 18 July 1982.

CONTRIBUTORS

TURNER, NAPOLEON "NAP." (4 March 1931–17 June 2004) Bass. Born in Tamms, West Virginia, he moved to Washington, D.C., in 1942, where he sang in church and listened to music on the radio and in the streets. As a teenager he would hang out at Washington, D.C.'s Howard Theater. Inspired by seeing a washtub bass player, he constructed one of his own, soon moving on to a real bass. He played local jazz and rhythm-and-blues clubs; he toured with several groups, then continued to play local clubs. He became a well-known radio personality and blues promoter through the 1970s and 1980s and continued to perform through 1990s as vocalist, storyteller, and music historian. Interviewed in Riverdale, Maryland, 25 April 1993.

TURNER, OTHA. (2 June 1907–27 February 2003) Drums, Fife, Guitar. Born in Jackson, Mississippi. Turner learned to play guitar, drums, and cane "fice" at an early age and began to play as a youngster for local fife-and-drum bands at picnics and parties. Later he played guitar at jook houses. Turner moved to Como, Mississippi where he began to host his own picnics or suppers. He recorded during the 1970s and has appeared in various documentaries. He was named a National Heritage Fellow in 1992. See George Mitchell, *Blows My Blues Away* (Baton Rouge: Louisiana State University Press, 1971), 18–47; David Nelson, "Drums Is a Calling Thing," *Living Blues* 100 (November–December 1991): 36–38. Interviewed in Washington, D.C., 29 June 1991.

WASHINGTON JUNIOR, GEORGE . (3 July 1924–) Guitar. Born in Malvina, Mississippi, and raised in Tunica, he made one-string guitars as a child and was then given a guitar. He worked on a farm and played at house parties. He played jooks from Greenville to Natchez through the 1940s, 1950s, and 1960s and played informally through the 1970s and 1980s. He is now on the local festival circuit. Interviewed in Clarksdale, Mississippi, 5 August 1991.

WATSON, EDDIE LEE "LOVIE LEE." (17 March 1917–23 May 1997) Piano. Born in Chattanooga, Tennessee. Watson grew up in Meridian, Mississippi, and taught himself to play piano, playing for different churches from age fifteen. He got into blues as a teen and played for vaudeville, rodeos. He worked with the Swinging Cats band in the 1950s and in 1957 moved to Chicago, where he playing with various bands, joining Muddy Waters in 1979. He continued to work through 1990s until his death in 1997. See John Brisbin, "Lovie Lee: I Can Entertain You," *Living Blues* 110 (July–August 1993): 22–28. Interviewed in Chicago, 9 June 1990.

WEBB, WILLIAM "BOOGIE BILL." (1924–23 August 1990) Guitar. Born in Jackson, Mississippi. Webb grew up in New Orleans, where his mother hosted weekend fish fries that featured blues legend Tommy Johnson. Webb learned guitar from Roosevelt Holts and returned to Jackson to work jooks. He recorded in the 1950s for Imperial, played house parties, and recorded for several other labels through the 1960s and 1970s. In the 1980s he put out an album on the Flying Fish label and began to tour and work festivals. Interviewed in Washington, D.C., 28 June 1985.

WESTON, JOHN "SO BLUE." (12 December 1927–) Guitar, Harmonica. Born in Lee County, Arkansas, he began music later in life after working in Arkansas and Chicago. He started playing guitar in 1958 and learned harmonica from Willie Cobb in the mid-1970s. He ran a nightclub in Smale, Arkansas, from 1967 to 1991. In 1989 he won a blues amateur contest and recorded later for the Fat Possum label. Today he plays guitar and harmonica and works various clubs and festivals. See James Tighe, "John Weston: Driving Down Highway 79," *Living Blues* 109 (June 1993): 43–45. Interviewed in Clarksdale, Mississippi, 4 August 1995.

WHEELER, JAMES "STRAWBOSS." (c. 1938–) Guitar. Born in Albany, Georgia. His brother, harmonica player Golden "Big" Wheeler, who brought him to Chicago in 1956, introduced him to music. By 1957 he was working with Freddy King and Magic Sam, and he formed the Jaguars in 1963. Wheeler led the house band at Chicago's Burning Spear Club, backing various national acts, and toured with Otis Clay, Otis Rush, and others. He is currently working with Mississippi Heat. Interviewed in Washington, D.C., 9 September 1995.

WHITE, JESSIE "UNCLE JESSIE." (1920–) Piano, Harmonica. Born in Terry, Mississippi. He played harmonica at local jooks and house parties. White moved to Jackson in 1940 and to Detroit in 1950. Between the years 1940 and l965 he stopped playing music and then began to play informally around his house in the 1960s and through the 1970s and 1980s. Jam sessions at his house on Twenty-ninth Street were legendary. Through the 1990s he toured and played at the Attic Bar in Hamtramck, Michigan. Interviewed 14 September 1999.

WILKINS, JOE WILLIE. (7 January 1923–28 March 1979) Guitar. Born in Davenport, Mississippi. Wilkins played several instruments as a youngster and worked the streets in Delta towns, billing himself as "The Walking Seeburg." Teamed with Sonny Boy Williamson, Number Two, and Robert Junior Lockwood, he performed over KFFA on "King Biscuit Time." Recorded as sideman for the Trumpet and Sun labels, he worked various jooks and clubs around Memphis and the Delta through the 1950s, 1960s, and 1970s. He played at the Smithsonian Folklife Festival with Houston Stackhouse in 1976. See Jim O'Neal, "Joe Willie Wilkins," *Living Blues* 11 (Winter 1972–73): 13–17. Interviewed in Washington, D.C., June 1976.

WILLIAMS, J. OTIS. (21 May 1939–4 April 1997) Drums, Guitar. Born in Grenada, Mississippi. His father hosted country house parties. As a teenager he worked in an uncle's barbershop, where he first began to learn guitar and saw various local musicians and visiting celebrities such as Magic Sam. He was influenced by visiting tent-show performers. He also briefly played drums with a cousin's band working local jooks. Following a stint in the service he moved to Baltimore, Maryland, where he worked as a writer, poet, singer, songwriter, storyteller, teacher, and blues preacher promoting various forms of African American traditional music. See Otis Williams, *The Blues Is: Darker Than Blue* (Baltimore: JOW Productions, 1982). Interviewed 15 April 1995.

WILLIAMS, MOSES "HAYWIRE TOM." (15 February 1919–) Born in Itta Bena, Mississippi. He learned the one-string early in life and continued to play it through adulthood, often working southern streets and house parties. For mobility's sake he constructed his "wire" on a hollow door that he could carry from venue to venue. He called this instrument a "traveling loafer board." In the 1980s he was living in Florida. Interviewed in Vienna, Virginia, 8 August 1981.

WRIGHT, ETHELEEN. Guitar. Born in Waterloo, Iowa. Her family was originally from Mississippi. Her grandfather played guitar; she taught herself to play as a youngster. She worked in various Waterloo groups, including her own band, Etheleen Wright and the Mixers. She plays jazz and blues and is currently working with Louis McTizic's Blues Machine. See Jim DeKoster, "Waterloo Blues: An Interview with Louis McTizic," *Living Blues* 105 (September–October): 18–25. Interviewed in Clarksdale, Mississippi, 5 August 1995.

YAWN, JESSE "BIG JESSE." (4 September 1937–) Born in Florida. As a young man he sang with several gospel quartets, and in the early 1950s he moved to Rochester, New York, to work with other gospel quartets. In the late 1950s and early 1960s he switched to blues, working various clubs. In the 1960s he worked with Bill Black, Bill Doggett, and other groups. In 1971 he moved to Baltimore, Maryland, developing a construction business and performing informally. Returning to music in the late 1980s and 1990s, he fronted various groups and now has his own band, the Music Men. He currently lives in Howard County, Maryland. Interviewed in Largo, Maryland, 19 September 1993.

NOTES

INTRODUCTION

1. Wiggins is half of the blues duo John Cephas and Phil Wiggins, today's leading exponents of the Piedmont or East Coast blues tradition. Cephas is also a National Heritage Fellow, and Armstrong was in town to receive the same award.

2. Lawrence Welk (1903–1992) was an accordion-playing bandleader and recording artist whose television show, "The Lawrence Welk Show," was on ABC for twenty-five years.

3. Heavyweight boxing champion and African American folk hero Joe Louis (1914–1983) knocked out Italian heavyweight Primo Carnera in 1935. At the time, Italy was involved in the invasion of Ethiopia, and Louis's achievement was seen as a moral victory throughout the African diaspora.

4. For more on this motif, see Pearson, *Sounds So Good to Me* (Philadelphia, University of Pennsylvania Press, 1984), 60–66.

5. Instrument construction, another major motif of the bluesman's story, works as a cultural indicator of musical talent, or a sign that one is destined to be a musician. See Pearson, *Sounds So Good to Me*, 49–52, 151; David Evans, "Afro-American One Stringed Instruments," *Western Folklore* 29 (October 1970): 229–45; and Gerard Kubik, *Africa and the Blues* (Jackson, University of Mississippi Press, 1999), 16–20.

6. For more on life story, see Pearson, *Sounds So Good to Me,* 29–45.

7. While no one knows exactly how long blues have been around, the U.S. Senate designated 2003 as the "Year of the Blues," commemorating its one-hundredth anniversary, based on two early references to blues by prominent blues popularizers, W. C. Handy, the so-called "Father of the Blues," and Ma Rainey, known as the "Mother of the Blues," who heard blues in St. Louis in 1902.

8. For more on blues humor, see Mel Wattkins, *On the Real Side: Laughing, Lying and Signifying; The Underground Tradition of African American Humor That Transformed American Culture from Slavery to Richard Pryor* (New York, Touchstone Simon and Schuster, 1994); Adam Gussow, *Seems Like Murder Here: Southern Violence and the Blues Tradition* (Chicago, University of Chicago Press, 2002), 39–45; Lawrence W. Levine, *Black Culture and Black Consciousness: Afro-American Folk Thought from Slavery to Freedom* (New York, Oxford University Press, 1977), 276–78.

9. Zora Neale Hurston also looked to the weekend dance as the source of the blues: "musically speaking, the Jook is the most important place in America. For in its smelly, shoddy confines has been born the secular music known as the blues." Zora Neale Hurston, "Characteristics of Negro Expression" in *Negro Anthology*, ed. Nancy Cunard (New York, Negro Universities Press, 1934), 44.

10. Nat Shapiro and Nat Hentoff, *Hear Me Talkin' to Ya: The Story of Jazz as Told By the Men who Made It* (New York, Dover, 1955) x.

11. Ibid, xii.

12. Robert Jeff and Tony Conner, *Blues* (Boston, David R. Godine, 1975).

13. James Fraher, *The Blues Is a Feeling: Voices and Visions of African American Blues Musicians* (Mount Horeb, Wisc., Face to Face Books, 1998), front dust jacket.

CHAPTER 1. BLUES TALK

1. "Trouble at Home Blues" was recorded for Excello in Crowley, Louisiana, in 1962.

2. Little Walter Jacobs (1930–1968) was Chicago's most popular harmonica player during its Golden Age of blues. Moving to Chicago as a teenager, he worked with various artists, eventually joining Muddy Waters's band. In 1952 he recorded "Juke" under his own name for the Chess subsidiary label Checker, and it became a smash hit, allowing him to form his own group. He recorded "Mean Old World" for Checker in 1952 in his first session, with Louis and David Myers on guitars and Fred Below on drums. See Tony Glover, Scott Dirks, and Ward Gaines, *Blues With a Feeling: The Little Walter Story* (New York, Routledge 2002).

CHAPTER 2. LIVING THE BLUES

1. "Easy to get into, hard to get out of," Parchman State Penitentiary is a notorious Delta institution; a prison farm located in Sunflower County at the intersection of 49 West and State Road 32. Commemorated in song and legend, its influence extends throughout the Delta and beyond, to Chicago and Detroit.

2. "Baby Please Don't Go," recorded by Mississippi artists from Big Joe Williams to Muddy Waters, became a staple of the Delta and Chicago blues tradition and later rock blues. It is based on the prison work song "Another Man Done Gone" and has been field recorded by that title by Vera Hall.

3. Chester Burnett, better known as Howling Wolf, was a major artist in the Delta-to-Chicago blues continuum. He recorded his hit record "Smokestack Lightning" for Chess Records in Chicago in 1954.

4. An eight-bar blues known by such titles as "Blood Red River" and "Bye-Bye Baby Blues," "Red River Blues" is possibly the most popular East Coast, or Piedmont, blues standard and has been recorded by Josh White (1933), Blind Boy Fuller (1937), and others.

5. In his autobiography, Edwards and his editors, Janis Martinson and Michael Robert Frank, describe the Hog Law as an 1876 Mississippi crime bill that redefined grand larceny to include minor theft, including theft of farm animals. The law also allowed police and local farmers to arrest blacks on vagrancy charges in order to put them to work in the fields. See David Honeyboy Edwards, *The World Don't Owe Me Nothing: The Life and Times of Delta Bluesman Honeyboy Edwards* (Chicago, University of Chicago Press, 1997), 226.

6. Work parties remained a mainstay of southern African American rural life from the grand-scale cornshuckings that took place during slavery, through the work feasts, woodcuttings, and cornshuckings that continued through the 1940s. See Barry Lee Pearson, *Virginia Piedmont Blues: The Lives and Art of Two Virginia Bluesmen* (Philadelphia, University of Pennsylvania Press, 1990), 31–32; and Roger Abrahams, *Singing the Master: The Emergence of African American Culture in the Plantation South* (New York, Pantheon Books, 1992).

7. Like the terms "dicty" and "hincty," "saddity" is an adjective connoting upper crust, high class, acting snobbish, or putting on airs. The prevalence of such terms in African American folk speech testifies to class tension and lower-class resentment towards those who acted "uppity" or "biggity."

8. Otha, or Othar, Turner was famous for his musical picnics. Even after his death and the death of his daughter, Bernice, his family still catered goat roasts as late as the Living Blues Symposium in February 2004.

9. Edwards is referring to Texas blues artist Blind Lemon Jefferson's 1926 Paramount hit, "That Black Snake Moan." Jefferson was the first popular guitar-playing, down-home, blues man, and his influence spread throughout the South, affecting countless guitarists, including white country musicians.

10. John Hurt Jr. is referring to his father, John Smith Hurt, better known as Mississippi John Hurt, who recorded in the late 1920s and was rediscovered during the blues revival of the 1960s. Willie Narmour was a popular Mississippi fiddler who also recorded for Okeh and Victor with his partner Shell Smith. Narmour supposedly was responsible for Hurt's initial

recording session. Hurt later recorded a song he titled, "Coffee Blues," which his son calls "Spoonful."

11. Noun, verb, and adjective, *jook,* or "juke" as it is often spelled, has a contested history. In *Africanisms in the Gullah Dialect* (Chicago, University of Chicago Press, 1949), linguist Lorenzo Turner connected the Gullah word *juk,* meaning "infamous or disorderly," to the Wolof *jug* or *dzug,* meaning to lead a disorderly life, and the Bambara or Bamana *dzugu,* meaning a wicked, naughty, violent person. There is also a Gullah personal name, *Jiku,* that parallels the Ewe word meaning excitement. Possible European sources include the French verb, *jouer,* to play, and *jouk,* to nestle and collect in a covey, as well as the Scottish words *jouk,* meaning a place of retreat or shelter and to "evade or play truant," and *jookerie,* meaning trickery or swindling. Tracing the terms through song titles paints an equally interesting picture that reinforces the Gullah connection. Similar terms date back at least to W. C. Handy's 1913 composition "Jogo Blues." In his autobiography he explained the term *jogo* was inspired by the humorous custom of the Gullahs, "and from there all the way back to Africa. . . . when they would say something not meant for outside ears they would invent words, or attach new meanings to familiar words." He cited *ofay,* meaning white, and *jigawawk,* meaning black, adding that *jogo* was a synonym for *jigawawk* and meant colored (Handy, 122). Novelist Rudolph Fisher also listed the term *jigwalker* among his current synonyms for *Negro* in "An Introduction to Contemporary Harlemese," appended to the end of his novel *The Walls of Jericho* (1928). These terms correspond to later usage of *jook* or the verb *jook* or *juking* as meaning doing things in African American style. In 1927 Edna Winston recorded "Joogie Blues," and in 1928 Tiny Parham recorded "Jogo Rhythmn." In the 1930s, references to "jook" appear in Walter Roland's 1933 "Jook It Jook It" and Cripple Clarence Lofton's 1938 or 1939 "Jook Joint Stomp" (Robert M. W. Dixon, John Godrich and Howard W. Rye, *Blues and Gospel Records, 1890–1943,* Oxford, Clarendon Press, 1997). The "juke" spelling comes in with the jukebox in the 1940s, as in Glenn Miller's "Jukebox Saturday Night." The term "jukebox" drew its name from the presence of jukeboxes in jooks or jook joints. Older musicians, by the way, tend to refer to these coin-operated music vendors by their brand names—Seeburgs, Rockolas, or Piccolos. But once the jukebox became an established term, *jook,* more often than not, was spelled "juke," and derivative words, such as the sports term *juke,* meaning a graceful, deceptive move, inherited the new spelling. As a political act, we should return to the original spelling, "jook," to perpetuate the subversion of dominant culture that Zora Neale Hurston initiated by elevating the jook tradition in the first place. Zora Neale Hurston, "Characteristics of Negro Expression," in *Negro Anthology,* edited by Nancy Cunard (New York: Negro Universities Press, 1969), 44.

12. Bessie Jones (1902–1984) was a National Heritage Fellowship recipient who promoted the music and folk traditions of the Georgia Sea Islands. From the 1960s, she toured festivals and recorded with the Sea Island Singers that included Doug and Frankie Quimby.

13. The Sunflower River twists and turns through the heart of the Delta from Moon Lake through Clarksdale, down through Sunflower County, meeting up with the Yazoo River in Yazoo County some 120 miles to the south.

14. (Aleck) Rice Miller, better known as Sonny Boy Williamson Number Two, fronted the King Biscuit Boys, who began as the King Biscuit Entertainers on radio station KFFA in Helena, Arkansas. Initially composed of Miller and Robert Junior Lockwood, the group included a veritable who's who of blues stars. The radio program, "King Biscuit Time," hosted by Sonny Payne, has run from 1941 to the present day.

CHAPTER 3. LEARNING THE BLUES

1. Leroy Carr and Scrapper Blackwell recorded a popular version of "Hurry Down Sunshine" for Vocalion in 1934. An earlier song, "Hurry Sundown Blues," was recorded by Madlyn Davis for Paramount in September 1927, and Sister Morgan recorded an unissued Victor side, "Hurry Down Sunshine" with "See What Tomorrow Brings" in February 1927. Townsend, who was born in 1909, moved to Missouri at about age seven, and his memories clearly predate these recorded versions, indicating the verse was traditional prior to any recordings.

2. Tommy Johnson (1896–1956) was a popular and influential blues artist who brought Delta blues back to his hill country community around Jackson. In 1928 he recorded six issued sides for Victor, including the classics Webb refers to. He did another session for Paramount in 1929, but these sides made less of an impact. David Edwards, in the following story, recalls hearing Johnson and his brothers Clarence and Mager playing the same pieces that Tommy recorded for Victor. For more on Johnson's impact, see David Evans, *Big Road Blues: Tradition and Creativity in the Folk Blues* (Los Angeles, University of California Press, 1981).

3. Johnson uses the term "diddley bow" for the one-string guitar, which is perhaps the most common name for the instrument, particularly among scholars. Blues artists, as you will see, have a remarkably varied list of names for the instrument, including "drum," "pulleydum," and "broom wire slim," indicating that a homemade instrument deserves an equally homemade name. My favorite name, as reported by a fellow blues scholar, is "rumpling steelskin."

4. Originally composed by Harold Arlen for the show "The Cotton Club Parade of 1933," "Stormy Weather" was a popular song and a 1943 film. It generated multiple covers by blues artists, including Walter Davis (1933), Ethel Waters (1942), Josh White (1934), and the Golden Gate Quartet (1939).

5. Roosevelt Holts was born in Tylertown, Mississippi. A guitar-playing blues singer, he recorded a number of sessions in the mid- to late 1960s, including duets with Bill Webb in 1969.

6. One of the most storied Delta blues artists of all time, Robert Johnson (1911–1938) entered a common-law relationship with Estella Coleman, Lockwood's mother. Although Johnson was only a few years older than Lockwood, the assumption has been that Robert Junior was Johnson's stepson.

7. Like "Baby Please Don't Go," "Rolling and Tumbling" is one of the best known and most deeply traditional Delta blues standards. Originally recorded by Hambone Willie Newbern for Okeh in 1929 under the title "Roll and Tumble Blues," it has been reworked by countless artists, and its melody has been used in dozens of songs.

8. While one might expect fife and drums in Mississippi tradition, the term *fice* reflects the preferred vernacular pronunciation.

9. Alan Lomax recorded the Hemphill family from Como, Mississippi, extensively. Lomax recorded Rosa Lee Hill's (or Rosalie Hill's) version of "Bullyin' Well" in Senetobia in 1959. According to Jessie Mae, Rosa was her aunt and Sid Hemphill's daughter.

10. Mississippi John Hurt recorded "Stack O'Lee Blues" and "Candy Man Blues" in December 1928. They were issued as the A and B sides of Okeh 8654. Later in life, in Washington, D.C., Edwards became close friends with John Hurt.

11. "Baza" is a phonetic spelling of what I think Mr. Hypolite said. It appears to be a Louisiana Creole term equivalent to "lala," "jook," or houseparty.

12. Elmore James (1918–1963) was a popular and influential Delta blues artist who recorded extensively. He played electric slide guitar, and countless rock and blues players have emulated his work. He is best known for his cover of Robert Johnson's "Dust My Broom." See Steve Franz, *The Amazing Secret History of Elmore James* (St. Louis, Blues Source Publications, 2003).

13. Both the Grand Ole Opry and WLAC were located in Nashville, Tennessee, and had the power to be heard throughout the South. The Opry, a country music program, began on station WSM in 1925 and was a favorite of many blues artists. WLAC began to feature black music in the late 1940s and sold blues record packages via mail order. Gene Noble was one of the

white disc jockeys that promoted black music in a format that ran forty-five minutes of blues and fifteen minutes of gospel. Blues artists mention these radio outlets, along with KFFA in Helena, most often.

14. Slim Harpo, born Thomas Moore, recorded "Buzz Me Babe" for Excello Records, December 1959.

15. Ella Fitzgerald (1917–1996) began singing with bandleader/drummer Chick Webb's band in New York in 1935. Her hit record, "A-Tisket A-Tasket" was one of the most popular songs of the era. She worked with Webb in New York and on tour until his death in 1939.

16. F. S. Wolcott's "Rabbit Foot Minstrels" from Port Gibson, Mississippi, and "Silas Green's from New Orleans" were touring tent shows that became southern institutions. The latter began in 1910 and ran up until 1959. These became black variety shows employing blues singers, as well as acts ranging from acrobats to magicians. Many of the early vaudeville blues artists began their careers working with these shows, but Williams is probably referring to the late 1940s or early 1950s.

17. *Corn songs* is one of many terms for secular songs before the term *blues* became popular. Most often the term *reels* was the pre-blues vernacular for non-sacred dance tunes, and early blues were often called reels by the older generation. The less common *corn songs* also refers to corn-shucking songs, and possibly even cornfield hollers.

18. Buddy Johnson (1915–1977) was a well-known New York–based band-leader who often worked the Savoy Theater. He had numerous hit records through the 1940s and 1950s and disbanded in the 1960s. Beginning in 1944 he recorded for Decca then switched to Mercury. His R&B hits often featured his sister, vocalist Ella Johnson. Like Ferguson, Johnson was born in South Carolina.

19. Big Joe Williams (1903–1982) was born in Crawford, Mississippi, and began to play guitar in the early 1920s. He called himself "a walking musician," playing the streets, stores, house parties, and jooks, moving throughout the Delta and from New Orleans to St. Louis. On one of these sojourns in 1932, he picked up Edwards as an apprentice. A prolific recording artist, he was the first to record, and may have written, "Baby Please Don't Go."

20. Little Walter recorded "Juke" and "Can't Hold Out Much Longer" while still with Muddy Waters in May 1952.

21. In 1936 Willie Dixon (1915–1995) moved from Mississippi to Chicago, where he sang and played bass with several successful bands. In the late 1940s he joined Chess Records as an A&R man, session musician, song-writer (writing for Muddy Waters and Howling Wolf), and talent scout.

Koko Taylor was his protégé, and her wrote her hit, "Wang Dang Doodle," which had been previously done by Howling Wolf. Taylor's reference to Sonny Boy Williams refers to Sonny Boy Williamson Number Two. It is not uncommon for southern blues musicians to shorten the name to Williams.

CHAPTER 4. WORKING THE BLUES

1. The "Forty-Four Blues" was originally a well-known piano instrumental. Roosevelt Sykes and Little Brother Montgomery, who called his version "Vicksburg Blues," added words in later recordings. It was later transposed to guitar, and numerous blues players from James Thomas to Howling Wolf recorded the piece. See Paul Oliver, *Screening the Blues: Aspects of the Blues Tradition* (New York, De Capo, 1968), 90–127.

2. Eurreal "Little Brother" Montgomery (1905–1985) learned piano in his father's Kentwood, Louisiana, barrelhouse. Leaving home at age eleven, he worked from New Orleans to Chicago. He moved to Jackson, Mississippi, in the early 1930s, and then to Chicago in 1942. He first recorded for Paramount in 1930, producing a two-sided hit "Vicksburg Blues" and "No Special Rider Blues." See Karl GertZur Heide, *Deep South Piano: The Story of Little Brother Montgomery* (London, Studio Vista, 1970).

3. Riley B. King (1925–), better known as B. B. King, is currently America's best known and most influential Delta-born blues artist. He moved to Memphis in 1947; in 1949, while working as a DJ for WDIA, he began a fifty-five-year recording career. An outstanding guitarist and powerful vocalist, he paid his dues on the chittling circuit, achieved international acclaim, and was inducted into the Rock and Roll Hall of Fame in 1987. See B. B. King and David Ritz, *Blues All Around Me: The Autobiography of B. B. King* (New York, Avon, 1996).

4. Robert Nighthawk (1909–1967) was born Robert Lee McCullum in Helena, Arkansas. Although he moved to St. Louis and Chicago, Helena remained his home base. In 1937 he began recording for Bluebird but was better known for his live jook-joint performances. In 1943 he began broadcasting for Helena's KFFA, and he and KFFA's other star, Sonny Boy Williamson Number Two, often competed for the best local musician.

5. Lee Magid worked for Savoy Records in Newark, New Jersey, as a song promoter and A&R man.

6. John Lee Hooker (1920–2003) was one of the Delta's most influential recording artists. Born in Clarksdale, he moved to Detroit in 1943. While working the house party and tavern circuit, he recorded "Boogie Chillen,"

which became a number-one R&B hit in 1949. Over the next fifty-three years he appears on a dozen or so labels and, along with Lightning Hopkins and B. B. King, was one of the most recorded blues artists of all time.

7. The case of the two Sonny Boys is one of the most celebrated in blues history. Sonny Boy Number One, John Lee Williamson (1914–1948), came from Jackson, Tennessee. He first recorded in 1937 for Bluebird and remained one of the label's stars until he was murdered in Chicago. After moving to Chicago in 1937 he became one of the most popular artists on the club scene as well. Sonny Boy Williamson Number Two, Aleck Miller (1910–1965), was the older harmonica player, and in many respects the more important musician. According to music folklore, he took the name Sonny Boy Williamson when he began to broadcast over KFFA in order to cash in on the Sonny Boy Williamson Number One's fame as a major recording artist.

8. Calvin Frazier (1915–1972) was a fine blues guitar player who worked with his cousin, Johnny Shines, in Memphis in the early 1930s. In 1935 he got in trouble with the law and, along with Shines and Johnson, left for Canada. He remained in Detroit, recording for Alan Lomax and the Library of Congress in 1938. Through the 1940s, 1950s, and 1960s, he worked with various Detroit-based blues groups, including Baby Boy Warren and Eddie Kirkland.

9. Peetie Wheatstraw (1902–1941) was the blues name of St. Louis pianist/guitarist William Bunch. An extremely popular recording artist, he worked for Vocalian, Bluebird, and Decca until he was killed in a car accident. He recorded "Good Whiskey Blues" and "More Good Whiskey Blues" in 1935 for Vocalian in Chicago. See Paul Garon, *The Devil's Son-in-Law: The Story of Peetie Wheatstraw and His Songs* (London, Studio Vista, 1971).

10. Rufus Thomas (1917–2001) enjoyed a long and productive career as a DJ, recording artist, and MC. A mainstay of the Memphis music scene, he recorded for Sun, Stax, and other labels, enjoying hits such as "Bearcat," "Tiger Man," and "Walking the Dog."

11. Myron "Tiny" Bradshaw (1905–1958) bridged the big-band era of the 1930s and 1940s, and the R&B era of the late 1940s and 1950s. He recorded for Decca and King. A bandleader, drummer, pianist and vocalist, he scored his biggest hits in the early 1950s.

12. The Atlanta street music scene was particularly strong in the 1920s, attracting several recording companies. The artists mentioned are guitarists Willie McTell, Buddy Moss, Barbecue Bob, Curly Weaver, and pianists Speckled Red and Piano Red. They worked the streets and also recorded but derived the bulk of their living from informal house party work.

13. Chicago's Maxwell Street market no longer exists, thanks to urban renewal, but at one time it was a central component of Chicago culture. At one time a primarily Jewish neighborhood, hence the name "Jew town" bestowed on it by blues musicians, it later became primarily black with Jewish merchants selling to black customers. On Saturday and Sunday it was packed, and musicians in the 1940s to the 1960s could make good money playing the streets. These included both blues and gospel artists who would get electricity from nearby stores and apartments. An open-air market, it was alive with vendors' calls, dancers, and the pungent smell of hot dogs and sausages.

14. "Pork Chop" was the nickname of a drummer who often played Maxwell Street and worked with various blues aggregations.

15. Otis Clay (1942–) is one of the Mississippi-to-Chicago soul blues artists. He began in the gospel field but switched to rhythm and blues in 1965. A prolific recording artist who tours the world, he is especially admired in Japan.

16. Johnnie Jones (1924–1964) was born in Jackson, where he met Uncle Jessie White. A piano and harmonica player, he moved to Chicago in the mid-1940s and worked with various artists, including Muddy Waters, Howling Wolf, and Elmore James, as well as recording on his own.

17. James Brown (1928–), known as the "Godfather of Soul," is also one of the most prolific recording artists of the last fifty years. Signing with King Records in 1956, his first release, "Please, Please, Please" on Federal, was a smash hit. During the mid-1960s, he was particularly popular with such hits as "Poppa's Got a Brand New Bag" and "I Feel Good (I Got You)."

18. Joe Liggins (1915–1987) was an Oklahoma-born bandleader who moved to Los Angeles. At the end of World War II he scored a monster hit with the 1945 release "The Honeydripper." Originally with the Exclusive label, he switched to Specialty and had numerous hits, including "Pink Champagne," which in 1950 scored number one on the R&B charts. "The Honeydripper" was covered and even claimed by artists ranging from Roosevelt Sykes to Muddy Waters. It's no wonder Williamson knew and could play the song.

19. Roscoe Gordon (1928–2002) was one of several Memphis blues artists known as the Beale Streeters. He recorded for Sun, Modern, Chess, and VeeJay, and in his later years was credited as one of the co-inventors of ska. See Richard Pearce's *The Road to Memphis,* 2002, a "Year of the Blues" film produced by PBS.

20. One of the legends of bandleader Fletcher Henderson (1897–1952) has Henderson ignoring, or snubbing, Fitzgerald while Webb steals her from under his nose.

21. Harmonica player Junior Wells (1934–1998), and guitarist Sammy Lawhorn (1935–1990), worked with Byther Smith at Theresa's Tavern and other Chicago venues in the late 1960s and early 1970s. Smith is speaking of Sweet Queen Bee Lounge, 7401 South Chicago Avenue, where Wells and Lawhorn also often worked.

22. Furry Lewis (1893–1981) moved from Greenwood, Mississippi, to Memphis as a child. A life-long member of the Memphis blues community, he worked with various jug bands and went out on the medicine show circuit. Between 1927 and 1929 he recorded for both Vocalion and Victor. Resurfacing in 1959, he recorded for Folkways and served as a blues elder statesman, appearing in several films.

23. Washboard Sam (1910–1966), born Robert Brown, moved from Memphis to Chicago in 1932 and began recording for Bluebird in 1935. An extremely prolific recording artist, he recorded well over a hundred sides for Bluebird, six for Vocalion, sixteen for Victor, and several for Checker in 1953. He often recorded with Big Bill Broonzy and various piano players, and worked as a sideman for many other recordings.

THE LAST WORD

1. Blind Boy Fuller (1908–1941) was born Fulton Allen in Wadesboro, North Carolina. Initially discovered and promoted by Carolina entrepreneur J. B. Long, Fuller recorded for ARC, Decca, and Vocalion from 1935 to 1941, working with Sonny Terry, Bull City Red, and Gary Davis, putting out 135 titles, both blues and gospel, in six short years. Fuller recorded "Little Woman, You're So Sweet" for Vocalion in 1940. Edwards, like most East Coast artists, performed a number of Fuller's songs.

SELECT BIBLIOGRAPHY

American Folktales. From the Collection of the Library of Congress. Edited by Carl Lundahl. New York: M. E. Sharpe, 2004

Broonzy, William, as told to Yannick Bruynoghe. *Big Bill Blues: William Broonzy's Story.* 1955. Rpt. New York: Da Capo Press, 1990.

Crow, Bill. *Jazz Anecdotes.* New York: Oxford University Press, 1990.

Fraher, James. *The Blues Is a Feeling: Voices and Visions of African American Blues Musicians.* Mount Horeb, Wisconsin: Face to Face Books, 1998.

Handy, W. C. *W. C. Handy: Father of the Blues.* New York: Collier Books, 1970. Rpt. 1991.

Lomax, Alan. *The Land Where the Blues Began.* New York: Pantheon, 1993.

Lomax, John, and Alan Lomax. *Negro Folksongs as Sung by Leadbelly.* New York: Macmillan, 1936.

Neff, Robert, and Anthony Conner. *Blues.* Boston: David Godine, 1975.

Oliver, Paul. *Conversations with the Blues.* New York: Horizon Press, 1965.

Pearson, Barry Lee. "CeDell Davis's Story and the Arkansas Delta Blues." *Arkansas Review: A Journal of Delta Studies* 33, no. 1 (April 2002): 3–4.

———. "Defining the Blues." *The Blues Project.* Edited by Isa N. Engleberg and Lyle E. Linville. Largo, Maryland: Prince Georges Community College, 1993. 5–7.

———. "Doctor Ross's One Man Boogie." *Living Blues* 99 (September–October 1991): 10–17.

———. "The First Time I Met the Blues: James Otis Williams (1939–1997)." *Arkansas Review: A Journal of Delta Studies* 30, no. 1 (April 1999): 29–42

———. "I Used to Walk Thirty Miles with a Guitar on My Back: John Jackson." *Living Blues* 163 (May–June 2002): 30–35.

———. "If I Couldn't Make a Quarter in a City, I Was Gone: Blues Stories of Life on the Road." *Arkansas Review: A Journal of Delta Studies* 34, no. 3 (December 2003): 219–28.

———. "Jook Women." *Living Blues* 169 (September–October 2003): 102–13.

———. "Jump Steady: The Roots of R&B." *Nothing but the Blues: The Music and The Musicians.* Edited by Lawrence Cohn. New York: Abbeville Press, 1993. 312–95.

———. "North Carolina Blues: John Dee Holeman: Bull City Blues." *Living Blues* 117 (January–February 1993): 31–32.

SELECT BIBLIOGRAPHY

———. "One Day You're Going to Hear About Me: The H-Bomb Ferguson Story." *Living Blues* 69 (1986): 15–24.

———. *Sounds So Good to Me: The Bluesman's Story.* Philadelphia: University of Pennsylvania Press, 1984.

———. *Virginia Piedmont Blues: The Art and Lives of Two Virginia Bluesmen.* Philadelphia: University of Pennsylvania Press, 1990.

———. "When You're Born and Raised in the Delta, You Just Write What You See: Delta Blues Stories." *Arkansas Review: A Journal of Delta Studies* 29, no. 1 (April 1998): 30–41.

Pearson, Barry Lee, and Alicia Hosmer. "An Interview with Eddie Burns." *DC Blues Society Newsletter* 1, no. 1 (October 1987): 3–4.

Pearson, Barry Lee, and Bill McCulloh. *Robert Johnson Lost and Found.* Urbana: University of Illinois Press, 2003.

Pearson, Nathan W., Jr. *Going to Kansas City.* Urbana: University of Illinois Press, 1987.

Shapiro, Nat, and Nat Hentoff. *Hear me Talkin' to Ya': The Story of Jazz as Told by the Men Who Made It.* 1955. New York: Dover, 1966.

Tracy, Steven C. *Going to Cincinnati: A History of Blues in the Queen City.* Urbana: University of Illinois Press, 1993.

Wood, Roger, and James Fraher. *Down in Houston: Bayou City Blues.* Austin: University of Texas Press, 2003.

INDEX

JOOK RIGHT ON was designed and typeset on a Macintosh computer system using QuarkXPress software. The body text is set in 10.25/14 Garamond and display type is set in Block Berthold. This book was designed and typeset by Kelly Gray and manufactured by Thomson-Shore, Inc.